PROSPERITY FOR ALL NATIONS

Prosperity
for _All_
Nations

A Call to Action

Raza Hasan

ISBN: 978-1-7344719-0-8 (hardcover) 978-1-7344719-1-5 (paperback); 978-1-7344719-2-2 (ePub); 978-1-7344719-3-9 (Kindle);

Library of Congress Catalog Number: 2020900125
Printed in the United States of America
First Printing: 2020
24 23 22 21 20   5 4 3 2 1

Designed by Mayfly Design

Prosperity Web
Prosperity for All
www.prosperityweb.org

Dedicated to my father
Shakir Hasan
A *political philosopher and my guiding light*

CONTENTS

6 WHY CORRUPTION OCCURS 109

7 ENVIRONMENT FOR PROSPERITY 129

8 SUCCESSFUL DEMOCRATIC STRUCTURE 167

INTRODUCTION

Dream

I share Dr. Martin Luther King Jr.'s dream, a dream of a world without corruption and injustice, a world where all human beings collaborate with each other to create equality for all people and justice worldwide. Minnesota Senator Paul Wellstone said, "We all do better when we all do better." I echo his sentiments. I dream of a world where only good deeds are rewarded and crimes are punished.

Belief

My core belief is that all human beings are created equal. We can all thrive and add to the benefit of one another. Harsh environments cause many of us to struggle in order to survive. Once people understand there is a system that enables them to thrive, they will work to implement this system and be prosperous.

Goal

My goal is to start an Internet-based revolution that connects people around the globe. This movement will prevent governments and politicians from implementing laws detrimental to prosperity. People across the world will connect with each other via a multilingual and crowd-funded website to facilitate the exchange of ideas on governance with checks and balances. The site will fund sponsors around the world to spread awareness in their own countries. Together we will back political leaders who will support this platform for the protection of individual rights.

Why This Book and the Movement

I grew up in Pakistan and moved to the U.S. in 1979 for college. My father was passionate about politics, and I was exposed to his thoughts from childhood. While studying at the Aligarh Muslim University, he participated in the Pakistan movement led by Mohammad Ali Jinnah. He shared with me his pain of seeing Pakistan in despair after becoming free from British rule.

Since I believe the Internet opens up great opportunities, I want to start a global web-based movement. I am writing this book to convince others that there is a way to achieve prosperity because it is already done in many countries. I want to use this book as a launchpad for the web-based prosperity movement.

Overview

The purpose of this book is to instill in you my belief in the goodness of all humankind and to implement a system that enables us to live free, prosperous, and peaceful lives. Freedom means living in a society of fairness, where we have equal access to opportunities and checks that prevent us from harming others. Just imagine a world where every individual is only allowed to do good and no one is above the law.

We need to start looking at the needs of every individual and understanding that the contribution of every person drives this world. We all act according to our environment. We cannot look at nations just as a group of people. Instead, we should focus on protecting the individual's environment, so that every person has the opportunity to thrive.

To maximize the human potential, we need to foster a feeling of well-being for every individual. If we can implement the system of government that protects the feelings of every individual, we will have thriving countries. As stated by the founders of the United States, the purpose of democracy is to protect the rights and serve the needs of individuals. The objective of democracy extends well beyond the actual selection of leaders.

I believe that a society can only thrive when a system of checks and balances works to deliver fairness. The best option we currently have is a democracy that limits the powers of leaders and their terms in office. It also distributes governmental power across many segments of society, again with the ultimate goal of limiting anyone's ability to cause harm to others.

This book uncovers the myths about what leads to prosperity. It shows that it is not education, it is not language, it is not culture, religion, race, natural resources, or geography that lead to prosperity. Most of the world's problems occur because corrupt leaders have the power to steal without being punished. Prosperity requires checks and balances in a system of government so that the natural instincts of human beings to assist each other are not thwarted by the corrupt acts of a limited number of people in positions of power.

I have cited examples from Pakistan based on my personal experience, knowing that similar situations are applicable to all third-world countries.

This book suggests a formula for creating a just and prosperous world. Please read on and join the movement.

WORLD IN A STATE OF CRISIS

1

"A person may cause evil to others not only by his actions but by his inaction, and in either case he is justly accountable to them for the injury."

— John Stuart Mill

The world is in crisis, with billions of people living in countries where their physical, mental, and financial well-being is constantly in danger. This book describes the reasons for the sufferings of these people and the changes required for achieving prosperity for all.

At a basic level, there are two groups of people in the world: under two billion people in free-with-rule-of-law countries and five billion people[1] in oppressed and/or lawless nations. Most people living in free-with-rule-of-law countries do not understand the experience of living under constant oppression and unfair conditions. They cannot comprehend a life where actions, beliefs, and even dreams are quashed by an all-encompassing cloud of hopelessness and depression.

People living in oppressed societies do not know what it is like to live in free-with-rule-of-law countries. They have never experienced life without violence, intimidation, and/or corruption. Instead of being able to pursue their hopes and goals, these individuals are forced to spend their time and energy on their daily survival. The mutual lack of understanding between these two groups creates a dangerous situation where people stop trying to perceive the realities of life in someone else's world, leaving little room for empathy and no room for effecting change. One of the goals of this book is to enable these two groups of people to not only understand each other's circumstances but also feel compelled to take action for those who need it most.

Out of the seven billion people living in our world, more than half are forced to live their lives in extreme poverty. More than five billion people live in countries where government officials consistently violate their inalienable rights. Inalienable rights are defined as the right to practice religion, equal protection under law, and freedom of speech. These five billion people live in nations run by overtly corrupt, unfair, and lawless governments.[2] These numbers indisputably demonstrate that the majority of people in this world live in desperate conditions. Their daily lives are filled with circumstances that most individuals in prosperous countries cannot even begin to imagine. They are constantly worried about meeting basic physical needs such as access to food and clean water, electricity and gas, and ensuring the security of their families. They have no opportunity to live a normal life, free to dream and work toward goals, without an oppressive environment that keeps them worried and depressed. All people should have a life in which their inalienable rights are not only recognized but also fulfilled.

Poverty

Global poverty statistics are extremely disturbing. Nearly half of the world's population, over three billion people, live on less than $2.50 per day.[3] The World Bank sets the poverty line at $1.90 a day, with more than 783 million people around the world living below it.[4] Many of us cannot even imagine living our lives with such limited resources, but this is the harsh reality that most of the world faces daily. Poverty creates an unfortunate situation where people are forced to fight for their sheer survival every day. These individuals do not have the luxury of choosing what they will eat for their one daily meal. They are unable to accumulate any savings or plan for the future. Instead, they continuously struggle to obtain the necessities of food, water, and shelter. Among poorer countries, more than 750 million people attempt to live their lives without adequate water. This is much more than the inconvenient lack of water for bathing. It is the life-or-death situation of not having adequate clean water to survive. More than 2,000 people lose their lives each day from waterborne diseases.

Lack of food is another one of the most prevalent poverty-based issues in the world. Hunger takes the lives of more people than malaria, tuberculosis, and HIV combined. According to the United Nations International Children's Emergency Fund (UNICEF), more than 22,000 children die every day from a lack of adequate food and nourishment.[5] Living with hunger is especially difficult for young children who are affected by a variety of issues. The absence of a nutritious breakfast negatively affects physical and mental development. As explained by UNICEF, these circumstances not only cause tremendous suffering for these children, but also are disempowering and detrimental to their futures.

Hopelessness

Though these statistics are deeply troubling, poverty is only one aspect of the tragic reality for most of the world's population. An issue which is often ignored is the mental strife of people living in these lamentable circumstances. In many areas of the world, individuals generally classified as middle class are forced to live their lives in a manner that stifles their pursuit of happiness. For example, even middle-class professionals in Pakistan wake up each morning with the burden of dealing with the lack of basic necessities such as reliable electricity, safe drinking water, gas for cooking, or gasoline or LPG (liquid petroleum gas) for driving cars. Instead of considering a better future, their mental capacity is consumed with worry over the safety of their children and the security of their limited possessions. Their challenging environment forces them to constantly think about basic day-to-day survival.

For the residents of a prosperous nation reading this, these circumstances may sound similar to those of many workers in your nation from lower income levels, living paycheck to paycheck. However, there is one glaring difference between these two populations: HOPE.

Equality of opportunity is a widely held value in the United States and other prosperous countries. Citizens are taught from birth that hard work and perseverance result in increased opportunity and financial success. When you grow up with this expectation, it's hard to imagine a life where your hard work amounts to very little or even nothing at all. But that is what happens to billions of people living in oppressed and poor countries.

Let's go back to the middle-class professionals of Pakistan. Even in the workplace, these individuals face the harsh realization that their most arduous efforts will not result in a promotion or better opportunities. This is a society where promotions are reserved for relatives and associates of powerful officials. In these nations, no matter your level of experience or ability, without the right connections or bribes, and in some cases both, you are relegated to your current job. In addition to this lack of opportunity, the average worker is also in a constant state of worry about the security of their job. Without the existence and enforcement of protective employment laws, upsetting the wrong person can result in a loss of employment or a transfer to an undesirable and remote location. These individuals are faced with an overwhelming sense of insecurity that leads to the continuous anguish of living in survival mode instead of pursuing bigger and better opportunities. Living in this type of environment forces people to focus on getting by rather than excelling in their professional lives. Such a person might appear to live a normal life, but on an emotional level, they are suffering from environmental depression. These people live in dire circumstances that suffocate their hope and deny their full potential.

The Unseen Victims of Terrorism

While many of us view terrorism as a distant problem that periodically makes its way to our secure nations, in reality, millions of people are surrounded by terrorism every single day. When terrorist attacks occur in Western countries, they take over the national conversation and become the most important issue of concern for governments as well as citizens. But many people around the world experience these attacks on a regular basis and must deal with them in addition to the already difficult circumstances of their impoverished lives.

The U.S. invasion of Iraq has had a profound effect on the number of terror-related deaths occurring around the world. According to the Global Terrorism Database, more than 61,000 incidents of non-state terrorism (acts perpetrated by individuals or groups that are wholly or partly independent of state governments) occurred between 2000 and 2014, claiming the lives of more than 140,000 people.[6]

In 2014, five countries experienced 78% of all terrorist attacks.[7] In one of the deadliest years on record, more than 32,658 people were killed at the hands of extremists. Suffering most attacks were the people of Iran, where 7,143 deaths occurred.[8] Nigeria came in second with 5,341 deaths, and Syria ranked third with 4,634 deaths. While these numbers give a general view of the problem, they do not come close to demonstrating the fear and intimidation that the citizens of these countries live with every day. This conversation often gets lost in the discussion over counterterrorism efforts and debates about the objectives of the most widely recognized terrorist organizations. But for the people who struggle to live and raise their families among these constant threats, the quest for survival takes its toll on a daily basis.

In Pakistan alone, more than 35,000 people have lost their lives in terrorist attacks since 2001. Of these fatalities, 5,000 were mostly poor members of law enforcement. In 2006, 657 terrorist attacks left 907 people dead and more than 1,500 injured.[9] The following year brought 1,515 terrorist incidents, including suicide attacks and assassinations. More than 3,400 people lost their lives, and approximately 5,300 were injured.[10] In 2008, the citizens of Pakistan experienced 2,148 terrorist attacks, causing more than 2,200 fatalities and 4,500 injuries. The darkest year in this period came in 2009, when 2,586 terrorist and insurgent-related incidents took the lives of 3,021 people and caused injury to 7,334 others.[11] These fatality numbers represent a 48% increase in deaths in comparison to the year before.

In November 2015, in a story ignored by most of the Western media, the people of Nigeria were forced to deal with the terror of multiple attacks within a 24-hour period resulting in 49 deaths.[12] First, a bomb exploded at a market, killing 34 people and wounding 80. Less than 24 hours later, two suicide bombers blew themselves up in the midst of a busy and crowded marketplace. Fifteen people were killed, and more than 100 people were injured. The attacks broke a three-week period of peace, which sadly had been quietly celebrated. Carried out by Boko Haram, these attacks added to the more than 20,000 fatalities already caused by this organization during its six-year reign of terror.

The lives of many people are affected by the life-changing unrest caused by terrorism. News media focus on the fatalities, but more importantly, these attacks create a sense of desperation for the survivors. Terrorism disrupts the lives of those that have lost loved ones or are now caring every day for their seriously injured and disabled family members.

For people living in affected countries, such as Nigeria, troops are as commonplace in the landscape as trees. Armored vehicles and even tanks patrol the streets, providing a constant reminder of the risk that continually lies in wait. People go to sleep in fear that their throats may be slit during the night. They send their children to school despite the genuine possibility that insurgents may kidnap them during the day, integrating boys into their armies and taking girls as their sex slaves. Even the simple task of buying food can elicit fear as individuals are forced to patronize marketplaces that have been bombed repeatedly by insurgents. Since most of the market bombings occur in the morning, shoppers choose to arrive later in the day in hopes of returning home safely. The possibility of a terrorist attack is a constant threat, and the citizens of Nigeria must continue to live in conditions similar to those that caused the deaths of their parents, spouses, and children. Each morning, crowds of young boys fight over a single loaf of bread. Many of them were displaced from their families when their relatives were forced to flee the city in fear of insurgents. Others have been orphaned at extremely young ages. All of them are permanently scarred by the persistent risk of terrorism.

The people of Syria also live in constant fear of terrorist attack. Almost half a million people have died since 2011.[13] Citizens have endured unthinkable atrocities at the hands of their government. More than 5,000 civilians were killed during the first half of 2017, including more than 1,000 children and 700 women. About 90 of these deaths resulted from indescribable torture. Living among the rubble of their destroyed cities, residents spend their days traversing demolished streets, scavenging for food. When attacks occur, victims are limited to the most basic level of care at unsanitary, makeshift hospitals. Though doctors try to provide treatment, they are compelled to operate without anesthesia or sterile instruments. Survivors carry the bodies of the dead to improvised graves, where residents hold mass burial ceremonies. Aleppo, which was once Syria's largest city, had a population of more than two million people.[14] It is estimated that the city has lost more than two-thirds of its population from death and desertion, as residents flee to the fields that surround the city in fear for their lives.[15] But even for those who flee, daily life is difficult with the constant need to search for food and shelter. In recent months, they have again become victims of violence, as bombs are now being used to target the fields as well. Humanitarian efforts do not reach the people who need supplies the most, as government officials and opposition fighters have developed systems of bribery, forcing victims to depend on corrupt smugglers. Thousands of refugees flee to neighboring countries for shelter and food, but resources are limited and cultural differences lead to tensions in their new countries as well. Many do not survive the long and arduous treks. For those who stay, chicken coops and sheds become houses, with a constant threat of sickness and disease.[16]

The effects of living in a terrorist-targeted society are varied and far-reaching. Even if the majority of people residing in these countries have not personally experienced a bomb blast, they live with the constant anxiety that an attack could happen at any time in areas they visit regularly. Places of worship, shopping malls, banks, hotels, and many other locations are frequent targets. This causes a sense of anguish to the people living in these conditions. For example, when a person in one of these war-torn countries visits a mosque on Fridays to pray, they are approached by a security guard upon entering the building. The guard checks to ensure that they are not armed or carrying any explosives. This is a necessary evil in these violent societies, and though it is meant to promote safety, it also instills a strange feeling of discomfort and danger among the peaceful residents. It sends the unmistakable message that one's place of worship is not safe and can be attacked at any time, just as so many other mosques have been attacked in the past. It's a harsh truth that keeps people in these areas of the world living in constant anguish even when they are visiting places of worship meant to provide peace and tranquility.

Human Rights

Inalienable rights are liberties that we are born with, by virtue of simply being human. In just societies, these are defined as the right to practice religion, equal protection under the law, and freedom of speech. In a just society, no one can take these rights away from its citizens. As far back as the sixteenth century, scholars recognized and wrote about inalienable rights and their importance to the maintenance of a moral society. The United States government has championed these rights as the fabric of the American way of life. The Bill of Rights lists these inalienable rights and directly prohibits state and federal governments from encroaching on them. But human rights should not be solely enjoyed by developed nations. All humans residing on this planet have the basic right to live free from oppressive governments.

In 1948, following the Second World War, the United Nations passed the Universal Declaration of Human Rights.[17] It was the first document to create a common standard of decency for all people, regardless of their location in the world. The preamble of the declaration states, in part, that "disregard and contempt for human rights have resulted in barbarous acts which have outraged the conscience of mankind, and the advent of a world in which human beings shall enjoy freedom of speech and belief and freedom from fear and want has been proclaimed as the highest aspiration of the common people." As explained in the declaration, the lack of respect for human rights creates a world where people are not free to speak and exercise their beliefs. Even more importantly, disregarding human rights creates a situation where individuals live in constant fear for their own lives and for the general safety and well-being of their families.

In addition to defining the rights that all humans share, the declaration also gives a directive for the way that people should treat each other. Article I states, "All human beings are born free and equal in dignity and rights. They are endowed with reason and conscience and should act toward one another in a spirit of brotherhood." When people fail to act in the spirit of brotherhood and don't treat each other with dignity, the consequence is a nation where human rights are disregarded, with people routinely treated as if they are less than human. All human beings have an innate need to do the right thing. We all have a built-in moral compass, and when we do something bad, our compass makes us feel shame and regret. People living in corrupt societies react to their environment driven by their political reality. When they participate in corrupt activities, they do it out of a need to survive. I believe that their participation in these activities does not make them happy or give them a sense of satisfaction. It only provides some semblance of security in an unpredictable and hostile environment.

Some countries have become notorious for routine violations of human rights by the government or by private parties with the consent of government officials. Each year, watch groups make a list of countries that have committed the most serious human rights violations. For example, Pakistan ranks fourth among nations with poor human rights records. Article XVIII of the Human Rights Declaration states, "Everyone has the right to freedom of thought, conscience, and religion; this right includes freedom to change his religion or belief, and freedom, either alone or in community with others and in public or private, to manifest his religion or belief in teaching, practice, worship, and observance."

Pakistan is known for discrimination against religious minorities, with attacks against Christians, Hindus, Ahmadiyya, Shia, Sufi, and Sikh communities. These attacks are typically blamed on religious extremists, but specific laws in the Pakistani constitution have caused these attacks to grow over time. The roots of religious discrimination were sown in 1974 when the parliament declared Ahmadis to be non-Muslims. Fundamentalists continued to be encouraged with this act of legalized discrimination. Religious persecution led by fundamentalists increased overtime, and now includes people from Shia and Bohra communities other than Christians and Hindus.

Though the Chinese government characterizes the country to the international community as a nation of religious diversity and freedom, the actions of government officials and representatives indicate otherwise. The United States Department of Labor's International Religious Freedom Report consistently includes China as a country where people are punished for loving God in the "wrong manner."[18] The 2014 report discusses the sentencing of Zhang Shaojie, a prominent Christian leader, to 12 years in prison for his religious advocacy work. Other incidents involved the government-sanctioned removal of crosses and steeples from church buildings, while the most appalling cases resulted in the complete destruction of churches, in spite of the human shields created by church members. Government officials tried to explain away these actions by asserting that the buildings were illegal and in violation of local zoning ordinances. However, when church leaders attempted to continue their worship in outdoor services, officials arrested and held them and the service attendees for hours, days, and in some cases even years.

Christianity is not the only religion under attack in China. Monasteries of Tibetan Buddhists routinely face interference when conducting religious ceremonies. A prominent monk died in custody after being detained and severely beaten for allegedly possessing politically undesirable writings, along with recordings of the Dalai Lama. Similar abuse has also been used to target members and leaders of Falun Gong, a Taoist-Buddhist sect. Government officials even offered rewards to citizens who provided law enforcement with information about Falun Gong worshippers.

China's Muslim Uighurs also face attacks from the government, which portrays the religion as extremist terrorists. Originating from Xinjiang in northwestern China, members of this religion lean more toward the culture of Central Asia than that of China. The government views these cultural and religious differences as dangerous to the security of China, which leads to clashes and oppressive actions against these Muslims. At security checks, Uighur men are forced to turn over their cellphones so officials can check for religious materials. Children are not allowed inside mosques in an effort to discourage religious teaching of the young. Men are not allowed to grow lengthy beards, and women are prohibited from wearing traditional Muslim veils. In addition, no public commentary or criticism of these government actions is permitted.

India provides another example of state-sponsored religious oppression. Under the guise of protecting religious sentiments, the state arrested a Muslim cleric for speaking out against Hinduism.[19] Some Christians have also been targeted by violent attacks, and the government refuses to denounce these actions or take any action to prevent them. Christians who convert from Hinduism are violently forced to convert back. There are numerous reports of church arsons and Bible burnings, nuns being raped, and Christian girls being locked away.

Sudan ranks second on the list of nations with a poor human rights record. Its former leader, President Omar al-Bashir, is wanted by the International Criminal Court for crimes against his people. In an election that was far from free or fair, he was reelected despite national and international protests. During his regime, the people of Darfur were killed or severely injured during armed conflicts. Land and personal property were taken without compensation. Political activists were detained without trial, and protests were squashed with incredible violence. The government censored the media in an effort to restrict free thought, while women and girls faced constant fear of bodily violation as the number of rapes and sexual assaults continuously rose.[20]

Article XXVI of the Human Rights Declaration lists free education as a fundamental right. Yet, in South Sudan more than half of all children are not in school. More than 800 schools have been destroyed during violent conflicts, leaving hundreds of thousands of children without classrooms. Adding to an already significant problem is the government's reluctance to spend adequate funds on education. But this is not an issue reserved to Sudan. Globally, more than two million children are robbed of this basic right due to war and conflict. These little ones learn very early that their governments are not willing to protect their rights.

The Universal Declaration of Human Rights states in Article IX, "No one shall be subjected to arbitrary arrest, detention, or exile." Syrian leaders violate this article on a daily basis via arbitrary arrests with no cause or proof of wrongdoing. Torture is a regular occurrence in Syria, as are executions of detainees. The Syrian government has openly defied numerous U.N. Security Council resolutions by dropping chemicals on its citizens and killing thousands of civilians in aerial attacks.

Women and girls in Syria are particularly vulnerable to incredibly horrifying violations of human rights. They continuously face the possibility of sexual assault, forced marriages, and domestic violence, all of which are sanctioned or ignored by law enforcement. Failure to comply with the will of the family can lead to "honor killings," where girls and women are killed by their family members for marrying without the permission of their families. The Movement for Solidarity and Peace in Pakistan reports that on average 1,000 Christian and Hindu girls there are forced into marriages with Muslim men each year.[21]

A less-reported but deeply disturbing incidence of war is the rape of women and girls. Sexual violence has long been used as a weapon. Not only is it often seen as a perk by some soldiers, it is also a tool of intimidation and control over a specific group of the population. In addition to the physical injuries, victims must also deal with psychological and emotional stress from being sexually assaulted. Post-rape counseling that has been proven to work in developed nations is unavailable in third-world nations. Many women in these countries are shunned by their families because they were raped. The stigma is so burdensome that reporting agencies are unable to establish accurate statistics due to the unwillingness of victims to report these crimes.

While many states recognize a code of rules of wartime behavior, as established in the Geneva Convention, many rogue nations choose to ignore these standards as women and girls are repeatedly raped and tortured in the name of a cause. These incidents are especially prevalent in situations where the fighting is occurs among militias or privately trained "armies."[22] Though struggles in sub-Saharan Africa are most often associated with this problem, a report by the University of Minnesota demonstrates that rape is also prevalent in Asia, Eastern Europe, and Latin America. Rape not only impacts the victim but also leaves members of the community with a feeling of helplessness and insecurity, which adds to the overall anguish of living in a society without basic human rights.

Mental Health

The National Institutes of Health (NIH) conducted extensive research into the connection between war and psychological trauma in Africa. One study of Uganda shows significant levels of war-related trauma.[23] Psychological disorders such as depression and anxiety are among the most prevalent disorders. In addition, Briquet's syndrome, a somatic symptom disorder, a clinical complaint of symptoms without evidence of disease, impacts an overwhelming percentage of the affected population. A separate study of displaced Kenyans determined that 80% of household heads suffered from posttraumatic stress syndrome.[24]

This data proves a very real problem that exists among individuals struggling to survive in war-torn areas of the world. Living with the daily risk of violence and outside attack creates a stress that many more privileged individuals cannot even fathom. *The New York Times* printed a series of articles regarding displaced individuals around the world.[25] According to these articles, there are nearly 60 million people worldwide who have been displaced from their homes due to war. Most disturbing is that half of these individuals are children. In Lebanon, displaced children who once spent their days playing and attending school are now forced to rise before dawn and pick vegetables from fields outside of rural Syrian refugee settlements. Tents of nylon and wood barely provide shelter from the elements, and the weight of winter snow places them in constant fear of a collapsed roof. These children are constantly plagued with memories of fleeing as bullets flew through the air above their heads. Others recall being held hostage in their schools as they were forced to watch while soldiers cut off a man's head. As reported by *The New York Times*, more than two million children have been displaced from their homes, seeking safety and shelter in tents and abandoned houses. When your childhood memories are filled with thoughts of unthinkable inhumanity and violence, there is a lasting effect on your psyche and emotional well-being as an adult.

Corruption

A vast majority of people in the world live in countries where corruption is expected as a normal occurrence. A general definition of corruption is fraudulent action taken by government officials, such as demanding unlawful charges as bribes for services to which citizens are legally entitled. For example, while living as a teenager in Pakistan, I wanted a driver's license and went to the government office to apply for it. I spent all day getting the runaround, forced to move from one window to the next. I finally realized that government employees were only interested in collecting a bribe. Finally, frustrated, I gave up on getting a driver's license.

I could have paid an official to obtain the driver's license or sought one through a family acquaintance or friend. Instead, I decided to drive without a license, under the assumption that my father had enough clout to shield me from punishment should I get caught. Without even thinking that I was doing something obviously wrong, I took advantage of my father's influence to do an illegal act. Without giving it much thought, I knew I could break the law.

This is a very simple example of how a corrupt system of government leads to illegal activities. This corrosive mentality develops from an early age, instilling a deep belief that illegal behavior is acceptable. As an individual matures, the normal course of development is to learn the lesson of consequences, which decreases the willingness to act inappropriately. However, when you come of age in a corrupt society, you learn that breaking the law in most cases is the only option. This dangerous mentality grows as you enter your adult years, leading you to participate in the misconduct that surrounds you. The environment essentially forces people to become slaves of corruption and to act counter to the basic human desire to behave morally.

India was in the midst of substantial economic gains during the early 2000s. In a country where 600 million people live in poverty, outsourcing to India by prosperous countries created financial opportunities and promising economic development for the nation. Yet, actual growth has been far less than expected. Reforms and programs could not outrun the pace of rampant corruption throughout the government. Reports show that half of India's public welfare budget ends up in the overseas accounts of politicians and business owners.[26]

For the citizens who struggle to live their lives each day, this translates into a never-ending cycle of poverty and lack of basic necessities. Some 300 million Indians are without electricity because of the government's refusal to properly fund and maintain infrastructure. Even in an important urban area such as Delhi, the struggle for a decent life is a daily challenge. For example, the owner of a small takeout restaurant must pay bribes to numerous officials every month in order to carry on business.[27] Police officers demand 10,000 rupees a month, in addition to free meals, for permission to stay open late. Also, the owner must pay about 5,000 rupees per month to government officials who are supposed to ensure health and hygiene standards for the protection of citizens. In reality, all that is necessary to comply with the health standard is a pay-off. On a monthly basis, one is likely to spend a third of one's earnings on bribes to continue business. But the corruption doesn't stop there. Personal matters, like seeing a competent doctor or avoiding confrontation with traffic officers, also require the payment of bribes. Bribes are even required to get children educated at a "free" public school. In a corrupt society, obtaining basic necessities is subject to the greed of people in power.

Life in Ukraine, where residents live in the looming shadow of corruption, is not much better. Transparency International ranks this Eastern European nation high on its list of the most corrupt countries worldwide.[28] Over $12 billion disappear from the Ukrainian budget each year without explanation. Law enforcement and the judiciary appear unwilling or incapable of taking any action against businesses and government officials who enjoy financial benefits at the expense of the Ukrainian people. Politicians, business leaders, and judges collude to pad their offshore bank accounts. When corruption is reported, prosecutors refuse to bring charges or pursue investigations.

Ukrainians deal with corruption in their daily lives.[29] Bribery is necessary to enroll a child in school. To receive a court ruling in your favor, you must be prepared to pay the judge more than your opponent pays. Even earning a good grade in class can depend on your willingness and ability to pay a bribe. Corruption is a part of their lives from birth to death, and even the most earnest attempt at stopping it is in vain. These residents are forced to support corruption for survival.

Conclusion

Billions of people across the globe live in conditions where they are constantly subjected to mental, physical, and financial harm. While individuals living in the middle of war, terrorism, and corrupt governments are painfully aware of their daily struggles, most citizens of developed nations understand little about the overwhelming mental strife that these oppressed individuals must endure in their efforts to barely survive.

SOMETHING HAS TO BE DONE

2

"The time has come for an all-out world war against poverty. The rich nations must use their vast resources of wealth to develop the underdeveloped, school the unschooled, and feed the unfed. Ultimately a great nation is a compassionate nation."

—Martin Luther King Jr.

All of us must feel the struggles faced by some of us. If we do not change our current view of the world, the status quo will persist. The belief that we are all equal should eliminate feelings of hate toward others. Hatred is spread to create fear of others. Muslims hate Christians. Sunni Muslims hate Shia Muslims. Protestant Christians hate Catholic Christians. Whites hate blacks, and so on. We are all the same people. Our differences develop from our environments, not from our physical makeup. Hatred is manmade; coupled with fear, it drives the world to spend nearly $1.6 trillion ($1,600,000,000,000) on the military every year, killing thousands of people.[30]

U.S. President John F. Kennedy once said, "Mankind must put an end to war before war puts an end to mankind."[31] Just imagine the state of the world if military funding were spent on helping people instead of killing them. This type of redirection of funds would have an escalating positive effect on the lives of all humans. The people of the world need to revolt against this senseless spending and demand that it be used instead for the improvement of all human lives. When addressing the struggles of people in poor nations, it is not a question of lack of money; it is a question of how the money is used.

Something must be done. The concept of a global society has never been more relevant than it is at this stage in our history. The nations of the world are continually becoming more interconnected and interdependent. Advancements in transportation, communication, and the economy are accelerating this trend. With air travel, you can be on the other side of the world in less than a day. International trade, borrowing, and investments promote a global economy where the finances of individual nations are directly and indirectly dependent on one another. But the most monumental influence on the evolution of a global society is the expansion of the Internet around the globe. According to a study by the United Nations, more than three billion people across the world regularly use the Internet. Internet use has increased more than 300% within the last 15 years, and the numbers are only likely to keep growing as access to technology continues to expand into less-developed areas of the world. So how does this growth in Internet usage apply to the concept of a global economy?

The world is becoming a much smaller place. Those of us living in developed countries can no longer ignore the pain that billions of people are forced to endure on a daily basis. Long gone are the days when we relied on the evening news to learn about the struggles of living in abject poverty or the horror of trying to survive under the constant threat of terrorist activity. We no longer need the Sunday paper to explain the travesty of corruption and disregard for human rights. We now live in a time where Internet access brings these shocking and disturbing realities right into our homes, complete with pictures, videos, and even live-stream. We live in a world where there is no justification for ignorance.

For individuals living in developing nations, Internet access offers an awareness like never before. Previous mysteries of everyday life in America and Europe have given way to up-to-date knowledge. The privileged lives that many of us are lucky enough to live are now widely known, resulting in a variety of positive and negative consequences. For example, while people in oppressive and corrupt countries have undoubtedly always been aware of their challenges, learning about the advantage of life in developed nations further salts their wounds. On the upside, they start dreaming of better conditions and greater opportunities. On the downside, this new awareness increases dissatisfaction and leads to revolts and uprisings, much like those the world witnessed during the Arab Spring.

We need to start looking at the whole world as one global society. I dream of a world where we can travel to any place, live in any place, have property rights in any place, and openly conduct business in any place. Imagine the economic activity that could take place if the resources of the world could be leveraged freely and comprehensively.

As unique as this hope may sound, in Pakistan I met a Caucasian farming family from Winnipeg, Canada, who were pursuing this dream. The family moved to Pakistan to purchase land at a lower price than in Canada. With their farming knowledge, they could grow more crops in Pakistan's fertile land and warmer climate. After trying diligently for over a year, the family packed up and went back to Canada. Their plan ultimately fell flat because they did not understand the challenges of running a Pakistani business. Their failure was caused by their inability and/or unwillingness to participate in the bureaucratic corruption that is necessary to sustain any business in Pakistan.

If we lived in a truly open global economy, the outcome might have been different for that Canadian family. They would have been given a fair and equal opportunity to succeed in their endeavors, which could have benefited Pakistani workers, the local economy, and by extension the country as a whole. If we could create a truly open global economy, opportunities would abound for the entire population of the world. Think about how many innovative thinkers, creators, and potential entrepreneurs are stifling in many areas of the world, with no opportunity to succeed or even dream of success. Lack of opportunity for some affects each one of us because we are missing out on their potential contributions and talents. The cure for cancer could be buried in the mind of a young girl who is fighting for her life in Sudan. An oppressed boy in Iraq may have the solution to end world hunger. An orphan in Syria could hold the key to unlimited space travel. There are no limits to the amount of talent that exists in these oppressed areas of the world, but if we continue to do nothing, it will continue to go to waste.

Even if we fail to acknowledge it, our connection with the rest of the world is evident when we examine past and current global economics. When some nations prosper from liberty and opportunity, other countries benefit. The opposite is also true when countries struggle and fail. Economists point to the shifting to the left of the aggregate demand curve caused by a decrease in consumption as the main culprit for recessions and depressions.

For example, the struggles that faced the United States during the Great Depression did not solely remain within its borders. Every continent on Earth felt the effects of this historic economic downfall. As the United States struggled to adequately handle a gross domestic product (GDP) that dropped by over half in four years, the rest of the world was also struggling. International trade fell sharply during this period, and national leaders tried to protect their financial interests by raising tariffs on goods imported from other countries.[32] Manufacturing not only fell sharply within the United States but also severely declined in other countries—for example, by 40% in Germany and 29% in France.[33] One financial crisis led to the next as world trade virtually collapsed.

After the 1931 closing of Australia's largest bank, people all across Europe rushed to withdraw their funds from their banks. The sudden high withdrawal rates caused even some of the wealthiest banks to fail, creating more problems for the European economies. Germany was unable to continue making payments on debts incurred during World War I, which placed a greater hardship on the countries that depended on those payments. Great Britain took the extreme measure of changing its currency and removing it from the gold standard in an effort to manipulate its value within the world economy.

International politics also shifted in response to America's Great Depression. Latin America was a major provider of raw materials to manufacturers within the U.S. As American businesses purchased fewer commodities from Latin American countries, jobs and financial opportunities significantly decreased. The citizens of these countries blamed the government, which led to social unrest. Instead of reasonably reacting to the concerns of the people, these governments created military-led dictatorships to quash the protests and maintain social order.[34]

Germany, Italy, and Japan reacted to the Depression with increased fascism. Adolph Hitler promised to rebuild Germany's economy and military forces. Japanese militarists took over government control and conquered parts of coastal China to end their country's economic depression. In Russia, Stalin used totalitarian communism to implement a collective economy.

European nations such as Great Britain and France relied on welfare capitalism to support their economies, and the majority of Europe recovered faster than the U.S. and Canada. However, some countries, especially Germany, continued to struggle for years following the Great Depression. As American banks withdrew their loans from Germany, unemployment skyrocketed, affecting more than 29 million residents. Banks were forced to close, causing people to lose their entire life savings and investments. Local businesses were unable to keep their doors open, and inflation drastically devalued German currency. Evictions occurred on a daily basis, and the simple task of buying food became virtually impossible. These extreme economic conditions led to widespread dissatisfaction and political unrest among the German people. History has shown us that these types of political situations open the door for extremists to gain power. When Hitler took control of the fledgling Nazi party, he built his support by appealing to the concerns and fears of the struggling working class. He convinced most Germans that their problems were caused by Jews in the country. The Nazi party leveraged the nation's instability to gain power and place Jews under years of unthinkable oppression and torture.

History is repeating itself and dangerous extremist groups are gaining control in vulnerable and poverty-stricken areas of the world due to the fears and concerns of the people. The Taliban and ISIS perfectly exemplify the types of organizations that can thrive in nations where individuals are struggling for survival due to poor governance, corruption, and oppression. When the Taliban began organizing, Afghanistan was a country broken by constant war among factions. In 1979, the Soviet Union invaded Afghanistan, sending thousands of troops to take over significant sections of the country. It was the Soviet Union's first time

invading a country outside the Eastern Bloc. Their intention was to secure and support the People's Democratic Party of Afghanistan in the
wake of a growing insurgency that threatened to give the United States a
stronghold in the country. At the height of the war, the Soviet Union had
more than 100,000 troops in Afghanistan. Since the Russians were backing the Communist party, a resistance army led by clerics erupted to
safeguard Islamic religious practices. Since the United States wanted to
curtail Russian influence and stop the spread of communism, it funded
and provided arms to these religious and fundamentalist Islamic clerics.
The movement was also supported by Iran, China, and Pakistan for their
regional political interests. Pakistan was directly involved as the main
ally of the U.S., channeling U.S. aid and arms to the Afghan mujahideen
(freedom fighters) and providing them with supply lines, training, and
refuge. In 1989, the Soviet troops were forced to withdraw from Afghanistan, leaving the country in the midst of a violent and deadly civil war.

During the war, thousands of Afghans left the country. Many worked
together to create organized freedom-fighter groups that evolved into
the Taliban, now categorized as a terrorist group. They set up madrasahs
(religious boarding schools) that were partially financed by Saudi Arabia and the United States. Thousands of children were educated in these
schools, away from their families and local communities. They were
taught obedience and conservatism that specifically excluded Western
ideals and customs. As these students aged, they were forced to fight for
the goals of the Taliban.[35] As civil war continued to ravage Afghanistan,
Taliban leaders used the struggles of the people to secure a foothold.
With promises to eradicate corruption and crime, Taliban leaders were
able to grow membership in the organization substantially. In November 1994, Taliban troops captured the capital city of Kabul. Most Kabul
residents sided with the Taliban, hoping to reduce corruption and crime.
The Taliban continued to spread its message, and by 2001, it controlled
more than 90% of Afghanistan.

The rise of ISIS follows a similar pattern. During the past 14 years,
the United States has spent upwards of $6 trillion on both the Iraq and
Afghan wars, making them the longest and costliest wars in U.S. history.
The U.S.'s stated objective in these conflicts was to secure democracy.
The rationale was that by forcing our way into someone's house, remov-

ing who we perceived to be the bad guy, and convincing the remaining inhabitants that democracy was the best, democracy would somehow take hold. It hasn't. It never will without a proper structure that protects individual rights and justice for all. Neither of those wars has established a successful democracy in the region. People are still suffering. Power is still frequently out. Water is still not clean. All that remains are the ashes of hope, which opens the door for the expansion of membership in extremist organizations.

ISIS began with the establishment of Al-Qaeda in Iraq (AQI) in 2004 by a leading jihadist insurgent protesting the continuous occupation of Iraq by American troops.[36] Sunni tribesmen began attacking and killing AQI members, prompting leaders to rename the organization the Islamic State of Iraq (ISI). Though its influence seemed to dwindle over the next few years, the organization reemerged around 2011 as U.S. troop presence surged in Iraq. The organization's leaders used instability in Iraq and Syria to gain support and carry out attacks.[37] In 2013, upon merging with an Al-Qaeda affiliate within Syria, the group changed its name to Islamic State in Iraq and Greater Syria (ISIS). The group ramped up its recruiting efforts, reaching more than 50,000 members within the borders of Syria. Leaders then began reaching beyond Iraq and Syria to influence individuals in many parts of the world.

A large part of their successful recruiting efforts are video productions. These videos promise to provide viewers with reward and purpose. They play on the fears of potential members and make them feel as though they will become a part of something larger and more significant than themselves. The success of these recruitment efforts is troubling. Some reports hypothesize that the group recruits 20 new members every day, with substantial numbers from Turkey, France, and the United Kingdom.

ISIS has also figured out a way to capitalize on the struggles and oppression of Islamic women. Leaders recruit women with offers of a devout marriage, even setting up marriage centers in some areas where women can register to become married to a jihadist. Marriage isn't the only option for a woman in modern terrorist organizations. An increasing number of women are being recruited as suicide bombers.[38] Some terrorist leaders use the concept of "feminine honor" to lure women into these positions. Sexual purity remains an extremely important virtue in many Middle Eastern countries. Women who had sex outside of marriage due to rape are viewed as disgraceful. They, along with their families, are shamed by their communities and treated as outcasts. Suicide martyrdom is presented as a way of restoring honor to themselves and their families.

Terrorist organizations thrive in countries where people are oppressed, unprotected, poor, and struggling for survival. Individuals who feel weak and sick experience a sense of camaraderie and protection within these groups. Terrorist organizations rise to power and stay there by filling in the gaps that governments leave open. They build schools in areas the state has ignored. They open hospitals for the sick and build housing for the poor. In exchange for these services, they successfully gain the loyalty of the people, who see them as heroes. While I don't condone the actions of these groups, I understand that many hold a deep-seated belief that what they are doing is right for themselves and their people. Their supporters view them as Robin Hood figures, defending their people from the corruption of their political leaders. Remember that desperate people will take desperate action. For example, I met a Syrian doctor living in the United States who visits Syria about four times a year to treat victims of war. I asked him why they continued fighting when it is causing so many civilian atrocities. His answer was, "We are fighting for justice, and it is more important to us than our lives."

Another common way for terrorist organizations to gain support and expand their respective agendas is through religion. As U.S. President Barack Obama once said, "People cling to guns and religion under desperation." Lack of opportunity for people causes them to find solace in religion and religious organizations. For residents of prosperous nations, it is mind-boggling to see terrorists blowing themselves up and killing countless numbers of innocent people. We wonder how religion can be used to promote such levels of violence. Religion provides comfort, and people in desperation are always looking for comfort. It's similar to a support group, where you feel as though you share common beliefs and challenges. In most cases, religious comfort is positive and productive, but sometimes it can become a support group that is akin to a criminal gang. People join such religious groups because of desperation caused by their unmet physiological and psychological needs. These distressing conditions can lead them to commit violent acts against their oppressors.

Religion and terrorism come together because these people have no hope for their lives. Even though it does not feed their families right away, religion gives people hope that they will live in paradise in the afterlife. A large part of jihadist recruitment involves the concept of martyrdom. Recruits are shown videos featuring statements of commitment by jihadists who are about to take part in a suicide attack. These videos are embellished with music and sentimental messages. The videos manipulate the words of the Qur'an to justify suicide bombings and spread the message that martyrdom and killing innocent civilians is a holy sacrifice.

Some of these suicide bombers live in countries that have experimented with pseudodemocracy, resulting in increased corruption and poverty. These people are left with no expectation that any type of democratic system would enable them to live a normal life. Our environment impacts our thinking, and living in an oppressed society under destitute conditions leads to drastic acts. For these people, without hope, desperation creates the drive to validate their existence. The only thing they feel they have control over is making a name for themselves in the afterlife, even if it means blowing themselves up. Some people are so fed up with their poverty-stricken lives and their inability to take care of their families and live peacefully that they resort to violence in the name of religion. Not only does it give them some sense of achievement and validation of their existence, but it can also provide food for their families. Many organizations provide funds to the surviving family members of suicide bombers.

Religion and violence have had a longstanding connection throughout history. Many great tragedies occurred due to misuse of religion. While the religion itself is not the primary driving force behind the violence, terrorists consistently use it to justify their actions and recruit new members.

In America, the Ku Klux Klan led a decades-long reign of terror throughout the southern states. Established during the U.S. Civil War, the organization touted a Protestant Christian ideology as its members engaged in lynching, arson, murder, rape, destruction of property, and vast intimidation. Their terrorist ways targeted African Americans, Jewish Americans, and other ethnic minorities. Leaders often proclaimed that Jesus was the first member of the organization. They were known for burning crosses, which was a method of intimidation but also a religious symbol. Members often congregated around a burning cross to pray and sing Christian hymns. Though the organization is no longer as visible as it once was, the Klan continues to operate within the United States.

The National Liberation Front of Tripura was formed in 1989 for the purpose of creating a Christian nation independent of India. Backed and financially supported by the Baptist Church of Tripura, the organization made death threats to Hindus in 2000 as they celebrated their religious festival. This militant group is accused of funding other terrorist organizations, while terrorizing non-Christian citizens of India. It is also accused of forcing the conversion of entire tribes to Christianity at gunpoint and opening fire on Hindu worshippers.[39] Some reports state that the organization is responsible for 1,000 murders of Hindus since its inception.

Boko Haram terrorizes the residents of Nigeria with the goal of establishing an extremist Islamic state. This Sunni Islamic fundamentalist sect champions a version of Islamic belief that forbids Muslims from taking part in any Western educational, political, or social activities, including wearing Western clothing. It spreads the belief that the Nigerian government causes the corruption and poverty because it is being led by nonbelievers who are not governing according to Islam. The group asserts that its violent attacks are required to promote the enforcement of Islamic laws within the country.[40] Since its inception, Boko Haram has killed more than 20,000 people, tortured thousands more, and displaced millions from their homes. In 2012, the organization burned down 12 public schools in the span of one night, leaving thousands of children without a place to learn.

Like other terrorist organizations, Boko Haram takes advantage of the grief and oppression felt by its target recruits. It uses religion to offer some commonality and feelings of community. The organization frequently recruits poor high school and university students, as well as destitute children. In 2004, numerous students from Borno and Yobe tore up their school certificates and joined the organization in protest.[41] The group uses religion in its recruitment endeavors, manipulating the principals of Islam to meet its needs and attract new members. It also takes advantage of the rampant poverty and unemployment that devastate the country.

Our emotions drive us. A person suffering from poverty and insecurity is in pain and looks for anything that can ease their suffering or at least make it more bearable. Religion provides solace to most people especially those who are hurting. These violent groups believe that using religion is the only option they have to fight injustice and end poverty. The violence never succeeds in the long run, but the attention that these groups gain through the use of violence is undeniable.

These people are suffering due to the injustice of their governments. Through religious terrorism, they are trying to fight back against the injustice of their rulers. Since they have no hope of getting justice through proper channels of government or law enforcement, they take the law into their own hands and resort to violence. The most extreme way to make a statement is to kill people, including oneself.

My dream is, with your help, to solve the issues that lead to terrorist actions like suicide bombings. But we need to understand that this is not a new concept. Martin Luther King Jr. said that it is better to die from physical death than psychological death. "If physical death is the price that some must pay to free their children and their white brothers from an eternal psychological death, then nothing can be more redemptive."[42]

The only way for nations to adequately fight these forces is with just and moral governing strategies. Ringing the bell of democracy is inadequate without extensive structural changes enforcing checks and balances. What better examples than Syria and Iraq? Both have dipped their toes into the pool of democracy but failed to eliminate the corruption that continues to run rampant within their borders. Within a few short years, both countries were rocked by attacks from thuggish terrorist groups. Weak governance invites terrorist organizations to come in and influence members of society. Without a strong government to protect the state, it will surely fail.

Thomas Hobbes talked about this in his *Leviathan* (1651). The social contract that exists between people and government must be one in which the people give up certain freedoms to ensure tranquility and peace, which is provided by their government. His argument lies in a person's natural tendency to be self-interested but rational. In order to live within a civil society, a person is willing to submit to authority. However, if their needs are not being met by that governmental authority, their self-interest takes over and they seek other ways to obtain what they need to fulfill that interest. This is exactly the behavior we are witnessing right now in our world, and it shows why *something has to be done.*

In the United States, slavery represents one of the most shameful eras in American history. Each of the large-scale problems that currently plague the majority of the world's population was present within this state-sanctioned, institutionalized system of forced labor. Slave owners compelled slaves to live in abject poverty, with nothing but the bare basics that some masters chose to provide. The destitution of slavery was so extreme that it has impacted generations of African Americans, even after slavery was abolished.

Slaves and even free African Americans within the South lived in constant fear of terrorist behavior. If their actions were not in line with their master's expectation, they were mercilessly beaten. Plantation overseers used whips and dogs to control the slaves and force them into the fields, where they worked from sunup until sundown, performing painful work. Discipline could come in a variety of harsh ways, including genital mutilation, imprisonment, or branding. In the act of branding,[43] as summarized by Frederick Douglass, who escaped slavery and became a leader in the abolitionist movement, the slave was tied to a post and a red-hot iron was applied to the quivering flesh. Those who tried to escape were lynched and left to hang from a tree as a warning to others. The daily life of a slave in the American South was marked with agony, torment, and torture at the hands of people who were basically domestic terrorists. White men assembled and marched with their muskets to intimidate slaves and suppress thoughts of escape. Slaves lived in constant fear of family members being sold away to other plantations. Babies and children were permanently separated from their parents at the owner's whim. Given this, many slaves worked tirelessly to please their slave owners and thus remain under the radar.

Despite America's Bill of Rights, the human rights of slaves were routinely violated without shame or apology. These people were stripped of their identities and punished for speaking their native languages. Practicing their native religion resulted in beatings, and masters forced their conversion to Christianity, which was ironically used to justify the conditions they were forced to live under. Rape was a common occurrence on plantations, where female slaves were forced to have sex with their masters and overseers. Owners used their authority to threaten slaves if they didn't obey. Even young girls were subjected to this violence and forced to bear their master's children. Owners routinely used rape as a tool for replenishing the slave labor pool once the importing of additional slaves was outlawed.

Though there were small movements to abolish slavery throughout the years, its continuation was often justified by economics. Slave labor was the basis of the Southern agricultural industry. Plantation owners capitalized on free slave labor and argued that abolition would destroy the entire country's economy with the collapse of both the cotton and tobacco industries. Cotton was a major export for the United States, which further supported the economic argument for slavery. Without free labor, the supply would diminish and this highly profitable business would cease.

As the South continued to make its claims, there was a growing sentiment against the institution of slavery in the North. An increasing number of influential people began to speak out against the moral wrongs of slavery, with evangelicals stressing the immorality of the institution. The arguments of these radical abolitionists differed from existing sentiments, which centered on gradual emancipation and the restriction of slavery to the Southern states. The new arguments against slavery called for immediate emancipation of all slaves, along with the prohibition of segregation and discrimination. Abolitionists began publishing their sentiments widely in newspapers and setting up antislavery chapters throughout the North. As these moral arguments gained traction, Southern slave supporters began to change their arguments and attempted to characterize slavery as a good practice in the best interests of the slaves themselves. Owners declared that the slaves were happy, asserting that they were living in better conditions than factory workers in the North.

The sentiments of Northern abolitionists continuously spread as speakers grew in popularity and antislavery literature circulated among the states. Abolitionists took positions of power within the community, establishing churches and founding schools. This growth in the private realm spilled into politics, with government officials feeling pressure from antislavery supporters. Nevertheless, President Abraham Lincoln tolerated the institution of slavery, as long as it did not spread into the new western settlements of the United States. It was only the seriousness of the Southern succession and the burden of the Civil War that finally compelled the federal government to take necessary actions to end such a tragic time in history. Lincoln legally abolished slavery on January 1, 1863, when he signed the Emancipation Proclamation. It was not until June 19, 1865, that the Union soldiers brought word to the last enslaved people that they were finally free.

The compassion and morality that drove the push to end slavery is the same level of commitment that we need when looking at the current plight of other human beings around the globe. We must recognize their value and stand up for their rights with the same level of devotion we would give to standing up for the rights of our relatives and neighbors. It's time that we extend our compassion beyond the limited borders of our homes, communities, and nations to develop a sense of responsibility for every human being across the globe. If we all work collectively toward the benefit of every individual, we will elevate the entire human population so we can all rise together.

When we remove constraints on human liberty and pursuit of happiness, we liberate people to contribute to making the world a better place. In the generations following the abolition of slavery, African Americans made significant contributions not only to the United States but to the entire world. Advancements in science, art, and medicine all sprang from the minds of people who were once oppressed and abused. We need only refer to the example of African Americans to appreciate the untapped potential of individuals who continue to feel the chains of persecution and tyranny. Given the opportunity, these people can and will contribute to the good of society. We need to work together as a global community to raise the majority of the world's population out of lives of limited freedom within corrupt societies. We would all benefit from their contributions and economic participation.

We are doing ourselves a major disservice if we fail to expand our horizons and look beyond our immediate families, tribes, and countrymen. In her book *Twelve Steps to a Compassionate Life*, Karen Armstrong states, "One of the chief tasks of our time must surely be to build a global community in which all peoples can live together with mutual respect; yet religion, which should be making a major contribution, is seen as part of the problem. All faiths insist that compassion is the test of true spirituality and that it brings us into relation with the transcendence we call God, Brahman, Nirvana, or Dao. Each has formulated its own version of what is sometimes called the Golden Rule, 'Do not treat others as you would not like them to treat you,' or in its positive form, 'Always treat others as you would wish to be treated yourself.' Further, they all insist that you cannot confine your benevolence to your own group; you must have concern for everybody—even your enemies."[44]

In order to fulfill the possibility of a truly global society, we must extend our compassion to everyone around the world.

In his "Letter from Birmingham Jail," Martin Luther King Jr. wrote, "Injustice anywhere is a threat to justice everywhere. We are caught in an inescapable network of mutuality, tied in a single garment of destiny. Whatever affects one directly, affects all indirectly." These eloquent words still ring true, exemplifying the bond that exists between us all, a bond that must compel us to act on behalf of our brothers and sisters.

I Have a Dream

Just like Martin Luther King Jr., I have a dream that we will love all human beings and will commit ourselves to their well-being. We will love all other human beings and will commit ourselves to their well-being.

We will love even the people we consider our enemies. Hate creates enemies, and once we begin to love everyone, we will no longer have enemies.

We will show compassion and love for all human beings and understand that no human being was born a bad person. It is because of circumstances, upbringing, and environment that people behave in negative ways.

We will believe that providing justice and rights to all human beings is not a zero-sum game. As we relieve some people from suffering, we will lift all people.

People who believe in God, and the justice of God, will believe that God would not create a human being inferior to anybody else just because of their race.

Just as King said, we need to relieve people living in the first world of a false sense of superiority and help people residing in the third world overcome the false sense of inferiority because of their circumstances. We understand the physical fact that all human beings underneath the skin have the same biology, and all the components of their bodies function the same way. We are all the same people with differences in skin color only to protect us from our environment.

We will not resort to violence as a way to solve problems. We believe that violence creates more violence. Just as treating a child violently because of bad behavior will most likely have negative results, using violence to solve problems will not lead to positive results, especially if the act is embedded in hatred.

We will see all other human beings as human resources. When all human resources are put into action, the entire human race will benefit. All human beings make up the human race, which is an interconnected system. Anytime you constrain one part of the system, the whole system is constrained. Whenever we lose one individual's contribution by limiting their potential, we are reducing the benefit of their contribution to our human race.

Instead of framing the future in expectations of gloom and doom based on religious thoughts of the apocalyptic destruction of the world, we will start believing that we can make this world a much better place with a plan for positivity. From the beginning of time, religious leaders and philosophers have made predictions about the end of the world and the destruction of humanity. I suggest that we focus on the teachings of our religions that drive us to help others. We should act now so that no one is suffering because of our inaction.

We will believe in the opposite of Armageddon—the "Peacegeddon."
We become what we believe, so let us believe that we can have a better world together. Let's believe that we can create a world of love where we don't hate anyone. Instead of limiting ourselves to success and survival, we will rise to a place where we care about improving the lives of others more than our own. This is no different than a business philosophy that focuses on improving customer satisfaction in order to succeed. As we all want a better life, we have to believe that we have a much better chance of achieving it by helping others rather than just focusing on improving our own lives.

Together we will create a new world order where every human being is dedicated to the success of all other people, regardless of race, religion, country, continent, or language. We will understand that we don't need allegiance just to our countrymen; we need devotion to all human beings because we're all in this together. As with any group, individual selfish behavior brings down the whole group; we need to stop being selfish and start caring for all humans as part of our group.

Believe and understand that we have more than enough resources. If we are ready to share, we will have tremendous opportunities for all to grow together and create a world where we all feel good about our actions and our lives. Just imagine a world where we wake up every day loving everyone and understanding that we are here to benefit others. Once we are engaged in others' problems, we will forget our own problems.

How we define our lives will be driven by how we feel at any point in time. Our feelings are driven by our experiences and our environment. For example, two people who eat three meals a day and have a place to sleep may have extremely different views of their lives if the first person is living freely and the other person is living in jail. Our feeling is enhanced when we have the freedom to focus our energies on helping others. This creates a tremendous feeling of well-being.

Why We Need to Act Now!

In his book *Thank You for Being Late*, Thomas L. Friedman analyzes the state of the world. He believes that three major issues will have the biggest impact on the near future of our globe.

- ▶ Technology, specifically the Internet
- ▶ Population growth
- ▶ Climate change

Technology

Technology, specifically the Internet, has significantly broadened individual capability to learn about other nations. According to Friedman, when people see their lack of freedom, they become increasingly frustrated with their circumstances. He states that the Internet provides the option for people to share their frustrations. He explains that, though struggling people want freedom from their country's shortcomings, they don't know where they want that freedom to lead them. He uses recent political revolutions, such as the Arab Spring, to support his point. The people who took part in these movements were frustrated and motivated enough to demand freedom from their situation, but they weren't clear about what that freedom would look like.

Another example of technology empowering ordinary people to do something is the ease of joining radicalized groups or even resorting to individual violence. This is evident in the widespread accessibility of improvised explosive devices (IEDs). These homemade bombs have been used to kill more than 3,100 people and injure more than 33,000.[45] The United States military has spent billions of dollars trying to fight a technology that is easily accessed by frustrated individuals.

Another example of technology empowering ordinary people to do great harm is the undetected drone flying onto the White House lawn. In 2015, a small drone was discovered on the White House grounds, where it had crashed into a tree. The incident caused security concerns because the drone had entered the secure grounds undetected by White House security. Safety officials questioned whether a widely accessible device could potentially harm the president. Another concern Friedman has about the Internet is that along with the power it provides for individuals to do good, this technology also amplifies a person's ability to cause destruction. He categorizes these types of groups as makers and breakers. He asserts that the breakers are able to find devastating technology on the Internet. We have no control over what information they access or how they might use it to harm large numbers of people.

Population Growth

In his discussion of population growth, Friedman shares the surprising fact that within his lifetime the population of the world increased from three billion to over seven billion, and it will soon reach nine billion—all within his lifetime. It took over 200,000 years of human history for the world's population to reach one billion and only 200 years more to reach seven billion.

Friedman contends that poor people in developing countries believe in having many children as financial assurance for survival. These families are often forced to deal with high mortality rates, so they feel compelled to have numerous children to make certain that they will have offspring to care for them during their elder years.[46] This is partly why birthrates tend to decrease as individuals move out of poverty. Without the challenges of extreme poverty, these families have more confidence in the survival of their children, so they no longer feel it necessary to have as many. The bottom line is that population growth is creating an increased population tilt toward people who are poor. The United Nations estimates that Africa's population will double by 2050. More than 400 million of these new people will reside in Nigeria.[47] Experts believe that these increases could potentially erode current efforts aimed at reducing poverty and protecting the planet.[48] The population of Asia nearly quadrupled during the twentieth century. Asia makes up 60% of the world's total population and continues to experience the highest rate of growth globally. This growth created substantial strain on resources, which culminated in high poverty levels. Though many Asian countries have made strides in reducing poverty levels, there are still more than 700 million people living in poverty in Asia.

Climate Change

Climate change is another issue altering our world. Friedman shows that, due to drought in many African countries, villagers who were once able to feed themselves through local agriculture are no longer able to sustain themselves and live in their villages. As a result, more and more people in drought-ridden African nations are moving to the cities. As they arrive in the cities, they encounter scarce employment and financial opportunities. Out of necessity, they look toward migration to prosperous countries. According to the United Nations, 244 million migrants are living worldwide. The migrant crisis is a huge problem that is not going to get better. In 2015 alone, the International Organization for Migration estimates that more than 1.3 million migrants arrived in Europe by sea and land.

The combination of the power of technology, tremendous growth in world population, and climate change are extraordinary problems that are not being addressed systematically. These enormous challenges reaffirm why *something has to be done*. We cannot continue using violence and force as our first option for addressing these problems.

Conclusion

Something must be done to ensure that all people are afforded their most basic human rights. The widespread growth of the Internet will continue to stoke the flames of dissatisfaction over the failure of corrupt governments to meet the needs of the people. Regardless of where we live in the world, when we do not consider everyone to be a valuable resource, we miss important opportunities to end injustice and create better standards of life for the world's population. Issues such as population growth, migration, and climate change will continue to exacerbate these problems, further illustrating the importance of taking action now.

WHY NATIONS FAIL

3

"Democracy is not freedom. Democracy is two wolves and a lamb voting on what to eat for lunch. Freedom comes from the recognition of certain rights which may not be taken, not even by a 99% vote."

—Marvin Simkin

There is no shortage of opinions and theories about why some nations fail while others prosper. This chapter examines several of these explanations, using real-world examples to demonstrate why I refer to them as myths instead of actual causes for the failing of a nation.

As of 2017, there are 196 countries in the world and the vast majority of them are failing, with horrific levels of poverty, unpunished crime, and rampant government corruption. When political experts attempt to analyze the causes of these problems, they usually come up with the same general reasons. The most prevailing theory asserts that a lack of democracy prevents the formation of a successfully functioning nation. However, global history abounds with historical and modern-day examples of democracies that have failed miserably to protect and support their citizens. Failing countries represent the entire spectrum of government formations, from dictatorships and monarchies to anarchies and democracies. Experts also seek to explain the situation by pointing to circumstances including inadequate education, insufficient resources,

overpopulation, and cultural or religious tensions. But all of these explanations fall short of the real problem. They are just widely held myths,
unsupported by fact or statistical data. Let's examine some of them to
better understand how I have reached this conclusion.

The Myth of Democracy

People living under a dictatorship often assume that if their government
were replaced with democracy, it would be more successful in meeting
the needs of its citizens. There is a widespread misconception that democracy is the sole answer to the struggles of people everywhere. While
the underlying principles of democracy can advance a more just society,
it is not an effective governmental system *in and of itself*, without additional structures in place to regulate the actions of all citizens equitably.
Most people have huge misconceptions about the effectiveness of democracy. The protests of the Egyptian people during the Arab Spring is
one recent example of this mistaken belief. Though Egypt successfully
ended a 30-year regime of dictatorial rule and held democratic elections,
the nation is no better at meeting the daily challenges of life than it was
under the authoritarian rule of former president Hosni Mubarak. Corruption continues to exist within the government, and individual rights
continue to be violated at the leadership's whim.[49] The country is presently operating under a system that many international scholars refer to
as a "managed democracy," in which formal procedures of democracy
are in place but one centralized regime still controls the nation. Egypt is
only one example of a failed democratic system. These managed democracies exist across the globe.

Let's look at India, considered the largest democracy in the world.
For most of its existence, India was governed under imperialism, where
familial dynasties maintained political control throughout multiple generations. In the mid-eighteenth century, European colonization placed
the citizens of India in the grip of colonial rule, where they remained
until 1947, when they gained independence as the individual nations of
India and Pakistan. This change in government ushered in a system of
democracy. In India, the national political parties put forth their candidates and elections are held for members of Parliament. The prime

minister is nominated by the party holding the majority in Parliament. The country's national government is divided into three branches, the executive, the legislative, and the judicial. The legislative branch is parliamentary, consisting of the Upper House, the Lower House, and the House of the People. Indian officials assert that the state is secular, with no state-sponsored religion. Citizens are theoretically free to practice any religion of their choice.

While these systems give the appearance that the democratization of India was good for its people, it is still a failing nation. Despite significant growth in the country's GDP, many of its citizens continue to live in abject poverty, with inadequate housing, insufficient healthcare, and a lack of educational opportunities. According to the country's 2011 Socioeconomic and Caste Census, a vast majority of India's more than one billion citizens live in financially struggling rural villages. More than half of all Indians reside in inadequate shelters, without working toilets or access to clean water. They cannot even earn enough income to pay taxes to the government. More than 85% of the villages do not provide their children with an education beyond elementary school. The country also has an enormous unemployment problem, and it is consistently embroiled in one type of corruption scandal or another. Hundreds of thousands of children live on the streets of India, and more than 90 million citizens earn less than a dollar a day.[50] For the people of India, who must live in these circumstances every day, the presence of a democratic government does nothing to alleviate their overwhelming struggles.

One reason for this failure is the lasting legacy of colonialism that plagues many countries around the world to this day. When colonialism ended, the new leaders of these countries took on the manners and techniques of governing employed by their former British colonial leaders. They moved into large and luxurious mansions and began living under the same system of extraordinary privilege. They continued with platoons of servants and conducted themselves in an entitled manner, as if their lives were more valuable than those of the people they governed. These leaders implemented methods of command and control, taking control of the nation's resources for their personal benefit, similar to the tactics used by their former colonial masters. This extension of colonial-inspired leadership helped develop and advance acts of corruption through human exploitation and repression. After living under these conditions for so long, many leaders and citizens had normalized these behaviors and accepted them as routine aspects of government, undermining and contradicting the basic principles of democracy—government for the people, by the people, and of the people.

In an article published in the *Times of India*, journalist John Elliott refers to democracy as "a fig leaf to cover India's failures."[51] He theorizes that government officials use democracy as a scapegoat, blaming it for the country's vast and plentiful failures. Opposing political parties are blamed for consistently delayed policy changes, which manifest as lagging economic development and a government that is ineffective at protecting and providing for its citizens. According to Elliott, democracy is also used as a cover-up for corruption and criminal activity throughout the Indian government. But his view of democracy, in general, is not one of blanket negativity. He recognizes the value of a democratic government as an outlet for citizens to complain and make changes in the country's leadership. Yet in India, as in so many other nations, the ability to protest is not enough to rescue the country from generations of failure.

Likewise, the political history of neighboring Pakistan exemplifies the myth of democracy as a solution to the problems of failing nations. Ironically, some historians point to ancient Pakistan as one of the world's earliest examples of democracy. The Indus Valley Civilization existed from about 5000 BC until 1500 BC. Geographically, it extended from northeastern Afghanistan into Pakistan and over to northwestern India. The highly organized system of governance within this civilization, along with what some historical experts see as a sophisticated rule of law, has led many historians to credit ancient Pakistan with one of the earliest models of modern-day democracy. Even with its rich history, the people of Pakistan have never since lived under a system where democracy and the rule of law work together for the benefit of all citizens.

When Pakistan was first established as a nation-state in 1947, Muhammad Ali Jinnah, the nation's first governor general, sought to have democratic principles as the driving force of its new government. But political conflicts quickly frustrated the goal of a democratic system, leaving the people of Pakistan to live under a fluctuating system of military and civilian rule for many decades. It was not until 1970 that citizens were allowed to take part in the nation's first direct election through adult franchise. Adult franchise means that the right to vote is given to all people regardless of caste, class, color, religion, or gender. In 2013, the country experienced its first transfer of power from one democratically elected government to the next. With the reelection of Prime Minister Nawaz Sharif, many people were of the opinion that the Pakistani government was finally representing the will of its citizens. On the contrary, corruption actually increased drastically, resulting in continued and unabated plunder of the impoverished country's resources. Elected government leaders have continued to strengthen the vertically integrated kleptocracy within every branch and at every level of the government, pushing the limits of corruption for their personal benefit. Similar to a Mafia organization, money moves from the bottom to the top. Every group operates within a sphere of influence. Everyone in the chain of corruption gets their share. Those benefiting from this chain of corruption have no desire for change. Instead, they prefer to maintain and strengthen the status quo. Some government employees resent the corruption but don't seem to know of anything better and don't have a way out, so they continue to play along for the survival of their families.

For the people of Pakistan, democracy has meant little for the betterment of their daily lives. Members of opposing political parties are arrested and openly harassed. Allegations of corruption and fraud within the government are constant. Citizens are forced to endure deplorable living conditions, as inadequate public services leave them without access to running water and basic sanitation. Systematic corruption helps maintain rampant lawlessness, which leaves citizens without adequate protection of their lives and property. Crimes often go unpunished, and justice is replaced by favors to those with the most money and/or power.

When citizens observe government leaders amassing vast amounts of personal wealth to the detriment of the nation, they become frustrated and enraged. Some individuals look to terrorist organizations for protection and to voice their frustration. The country's systematic corruption only adds to growing membership in these groups and makes its own citizens a target for attacks. Many violent incidents, in both poor and upscale venues, have caused the demise of innocent people in a country where the corruption continuously fuels terrorism—and all of this occurs under a democratic government. For example, one of my cousins was at the Marriott Hotel in Islamabad on September 20, 2008, for the opening of the fast during Ramadan, when a bomb blast killed 54 people and injured another 266.[52] This is only one example of the unimaginable hardships endured by the people of Pakistan on a daily basis, and the presence of democracy has done little to solve these disastrous incidents.

At first glance, the Middle Eastern nation of Tunisia appears to be an exception to the rule of failure of democracy. It is the first Arab country in 40 years to be classified as "free" by the group Freedom House, a democracy advocacy organization. A widespread revolt led to the ousting of the country's last dictatorship in 2011. Since that time, the Tunisians have proudly participated in two democratic elections for national leadership. While these gains are significant, numerous issues are keeping Tunisia in the category of a failing nation. Income disparities between the wealthy and poor have continuously increased, leaving impoverished citizens angry and creating a breeding ground for extremist organizations. A lack of adequate infrastructure and threats of unrest frustrate efforts to build economic opportunities, which would bring much-needed jobs to the masses of unemployed Tunisians.

Egypt, India, Pakistan, and Tunisia provide us with modern examples of how democracy, without an underlying system of checks and balances, does little to elevate the daily living conditions of a nation's citizens. Let's also not forget that some of the cruelest and most tyrannical dictators in history gained their positions through democratic elections. Adolph Hitler is the most notorious of them all. His rise to power started in the 1930s as the world struggled with economic depression. Germany was hit especially hard, leaving millions of people without jobs, savings, or means to care for themselves and their families. Hitler was the head of the National Socialist German Workers' Party (Nazi party). In this capacity, he spoke to masses of people, mostly appealing to the unemployed and the younger generation. His popularity snowballed, and the Nazi party went from virtual obscurity to a booming political force among German voters. In 1932, the party won the majority of the popular vote, though Hitler lost his bid for president.

Paul von Hindenburg was democratically elected in 1925 as the second president of Germany. Even though the Nazi party was a minority, under pressure from his former supporters, he appointed Hitler as the chancellor of Germany. Though Hindenburg was the elected president, he had little power compared to the chancellor, so naming Hitler as chancellor was essentially handing him control of the country. Hitler wasted no time in turning the country's leadership into a dictatorship and ending all individual freedoms, including the right to vote. In 1933, all opposing political parties were abolished, leaving the Nazi party as the sole governing body. Upon the death of Hindenburg, Hitler successfully merged the office of president and chancellor into one. The atrocious system of oppression that he went on to create is well known. It is an undeniable fact that Hitler's democratic rise to power was instrumental in the failure of Germany to serve the interests of all its citizens.

Ferdinand Marcos was another tyrant who came to power through a democratic election process. A lawyer and military officer, Marcos rose through the ranks of the Philippine government, serving in the House of Representatives and the Senate. In 1965, he was elected president as a member of the Nationalist Party. His first term in office brought the people of the Philippines considerable progress in manufacturing and agriculture, yet not all citizens supported him and some openly protested to show their disdain. Despite pervasive dissatisfaction, four years later he won reelection and became the first person to ever serve a second term as president of the Philippines. In response to widespread protests and violence, Marcos declared martial law across the country, ushering in a decades-long era of authoritarian rule. This democratically elected leader jailed politicians who opposed him and used the power of the military to serve his purposes. Protestors were killed to "salvage the regime." His time in the office substantially expanded the economic gap between wealthy and poor citizens, as the rich continuously benefited from the corruption of government officials. Meanwhile, economic stagnation kept most citizens from making any headway out of poverty. The reign of Marcos lasted until the majority of the people grew dissatisfied with him. He fled into exile in 1986.

Moeed Yusuf, associate vice president of the Asia Center at the U.S. Institute of Peace, speaking on a panel sponsored by the Middle East

Institute on the future of democracy in Pakistan and Afghanistan, talked about elected dictatorships supported by patronage.[53] Patronage is the use of rewards and favors to gain public office and influence. In its most extreme form, patronage becomes a system of bribery and corruption. Yusuf states that these leaders work to defend their patronage, even above the national interests. Patronage persists due to compromised law-enforcement institutions. When law enforcement is controlled by an elected dictator, the members know that they will gain unfair advantage once their party is in power.

A commonality between these countries is that democracy alone does not adequately address the overwhelming issues of poverty in a failing nation. The democratic election of officials does not guarantee justice and the equality of all citizens. When democratically chosen leaders are allowed to maintain a system of corruption, little changes in the struggle of an average citizen for daily survival. In failing countries, democracy is reduced to a process of selection of leaders by popular vote; after the elections, however, there is a lack of structural checks on governance to stop leaders from looting the country's resources.

The Myth of Education

There is a widespread belief that higher literacy rates equal elevated levels of national success. It sounds like a plausible argument. We are taught the value of education from day one and assured that successful schooling will lead us down the road to a successful life. However, when you compare literacy rates and GDP in some countries, you will find that this assumption often does not hold water. The world offers numerous examples of nations where the citizens are literate, but the country's economic condition shows little evidence of citizen prosperity. The GDP is an indicator commonly used to measure the economy of a nation. As defined by *Investopedia*, it is the total dollar value for all goods and services produced by a country within a specified period. Let's compare the economic performance of multiple countries to their literacy rates, using the economic value created per person, or GDP per capita, as an objective measure normalized for the size of the population.

Most readers expect a positive correlation between high national literacy rates and high GDP per capita. But analysis of the actual data proves otherwise. Some economists suggest the use of purchasing power parity (PPP) for comparing economies. However, PPP also has its limits due to questions about the accuracy of the price of a basket of goods. For a more straightforward argument, GDP per capita is more objective.

Comparing the 20 countries with a 100% literacy rate, GDP per capita varies from a low of $820 for Tajikistan to $101,715 for Luxembourg, 124 times higher.[54]

GDP of Countries with 100% Literacy Rate

Country	Literacy Rate	GDP per Capita
Luxembourg	100%	$101,715.00
Norway	100%	$73,450.00
Finland	100%	$42,612.00
Slovenia	100%	$21,062.00
Estonia	100%	$17,891.00
Barbados	100%	$16,938.00
Slovak Republic	100%	$16,412.00
Lithuania	100%	$15,090.00
Latvia	100%	$14,188.00
Poland	100%	$12,722.00
Russia	100%	$10,885.00

For example, Ukraine, with a population of 45 million (in 2016), has a near 100% literacy rate but a very low GDP per capita of $2,262. The high literacy rate has not translated into financial success for the masses. One of the main reasons for Ukraine's poverty is systematic corruption. For example, 34% of the nation's GDP is attributed to a shadow economy, with businesses operating underground to avoid taxes.[55] It is estimated that Ukraine's most profitable shadow economy is the production of alcohol, with a worth of about $1.1 billion.[56] Shadow-industry-manufactured oil products are valued at $550 million, while illegal amber mining is valued at $330 million. In total, Ukraine's shadow economy earns more than $2 billion that is never taxed by the government for the benefit of the people. Corruption runs rampant within the government, with current leaders claiming that $37 billion went missing during former president Viktor Yanukovych's rule.[57] News reports out of Ukraine estimate that he took more than $2 billion in bribes during his time in office, yet not a single criminal charge has been brought to hold him accountable for his corrupt activities.[58]

With a 91% literacy rate, Zimbabwe has one of the highest literacy rates in Africa. Yet the GDP per capita is $1,027.[59] Most citizens have no access to drinking water, and most rural residents have no source of transportation. Medications and health care are extremely limited, which only adds to the high rates of deadly diseases such as malaria, typhoid, and polio. Despite international gains in the treatment and prevention of HIV and AIDS, Zimbabwe continues to experience high rates of illness and death related to HIV. The nation's poorest residents sleep on concrete floors, unable to afford basic furnishings. Failing infrastructure sends sewage flowing through these poverty-stricken residential areas, polluting already limited water supplies. Many in Zimbabwe face a daily struggle to feed their families.

Let's analyze global educational data to understand the relationship between literacy and GDP per capita. The following chart shows the GDP per capita versus the literacy rate of all countries. It demonstrates a positive correlation between literacy rate as a measure of the educated percentage of the population with the increasing GDP per capita. However, note that the correlation coefficient (R^2) is weak.

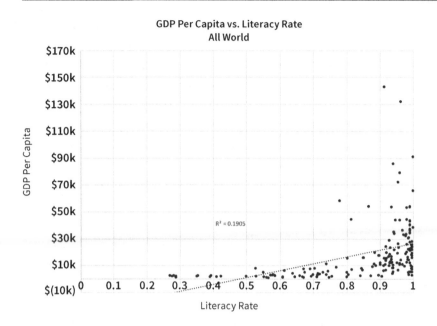

To understand the causality, the next chart shows the relationship between the top 110 literate countries versus the GDP per capita. As you
can see, there is a weak correlation between the rise of GDP per capita
and the literacy rate.

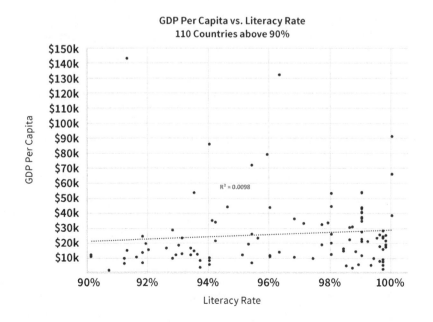

Lack of education is not the main cause of poverty. Countries such as Tajikistan, with its 100% literacy rate, and Zimbabwe, with a 91% literacy rate, are still extremely poor. As these examples show, high literacy rates do not equate to healthy economies. Education by itself does not create jobs and economic growth. Most people pursue formal education for better financial opportunities. If you invest the time, money, and effort necessary to earn a degree, you expect that investment to pay off in the form of employment opportunities. Unfortunately, for people living in failing nations, receiving an education does not always equate to a better standard of living. Instead, these individuals are forced to take their knowledge and talents to other parts of the world with greater economic opportunities.

The elite medical school of Pakistan is the Aga Khan Medical University. More than 2,000 students attend this prestigious institute, with aspirations of helping their fellow citizens. However, a lack of attractive opportunities keeps the cream of the country's crop from staying within Pakistan. Instead, over 80% of the medical school's graduating class moves to the U.S. The *Journal of the Pakistan Medical Association* researched the number of Pakistani physicians working abroad. Their studies showed that these doctors moved overseas for various reasons, one of which was to pursue professional careers for higher compensation. Since these doctors are paid five to ten times more than they would be paid working in Pakistan, the decision to move and work abroad is obviously much more lucrative. Another common reason for the relocation of these physicians to other countries is a lack of law and order within Pakistan. Doctors continually face increased levels of hostility. According to one study, acts of terrorism have killed as many as 50 doctors within the last ten years.[60] Frequent kidnapping of physicians is also causing doctors to leave the country.

Education is required for the success and prosperity of a nation, but lack of it is not the fundamental cause of a nation's failure. Once a country has dealt with the fundamental cause of poverty, which is a lack of justice, people of those countries will become educated and pursue economic opportunities. Many political scholars continuously use literacy and education in their attempts to explain the successes and failures of nations, but the facts do not support this myth.

The Myth of Geography

Geography is another reason often put forward to explain the poverty of some countries. Some political experts argue that lack of adequate natural resources prohibits a nation from flourishing economically. An additional argument asserts that countries located in certain geographic regions are naturally more prone to economic failure than others. For example, people in numerous parts of Africa face insurmountable poverty and deplorable acts of political violence. Without adequate analysis, there is a tendency to assume that the mere location of these nations on the continent of Africa is a major factor for the poverty faced by its people. However, real-world examples from across Africa and around the globe disprove such theories. Geography does not necessarily explain the failure of a nation. Countries rich in natural resources can still fail, while countries poor in resources can thrive. Also, many of these failing and thriving nations are located on the same continents and even share the same basic geographic characteristics.

Japan, a country of minimal natural resources, is an excellent example of success without geographic benefits. The United States Central Intelligence Agency (CIA) lists fish as Japan's only valuable resource. Its lack of natural energy sources makes Japan the world's largest importer of natural gas and coal, as well as the second largest importer of oil.[61] Despite these geographical limitations, Japan is the world's third-largest economy. Income levels have significantly increased over the past 20 years, with greater numbers of Japanese enjoying a higher quality of life than ever before in the country's history. Even without an abundance of natural resources, the country's leaders have found innovative and effective ways to grow the nation's economy and provide for its citizens.

A diametrically opposite example is that of Afghanistan, which is rich in natural resources but failing in economic success. Afghanistan is rich in natural gas, petroleum, coal, copper, sulfur, salt, precious stones, and numerous other natural resources. It has enough resources to make it one of the richest mining countries in the world, yet the people of Afghanistan go without the most basic government services. Poverty is the biggest killer of the Afghans, with more than two-thirds of the population unable to meet their most basic needs.[62] Infant mortality is extremely high. Out of every 1,000 births, 460 mothers and 119 infants die. These tragic statistics are due to a lack of healthcare and more than half the population living without access to clean water. The low standard of living experienced by the Afghans directly contradicts the asserted relationship between rich geography and economic prosperity. Even with some of the most valuable natural resources on Earth, the people of Afghanistan are forced to live in abject poverty.

The poor conditions in some countries of South America also debunk the myth that geography is responsible for the failure of some nations. All these countries share similar geographical characteristics. Mountain ranges span from one country into the next, while several of these countries have miles and miles of beachfront due to their location along the Caribbean Sea and the Pacific Ocean. Even with all these similarities, vast differences are evident in the living conditions of denizens of these lands. While most South American countries suffer from significant levels of poverty, for some of these countries, the statistics are strikingly grim and seemingly out of control.

Bolivia is a nation that contradicts the myth of geography determining a nation's wealth. The country is extremely rich in natural resources such as gold, lead, silver, petroleum, and natural gas. Yet it is one of the poorest countries in South America, with almost half of its population living in extreme poverty. Most of the impoverished citizens live in the rural areas of the country, where the government refuses to provide the infrastructure they need to transport their crops to the urban areas of the country where they are more likely to find paying customers. They are also denied the technology that would allow them to mass produce their crops. The lack of infrastructure to provide water for crops also yields lower prices and impoverished farmers. These problems have contributed to Bolivia's income inequality being the highest in Latin America. Economic instability is a constant issue for the country, largely due to the collapse of its mining industry in the 1980s and vast dependency on foreign lending. Though the economy has shown some recovery over the past few decades, its growth remains slow and inequitably beneficial to the wealthiest citizens. As members of a failing nation, Bolivians deal with high death rates, particularly for children under the age of five. Many also lack access to clean drinking water, which causes the country to be ranked as a nation with one of the highest malnutrition rates in Latin America. The abundance of natural resources has been of little benefit in addressing the poverty of the country.

The United Arab Emirates (UAE) also provide a real-world argument against the myth of geography. Geographically, Dubai is the poorest state in the UAE, with much smaller oil revenues than the rest of the Emirates. For example, Abu Dhabi claims to have oil reserves of 92 billion barrels compared to Dubai's four billion barrels.[63] Despite this vast difference in oil production, the economy of Dubai is much more vibrant, thriving with international investments and a flourishing tourist industry. While 85% of the UAE's overall wealth is attributed to oil revenues, Dubai has become far more successful by relaxing the historically restricted policies prevalent in Arab countries. To attract foreign businesses, the country has established economic free zones that offer international companies such benefits as 100% ownership of their enterprises, no taxes (though there are significant tax-like fees), relaxed labor laws, and quick-turnaround document clearance. This business-friendly environment makes Dubai very attractive to international businesses, which has helped the country establish its economic success within the UAE despite its comparative lack of natural oil reserves.

Africa offers numerous examples of nations rich in natural resources but economically poor. Zambia is extremely rich in copper, with mining operations producing hundreds of thousands of tons of the metal each year. While this highly sought-after metal should create wealth for the citizens of Zambia, it is instead extracted for the benefit of foreign nations. None of the top four mining companies working within the country is owned by citizens of the country or even the government of Zambia.[64] Though the government does maintain a small share in each of the companies, the financial benefits of this investment are not distributed among the citizens. Glencore, a Swiss company, makes billions of dollars from the extraction of copper from Zambia.[65] As the owners of these mining companies get richer, the standard of living of the people of Zambia has been steadily declining. More than 60% of the population lacks adequate food and water. The nation's children are highly prone to cognitive and physical impairments due to malnutrition. Life expectancy is only 37.5 years, and maternal mortality is 729 per 100,000 live births. In addition, the copper-mining operations have created an extensive problem with pollution within the country, resulting in unsafe drinking water and causing serious illness to the people of the nation. Entire rivers have been polluted with heavy metals and sulfuric acid. Zambia exemplifies the disconnect between a rich geography and economic success. Despite its abundant supply of copper, Zambia has failed to provide for its citizens adequately.

Zimbabwe is rich in precious minerals, but its people live in extreme poverty. Not only do they not benefit from the revenues of their natural resources, they are actually harmed by them. Mining activities have caused devastating pollution of the nation's waterways, leaving residents without access to clean water. Most of Zimbabwe's rivers and dams are polluted with such metals as iron, copper, zinc, and nickel.[66] When consumed in excessive amounts, iron can cause severe stomach pains and even result in damage to the brain. Water contaminated with zinc can damage the central nervous system. Nickel exposure can cause skin rashes, bronchitis, and diminished functioning of the lungs. Further complicating the matter is the fact that many mining operations use chemicals such as cyanide and mercury to process the extracted minerals. These toxins have been linked to kidney and brain damage as well as the failure of the central nervous system. The people of Zimbabwe do not benefit from the rich geography of their country. They are dying from it.

Geography does not guarantee economic success. Some of the most geographically rich nations in the world have failing economies with life-threatening levels of poverty. Further supporting my point is the fact that many thriving and failing countries share the same geography, with some of them located directly adjacent to one another. Like the myths of democracy and literacy, the argument of geography as an explanation is flawed.

The Myth of Race and Culture

For more than 200 years, scientists have attempted to prove the superiority of one race over another. In 1851, physician Samuel Cartwright wrote about a condition called "drapetomania," which he described as a mental illness that affected African slaves, causing them to go crazy and attempt escape.[67] Though his theory is widely disregarded today, his writings were wildly popular among slaveholders and essentially opened the door to scientific racism. During the early 1900s, anthropologist Margaret Mead asserted that tribes of the Samoan islands were more civilized than and superior to the people of Europe and America. One of the most controversial theories of scientific racism was written in 1994 by Richard Herrnstein and Charles Murray. This duo asserted that class differences between blacks and whites in America can be explained through innate differences in their intelligence quotients. They essentially argued that blacks are born intellectually inferior to whites. Though not to the same level of severity, it is this type of thinking that drives the myth of race as an explanation for the failure of many nations. Subscribers to this theory believe that certain races are just unable to govern themselves and create successful governments. However, there are numerous examples throughout history and around the globe that negate this flawed hypothesis and demonstrate how people of any race can create an entity that succeeds, just as people of any race can run a governmental body to ruin.

In the book *Why Nations Fail: The Origins of Power, Prosperity, and Poverty*, authors Daron Acemoglu and James A. Robinson discuss the localities of Nogales, Arizona, and Nogales Sonora, Mexico. These two cities encompass one vast area of land that is separated by a fence at the U.S./Mexico border. The majority of the residents on both sides are of the same Hispanic heritage. On the American side of the fence, most adults have earned at least a high school education and almost all children attend school regularly. The average yearly income is approximately $30,000, and residents have homes with running water, working electricity, and various other amenities. They drive on state-funded roads and use infrastructure developed for their convenience. The residents of Nogales live their lives with an expectation that their government will protect them and punish anyone who illegally encroaches on their rights as citizens of the United States. Life in Nogales resembles the lives of most Americans across the country.

On the other hand, life on the Mexican side of the border tells an entirely different story and exemplifies a much more challenging existence for its residents. The average income is only $10,000 per year, and most adults did not complete high school. Most people work industrial jobs, making cellphone parts or airplane parts. Older children do not attend school, and infant mortality is a significant concern. Unlike their neighbors north of the border, residents of Nogales Sonora do not have access to adequate roads or necessary infrastructure. They are reminded on a daily basis that the government cannot or will not protect them from the crime that runs rampant within the city as murderous drug cartels go unrestrained.

The circumstances of these two groups of people of the same race exemplify how insignificant race is as a reason why some nations fail or succeed. The only difference between the two is the fact that one city lies within the United States and the other one lies within Mexico.

North and South Korea also debunk the myth of race and ethnicity as a reason for the failure of nations. These two countries started out as one country under the rule of the Japanese government. An industrial revolution took place in the northern sections of the territory with Japan's development of mines, steel mills, and manufacturing plants. While this expansion was occurring, a growing communist movement began challenging Japan's authority. On August 8, 1945, the Soviet Union declared war on Japan. As Soviet troops began to invade Korea, the United States government proposed a division of the territory, with the north falling under Soviet control and the south falling under U.S. control. This division was incorporated into Japan's surrender, placing about 16 million Koreans within the southern section and roughly nine million Koreans in the north. The south eventually became the Republic of Korea, with a democratic government that is similar to that of the United States. The north became the Democratic People's Republic of Korea, though there was little democratic about the way it was run. The north took on communist ideology, led by then Prime Minister Kim Il-Sung. In 1950, backed by China and the Soviet Union, North Korea invaded South Korea. Though millions of lives were lost in the Korean War, neither side gained any territorial advantage. The line of demarcation remained the same, separating cousins, siblings, and entire families into two different countries.

For more than 50 years, North Korea has been governed in virtual isolation, allowing for little communication with other countries. This isolation has starved its economy. The economy of South Korea is more than 30 times that of North Korea.[68] The country's GDP per capita is about $33,000, compared to $1,800 in North Korea. The people of South Korea enjoy a higher quality of life with better educational opportunities and health care. In North Korea, a chronic shortage of food leaves children malnourished and also contributes to the high infant mortality rate. In 2012, the infant mortality rate in South Korea was about four deaths for every 1,000 live births, compared to 26 deaths for every 1,000 live births in North Korea. The citizens of North and South Korea are people of the same race and, historically, the same culture. Yet the political policies of each country have led them to remarkably different economic outcomes. The people of North Korea are forced to suffer and struggle through their daily lives, while the people of South Korea are afforded a prosperous society.

Summary

Again, the use of real-world data and examples dispels a widely held myth about failing nations. Race and culture are of no significance for a country to thrive. Many philosophers, including Martin Luther King Jr., have asserted that all human beings are created equal. For the people who may disagree with this assertion, it is an irrefutable fact is that we are all biologically the same underneath our skin. There are only four types of human blood, and the blood of an African man from Ghana can be transfused to a white woman from Iceland. As we see from the examples mentioned above, people of the same race can live in drastically different levels of poverty. Even when the people share remarkably similar cultural identities and practices, the health of their economies can be drastically different.

As political scientists have sought to explain why some nations succeed and others fail, they have relied on numerous theories. These traditional ideas are myths that fail to accurately identify the common problem with failing nations. Democracy may be a step in the right direction, it but alone will not improve the quality of life for all people living in those countries. The world is filled with examples of failing democratic countries. Likewise, the theory of education as a root cause is also false. Without economic opportunities, education is of no consequence. In many instances, these countries educate their best and brightest citizens for the benefit of other countries with better employment opportunities. Geography is also an inadequate explanation for the failure of a country to attain prosperity. Some countries with fewer natural resources are more prosperous than countries that have more natural resources. Many countries do much better than their immediate neighbors even though they possess basically the same level of resources and similar climates. The final myth, and perhaps the most insidious, is the argument that countries made up of certain races and cultures are more susceptible to failure. The global landscape is filled with examples of similar races and cultures with hugely different levels of prosperity. These myths lead us away from the real problems of failing nations and keep us from identifying viable solutions.

HOW DID WE END UP HERE?

4

"A wise and frugal government which shall restrain men from injuring one another, which shall leave them otherwise free to regulate their own pursuits of industry and improvement, and shall not take from the mouth of labor the bread it has earned. This is the sum of good government."

—Thomas Jefferson

Introduction

The previous chapters illustrate that many of our existing government structures, including some democracies, fail to provide even the most basic necessities for their citizens. Now that we have identified the problem, it is essential to present why the problem exists and what historical factors contributed to these failing governments, leaving over half the world's population without the most basic necessities. In this chapter, we will review the crucial question: "How did we get here?"

It's an entirely valid question with no simple answer due to a multitude of contributing factors. However, a historical view of the world's modern political systems reveals a common thread. Most governmental structures evolved so that rulers, mostly kings and dictators, were able to command and control the population for their own benefit. These same principles were applied to conquer and dominate foreign lands. The governmental organizations in these countries were not created out of any concern for or loyalty to the people. Instead, they manifested from an intention to control resources and stay in power. For the purpose of this discussion, I refer to these efforts as "command and control," as used by the authors of the book *Why Nations Fail* in their analysis of political history, a theory referring to the type of relationship that exists between these dictatorial leaders and their nations.[69] Command refers to the act of taking full or partial authority over the country.

This structure further evolved to command and control captured nations. The invaders used the authority of force to take control of the occupied country's most valuable resources. Recent history is filled with examples of European nations asserting authority over colonized nations. The common goal was to colonize the geographic area, controlling it with the conqueror's military and extracting its valuable resources for the benefit of the king or dictator. Whether it was the British colonizing regions in Asia, the Spanish colonizing South America, or the French colonizing Africa, these examples of command and control offer a useful explanation of prevalent government structures and why most run via a centralized system of control.

Ruling Dictatorships in Modern History

Tyranny has been a consistent fixture of world history. Most of the world's nations are or were ruled by dictators, and many of these rulers used their country's resources for their own benefit and personal wealth. It's not a huge mystery. From the beginning of time, individuals have sought to gain exclusive political power and use it to their advantage. When opposition does raise its head, unjust rulers use the backing of the military to quash it. If a person or group somehow amasses enough support to become a serious threat, the ruler will persuade them to join their corrupt system by sharing limited power and wealth extracted from the people. This type of bribery essentially buys the cooperation of the opposing party while allowing them to maintain their public image. Since the goal of the dictator is to stay in power and control wealth, there is no benefit to sharing the power or the wealth with the masses. It is not in the ruler's interest to help the people or create policies that will lift the majority of the population out of poverty. I see this as another form of slavery that currently is not categorized as such. If the majority of a country is not allowed a beneficial life and the pursuit of happiness while the ruler is living like a king, it is slavery. Most people living under these rulers have little to no access to wealth or opportunities within their countries. To make matters worse, they must endure daily life without any protection of their fundamental human rights because, under an unjust and corrupt ruler, rights are given and taken away at the leader's whim.

Unjust rulers implement the same tactics when they set out to conquer other countries, using their wealth to bribe and influence local leaders to give up power and valuable economic resources. If leaders resist, the dictators use military force to demand compliance and stop the opposition. Religion has been used to enforce the ruler's authority and seek the people's submission. The people are told that their miserable existence is God's plan for them. Rulers fund the clergy to propagate their message, including the idea that suffering is a test by God and if you don't complain, you will be rewarded in the afterlife.

A large number of countries are categorized as third world. Whether these countries are in Africa, South America, Latin America, the Middle East, or Asia, they share a common legacy. Starting in the sixteenth century, they were colonized by European nations. Countries such as Spain, Portugal, France, Britain, the Netherlands, and Belgium established colonies throughout the world. Their prime objective was to extract natural resources from the colonized nations. In the worst instances, they kidnapped prisoners from the colonized nations of Africa and sold them as slaves in the United States, Latin America, and other nations. Since the European conquerors did not provide democratic institutions to their colonized people when they left, most of these developing countries have been ruled by corrupt leaders with networks of political henchmen.

Virtually every nation that set out to command and control other areas of the world ruled through some form of dictatorship, granting very limited rights to the citizens of the colonized countries. France, Spain,

Portugal, and Great Britain provide relevant examples, as some of the most active colonizing nations.

France

The rise of the Bourbon Dynasty began an extensive history of French colonization in foreign lands and a long legacy of exclusionary family rule over the nation of France. Successors of King Henry IV controlled the country for more than 150 years. Perhaps one of the most infamous of these rulers was King Louis XIV, who proclaimed himself "The Sun King." The king declared that he was a direct representative of God, with the ordained power to rule without interference or assistance from any other member of society. He used bribery and payoffs to quiet the raging dissatisfaction of the nobles. He also shamelessly depleted the nation's wealth with the building of lavish palaces, where he hosted exorbitant festivities for international dignitaries and the country's wealthiest elite. During this time, the French people were divided into hierarchal classes by the monarchy and treated according to their classification. The highest class was referred to as the First Estate, and it consisted of clergy members, who exercised some level of control over the Catholic Church as well as certain state functions, including the power to levy a 10% tax on the people.[70] This mandatory payment was referred to as a tithe to the church. The Second Estate consisted of the country's nobility. While the king rose above any classification, the rest of the royal family was included in this group. Members of the Second Estate enjoyed a variety of unique privileges, including exemption from paying taxes. However, they were allowed to collect taxes from members of the lowest classification, which was the Third Estate. This level included everyone else, which accounted for about 97% of the country's population. It included everyone from farmers to the wealthy bourgeoisie. These individuals enjoyed none of the rights held by the other two privileged estates and yet were subject to their taxation.

This same intent to provide privileges to an elite class, while limiting the rights of the masses, carried through to France as colonizer. During his 72 years in power, Louis XIV ordered the military to engage in numerous expansionist campaigns, using force to take control of foreign territories. In 1664, he ordered the colonization of Saint Dominique in the western half of Hispaniola, a country now known as Haiti. As in other West Indian food-producing colonies under French rule, the command and control of Saint Dominique was accomplished through the suppression of the natives and the introduction of African slaves to work the land. Under French rule, Saint Dominique became one of the greatest wealth-generating colonies in the Caribbean. But this wealth was not used to benefit the people or promote self-sufficiency; this wealth was used for the benefit of the king.

Upon his death, Louis XIV was succeeded by two heirs before the French Revolution ended the Bourbon Dynasty, but that was not to be the end of tyrannical leadership within the country. Napoleon III successfully ended the revolution and became the head of France in 1804. Under his rule, French colonization more than doubled with the assistance of a new state ministry that he implemented for the express purpose of increasing colonization. Napoleon also attempted to establish a strong French presence in Japan, Korea, and Mexico. This was unsuccessful, but expansion into Africa was a significant initiative during his rule. He set out to colonize Senegal within the western area of the continent and Algeria in North Africa. Though some historians prefer to paint Napoleon as sensitive to the plight of Algerians, the devastating impact of French colonialism cannot be overlooked. Though he allowed Algerian Muslims to join the French army and relocate to France, he also required them to give up critical aspects of their religion in return. His changes to land ownership laws effectively unraveled generations of tribal land ownership traditions, leaving many native Algerians without land that was rightfully theirs. French colonists were allowed to purchase the most fertile lands, while Algerians were left with arid, desert regions of the country. Under Napoleon's reign, tribal leadership was awarded based on loyalty to the crown instead of loyalty to the tribe and its members. When Algerians revolted, they were defeated by harsh military force.

The French reign in Algeria lasted for over 100 years. During this time, the ruling class gained significant wealth from the country's rich agriculture. They took over tribal lands and cultivated them, producing lucrative crops such as olives, tobacco, and citrus fruits. Wine was a successful export, along with rich mineral resources, like oil and phosphates. French rulers benefited by extracting resources from Algerians, leaving them poverty-stricken, with food shortages due to the loss of their fertile homelands.

Spain

The history of Spain is also filled with the rule of monarchs. Under the House of Habsburg, which reigned throughout the sixteenth and seventeenth centuries, the country enjoyed a high level of financial success and international influence. While the colonization of foreign lands began during this period, it was under the House of Bourbon, throughout the eighteenth century, that the Spanish empire greatly expanded. King Philip V, a Frenchman, ruled the country from 1700 to 1724. During his reign, he changed the structure of the government for the purpose of expanding the power of the crown to resemble that of the French monarchy. The classification of people within the country also resembled that of France. Spanish nobility received numerous privileges, including exemption from taxes, while peasants were left to bear the brunt of the country's financial obligations.

Part of Philip V's mission included strengthening the Spanish presence in several previously established colonies. In Honduras, the Spanish Empire took advantage of the country's rich mines and developed a lucrative precious metal mining industry. The Spanish used indigenous Hondurans to work in the mines. To maintain production, they were forced to migrate from their homes and work in the mines under deplorable conditions. In defense of their people, tribal members revolted against the Spanish, resulting in the massacre of many native Hondurans.

Spain first colonized Cuba during the sixteenth century. The monarchy ordered invaders to command and control the island to extract the resources. Initial attempts were met with resistance from the native Taino people, who had relocated to the island to flee the savagery of Spanish rule in other parts of Hispaniola. Under the direction of Philip V, the Spanish fought violently with tribal members. Tribal leaders were caught and burned alive. Tribal members were also reportedly butchered, even if they made attempts at peace with the Spanish colonists.

Those who did survive either fled into the wilderness or were forced to live on reservations inside their native land. As the Spanish leaders sought to farm the land and cultivate tobacco, they unsuccessfully attempted to force natives into working on the farms. The natives refused to cooperate, and many became sick with the diseases brought to the island by the Spanish. In response, Spain imported African slaves to work in the fields. Philip V established separate naval ministries for Honduras and Cuba to ensure that colonization continued and Spain maintained a stronghold on its territories.

Like so many government legacies throughout history, Spanish colonization plundered occupied nations to expand Spain's influence and wealth, while leaving its citizens without basic necessities. In Honduras, the Spanish government took control of the mines, extracting precious metals from the land for the benefit of the leaders. In Cuba, the fertile land was used to cultivate an extensive tobacco industry, in which natives and African slaves were forced to labor. Both of these circumstances exemplify Spain's historical legacy of command and control.

Dutch Control of the Spice Trade

During the sixteenth, seventeenth, and eighteenth centuries, spices were so valuable that countries were willing to fight each other for control of the trade. Pepper, cinnamon, cloves, and nutmeg were as coveted as gold and silver during this period. Since these spices were not grown in the West, monarchs enlisted their most trustworthy military commanders to find new sea routes to the Orient and take control of this valuable commodity. For centuries, the spice trade routes were controlled by the Ottoman Empire. The control of the spice trade shifted in the early 1500s when the Portuguese discovered a new sea route to India. European battle for control of the spice routes disrupted spice-rich sovereignties, such as the Banda Islands and the Moluccan Islands, part of the Indonesian archipelago. For the people who lived in some of these nations, the arrival of the Dutch would forever change the course of their lives.[71]

The Banda and Moluccan Islands, though small in size, were the sole producers of clove, nutmeg, and mace. Instead of competing with other

Europeans for the control of the spice trade, the Dutch set out to be the sole distributors of these valuable spices. They coerced one of the Moluccan rulers into signing an agreement that granted them an exclusive monopoly over the clove trade. The signing of this agreement marked the beginning of the Dutch East India Company, complete with its own Dutch-backed military with the power to wage war when deemed necessary or set up colonies as ordered by the king. The Dutch not only waged war against European countries competing to extract spices from the area, but also attacked other Moluccan islands in an attempt to expand their control of spice production. They forced the people of these nations to abandon their rightful production of the valuable cloves and even burned clove trees in hostile territories.

Once cloves were securely in their stronghold, the Dutch monarchy set out to control the mace and nutmeg markets by attempting to control Ambon. Ambon is the main city and seaport of Ambon Island and is the capital of the Moluccan Islands. Ambon had many small, noncentralized governing bodies to bribe or force into compliance. The lack of a central government frustrated the efforts of the Dutch, and their response was deadly. In 1621, the king ordered the massacre of more than 15,000 Ambon residents. While every leader was executed, the Dutch strategically kept enough residents alive to teach them how to produce the mace and nutmeg. The islands were divided into parcels and given to Dutch men to set up plantations. Slaves were brought in and taught how to work the fields. By the end of the seventeenth century, the Dutch controlled more than half the world's spices, effectively doubling the price of nutmeg.

While the immediate effect on the conquered islands was destruction and control, the actions of the Dutch also affected other islands. Rather than face the violence and coercive tactics of the Dutch, their people chose to completely abandon their spice production, which left them without a viable economic source that might have sustained them for generations. There is no telling how successful these nations could have become without the command and control policies of the Dutch monarchy. This is just one of many examples from around the globe of how the self-serving interests of the ruling European monarchies destroyed entire nations and populations.

The British Empire

The Dutch were not the only Europeans who were competing to control trade routes. Similar interests caused the expansion of Britain's colonial empire. The East India Company was chartered in 1600, creating a monopoly on all trade between the Cape of Good Hope and the Straits of Magellan, a passage that separates Tierra del Fuego and other islands from mainland South America, connecting the Atlantic and Pacific oceans. The spice trade was challenging for the British to control due to the stronghold of the Dutch. By leveraging their power within India, the British took control of trade of other valuables such as silk, indigo dye, and cotton. In exchange for exclusive rights to set up factories, the Indian emperor was bribed and promised rare commodities from Europe. Over the next century, the English monarchy strengthened its control over Indian trade. By 1720, 15% of British imports were from India, supplied by the East India Company.

During this same period, the British were also expanding their empire to include the Americas. In the Caribbean, colonies were formed with no regard to the native populations. The islands of Barbados and Saint Kitts were extremely lucrative for the crown due to sugar production. Initially, indigenous inhabitants were forced to work the plantations, but many died due to illness and violence suffered as slaves. Indentured servants were used next, but they were unable to endure the harsh conditions of the work. In subsequent years, after the indigenous population had been virtually eradicated, African slaves were bought and made to work on plantations under atrocious conditions. The English leader's rationale was that Africans were better suited for the work due to the climatic similarities between the Caribbean Islands and their West African homeland. The islands became a place of immense wealth, thanks to the sugar plantations that covered most of the island.

The history of colonization in South America provides additional examples of the constant struggles that resulted from an instituted system of command and control. The arrival of Christopher Columbus in the Bahamas marked the beginning of Spanish colonization of the Americas. The Portuguese had already completed several expeditions into South America. As Spain's leaders witnessed the resources that the Portuguese were able to take from the area, they set out to lay their own claim to the riches. The Spanish monarchs, Ferdinand of Aragon and Isabella of Castile, contracted Columbus to sail west across the Atlantic Ocean. While Columbus was chasing fame, the Spaniards were chasing spices, gold, and silver. In his attempt to secure these gifts for the throne, he took the stance that the indigenous people, who had lived in these areas for decades, should be enslaved and made to work for his benefit and that of the Spanish monarchy. In 1501, the Spanish government implemented the encomienda, a labor system rewarding conquerors with the labor of local people, a form of communal slavery. In many cases, natives were forced to do hard labor and subjected to extreme punishment and death if they resisted. Many of them died from war-related injuries or diseases such as smallpox, which were brought over by the Spanish colonists.

Though Columbus made only two more voyages, the seed was planted and the Spanish government continued to assert its control over the lands of South America. The discovery of silver in Bolivia cemented the Spanish government's desire for financial gain within all South American countries. Bitter battles broke out between the Spaniards and the natives across the continent. In the area we now know as Mexico, it is estimated that more than 90% of the indigenous population was killed or died from illness during the first 100 years of Spanish colonization. Over the next three centuries, Spain's efforts led to its control over most of Central America and half of South America. Conquistadors warred with each other for the control of the region, completely ignoring the ownership rights of the natives. Colonists were placed under tight trade restrictions to ensure that the monarchy benefited from all economic activities. Just as we have seen in so many other areas of the world, much of the region's potential earning power was stolen and used mostly for the benefit of the king. For entire generations, most resources were stolen from the land and from the people, leaving us to wonder what might have been.

The Legacy of Command and Control

The majority of Central America is classified as "developing," with a lasting legacy of poverty, illiteracy, and low-quality health care.[72] Among the six countries, Nicaragua is considered the poorest, followed by Honduras. Costa Rica and Panama are ranked as the most developed countries in Central America based on a higher GDP. Many scholars attribute poverty in these countries to the larger population of indigenous people at the time of Spanish colonization. In the areas where indigenous people were present, mistreatment by the Spanish created a two-tier society with the indigenous on the bottom and the Spanish on the top. Unjust treatment forced many indigenous people to flee into the mountains and jungles, where there was no economic opportunity. All Central American countries have a skewed distribution of wealth, with a small group of individuals holding most of the wealth and the majority of the citizens impoverished.

South America is also classified as a "developing" area of the world. The regional economy only started to improve after World War II, when the nations began gaining greater independence over their affairs. The poorest countries are Guyana, Paraguay, and Bolivia. As we discussed earlier, Bolivia was a land rich in silver mines. The Spanish colonists extracted this metal and used it for the benefit of Spain without sharing any financial gains with Bolivia. The majority of Bolivians are indigenous, and they overwhelmingly live below the poverty line. The rural areas in which they live continue to be ignored by leadership and kept out of economic development plans. They are excluded socially and politically, just as they were when the Spanish conquistadors ruled the colonies. The same circumstances exist in Paraguay and Guyana. While Guyana was chiefly colonized under British rule, the same system of command and control was employed. This system, which included the maltreatment of indigenous people, created a legacy of high poverty rates within each of these countries today.

Revolts against Command and Control

The history of the world is filled with examples of people growing tired of oppression and restricted human rights. When collective frustrations grow and fester, the resulting reaction is often revolt against those in power. One of the earliest and most famous examples of the repressed asserting their rights is the Magna Carta. In the early 1200s, the British were under the rule of King John, widely considered one of the worst rulers in their history. He imposed unfair taxes on his subjects and killed people at will. Those who opposed his actions were punished severely with imprisonment and confiscation of their property. The barons of the country demanded that the king follow the laws of the land, but he refused. In response, he was captured and forced to negotiate a list of demands that they had created. These forced negotiations ultimately resulted in the creation of the Magna Carta, which is considered one of the first written constitutions in European history. The document listed specific rights and liberties that could not be violated by the king. While much of it dealt with the individual grievances of the country's residents, it also included clauses that would become the cornerstone of individual freedoms throughout history. One of the most famous clauses guaranteed the right to justice and fairness for all free men: "No free man shall be seized or imprisoned, or stripped of his rights or possessions, or outlawed or exiled, or deprived of his standing in any other way, nor will we proceed with force against him, or send others to do so, except by the lawful judgement of his equals or by the law of the land. To no one will we sell, to no one deny or delay right or justice."

Though this clause has become an example for generations to come, at the time of execution there were very few free men to whom this applied. The majority of residents were unfree peasants whose "justice" was handed down by their lords. Though the immediate practicality of the Magna Carta was questionable, its lasting significance is undeniable. Its principles of justice and equal treatment under the law can be seen in the United States Bill of Rights. The document's influence is also evident in the Universal Declaration of Human Rights written after World War II.

The French Revolution of 1848 was part of a series of revolutions taking place throughout Europe during this period. Citizens from several countries, including France, Germany, the Austrian Empire, and the Kingdom of Hungary, all took up arms against their rulers in protest of their treatment and arbitrary government actions. The revolutions were so common that this year in history is often referred to as the Year of Revolution or the People's Spring.

In the years leading up to the revolt, France was particularly hard hit with unfavorable weather, placing a substantial burden on the country's agricultural market. The secondary effects were widespread unemployment, fueling frustration among citizens. While elections were held for certain government positions, the majority of French citizens were disenfranchised, denied participation in the political process. There was a universal discontent with the rulers, but people felt helpless to change the situation. During most social gatherings, Frenchmen would voice their concerns about the government. One such meeting was scheduled for January 1848. Officials banned the meeting, stating that permission was required for any assembly attended by more than six people. The meeting was postponed to February, only to be canceled by officials at the last minute, leading to demonstrations and protests in the streets of Paris. Further complicating matters for the government was the refusal of the civilian national guard to take any action against the protestors.

Later in 1848, faced with the growing unrest, King Louis Philippe relinquished the throne, but the naming of the new king was abruptly interrupted when the national guard, students, and workers took over the parliamentary chamber in protest. Tens of thousands of citizens circled the building, many armed and prepared for a fight. In response, the Chamber of Deputies refused to accept the new king and instead created a provisional governing body charged with overseeing reforms. Part of those reforms was the overthrow of the established French monarchy in favor of a new French Republic. As a step toward political reform, capital punishment for political crimes was abolished and numerous political prisoners were released. They also granted the right to freedom of speech, assembly, and association. The provisional government announced that it would recognize the rights of French workers and undertake the tall task of providing paid employment opportunities for all citizens. To that end, the National Workshops system was set up to offer constant work, though at low wages. The number of employees grew, and they were tasked with such duties as planting trees and building roads. Universal male suffrage was enacted, giving all men, regardless of land ownership, the right to vote in French elections.

Though the revolt had a significant impact on the immediate circumstances of the French, the future of the nation was very much in question, with conservatives urging a return to a monarchy and radicals fighting for a republic where elected representatives would govern. The urban and rural workers who once fought side by side for change were now pitted against one another over the appropriate course of action for the country. Out of this controversy emerged Louis Napoleon, or Napoleon III. His proclamation that he was "all things to all people" was accurate in that he was able to garner significant support from each of the various classes. His election to office effectively ended the revolution, and the National Assembly was eventually dissolved under his dictatorship. He ultimately named himself emperor, beginning the rule of the Second Empire.

I hope that you can see a stark similarity between the revolt in England and the French Revolution of 1848. Though each of these actions was undertaken with the intention of creating change and bettering the condition of the people under monarchical rule, both ended with a return to the status quo. The influential Magna Carta was born out of an English revolt, but it did nothing to prevent future centuries of maltreatment of individuals and denial of their rights. The French Revolution started from dissatisfaction with the monarchy and ended with the election of a new and even more oppressive monarch.

While these citizens dared to take up arms and fight for their rights, they did not have the forethought to adequately plan for political change and implement new forms of government. Leaders lacked an adequate understanding of the structure of government required for the protection of citizens' rights. Therefore, they proceeded with the existing structure of command and control, in which the government fails to provide equality and justice to all individuals. This same lack of understanding is repeated in recent revolts.

Modern Revolts

The "Arab Spring" refers to the spring of 2011 when the Arab world experienced a wave of protests and demonstrations by citizens dissatisfied with their living conditions, extreme unemployment, and the corruption of government leaders. The ousting of the Tunisian president is widely viewed as the starting point for the Arab Spring. His ejection was initiated in response to the suicide of Mohamed Bouazizi, a street vendor who set himself on fire in protest of harassment that was mercilessly inflicted on him by a high-ranking local official and his aides. His very public death ignited widespread demonstrations and a call for the ousting of then-president Zine El Abidine Ben Ali, who had been in power for more than 23 years. As residents took to the streets, leaders responded brutally, with police and security forces taking up arms against the demonstrators, inflicting many injuries and even deaths. But these violent measures proved unsuccessful, and the protestors continued their revolt against the president. Under increasingly mounting pressures from citizens and the military, he fled to Saudi Arabia, where he remained in exile. A state of emergency was declared and a temporary government was put in place to address reforms, but all members resigned almost immediately under pressure from dissatisfied protesters.

In October 2011, Tunisian citizens voted in their first postrevolution election to name a Constituent Assembly to rewrite the nation's constitution. Sadly, this was a short-term victory, failing to have the lasting effects that protestors fought to achieve. As of 2016, Tunisians still deal with rampant corruption, high unemployment, and overwhelming economic struggles. Violent protests continue, and the response of the government continues to be questioned.

The changes in Tunisia inspired citizens in other Arab nations to rise up as well. Protests in Egypt began in October 2011, and the world watched as they continued for more than two weeks. The government tried brutal force in its attempt to end the protests. Demonstrators were met with riot gear and tear gas. The world watched as Tahrir Square exploded in violence between citizens and heavily armed law enforcement officials. Approximately 900 Egyptians were killed during the first few days of the revolution, and more than 6,000 were severely injured. It was later proven that the government was responsible for these atrocities.[73]

Another government tactic was to inhibit international support by cutting all Internet access. Many people across the globe supported the people of Egypt. Local bloggers and reporters used the Internet to broadcast videos showing the government's cruelty, causing tens of thousands of protesters to gather on the streets throughout the day and night. In response, then-President Mubarak dismissed his entire government and appointed a new cabinet. He gave all presidential power to his

vice president but attempted to retain his position as president. Protestors were not satisfied and demonstrations continued, forcing Mubarak
to resign and transfer all power to the country's military leaders. A new
prime minister was appointed, and the military made numerous promises of reform. Mubarak was convicted and sentenced to life imprisonment. Though Mohammed Morsi was elected by the people in their
first democratic presidential election, new protests and demonstrations
in 2012 led to his removal as well. Since that time, numerous violent
protests have occurred as Egyptians struggle to find a consensus about
the future of their nation. Five years after the revolution, the economy
remains stagnant due to government corruption. Poverty rates continue to rise sharply while the value of the nation's currency declines. For
many Egyptians, life is worse now than prior to the revolution.

In 2011, the Pakistani immigrants living in Bahrain agitated as part
of Bahraini uprising against lack of civil rights and political freedoms.
They also called for an end to the monarchy of Hamad bin Isa Al Khalifa.
The government responded with unspeakable violence against the protestors, leading to multiple deaths and injuries. The king declared martial law, which lasted more than three months. Protesters began holding
weekly demonstrations after martial law was lifted, but in the end, the
king prevailed, with unrest continuing among the people.

These modern-day revolutions were filled with so much commitment and belief. The entire world seemed to watch in awe, and many
hoped for the success of the movements. The people's efforts were real,
and they put their lives on the line to change their circumstances. But,
unfortunately, all of these revolts were unsuccessful in the long term.
Like many past revolutions, none of these recent rebellions resulted in
long-term advancements for the citizens, and some even exacerbated
the injustice. Why? Once again, there was a lack of comprehension of
the intrinsic connection between government structure and the quality
of daily life for the nation's citizens.

Have you ever heard the phrase "of the people, by the people, for
the people"? These words from Abraham Lincoln are much more than a
famous quote. They state with perfect clarity that a government established by the people works in the best interest of the people. Changing
leadership without addressing the governmental structure is inadequate

for reducing injustice and corruption. The revolutionaries failed to recognize that fundamental change in the governing structure is necessary for any real progress to occur. Even in situations where the people gained the right to vote, elected leaders ultimately abandoned the interests of the people for their own interests. This lack of understanding manifested itself among the revolutionaries as an absence of direction. Demands were generalized, and though the protestors collectively wanted change, there was no common accord about the most efficient manner of making that happen.

Unfortunately, most people lack understanding of government structures and how these can affect the everyday experiences of a country's citizens. Even when citizens choose to protest, they do so with the belief that their leaders are merely bad and need to be replaced. However, this is not an adequate approach to achieving justice for all and lasting prosperity. Change is difficult because it requires the current beneficiaries to lose their power. Their resistance to change is supported by strong bureaucracies backed by powerful military systems. Since the top few percent of every country are benefiting from the underlying structure, ordinary people without a clear goal are unable to make change.

Revolts against tyranny have taken place many times. However, there is no history of people coming up with a completely new system of government and redesigning the whole bureaucracy, the judiciary process, and the structure of law enforcement until the United States Constitution was ratified on June 21, 1788—the only system developed to achieve government of the people, by the people, and for the people.

Like most other countries, the United States also began under a system of command and control. Before 1776, the United States was not a country but individual British colonies. The colonists were not treated as British citizens and had no representation in the British Parliament. The British controlled the distribution of land, awarding property only to colonists loyal to the king. They restricted the colonists' ability to trade freely to ensure their reliance on Britain for most goods and services. As colonies began expanding into the western regions of North America, the British placed restrictions on them by prohibiting western settlements and forcing those who had already moved into these areas to return east.

But the most contentious aspect of British control was the taxation of the colonists. Following the French and Indian War, the British wanted to raise money to pay war debts and decided that the colonists should be held financially responsible. The British government enacted the Stamp Act, which required the colonists to purchase special paper for legal documents. The colonists began resisting these unfair levies by boycotting and refusing to buy British goods. Tensions came to a head in 1773 when colonists snuck into the Boston harbor and dumped imported teas into the water, which came to be known as the Boston Tea Party, one of the primary events leading to the American Revolution. Like colonists in so many other areas of the world, American colonists revolted against the unfair policies of the crown and the restrictions on their individual rights. But unlike the other colonists, Americans did not seek to change only their immediate circumstances. Instead, they created an entirely new system of government.

As American colonists worked to build a new nation, the underlying goal was always to prevent the centralization of power in the hands of one or a few. In revolt against the overreaching authority of the British government, the colonists created a governmental structure that would always ensure a balance of power and a sharing of that power with the people. For example, the United States Constitution is referred to as the Supreme Law of the Land. No citizen is above the provisions of this document, and the process to change it is intentionally challenging to ensure that no leader can modify it to drive his or her agenda. The goal of decentralization is also evident in the role of the president. Term limits restrict the length of time that a person can serve in the office. Also, the Constitution expressly limits the power of the president, and various independent authorities lie with other branches of the government. The colonists did an excellent job of creating a federal government structure that dispersed powers between the executive, legislative, and judicial branches—called the separation of power.

Supporting this structure is the system of checks and balances, where each branch has the ability to override certain decisions of other branches. Collectively, the entire structure of the American government is designed to prevent the concentration of power and place as much control as possible in the hands of the people. The primary goal of the Constitution is to protect the individual's rights.

Another significant factor in the government structure created by the American colonists is the creation of law-enforcement agencies tasked with protecting the interests of all individuals. Throughout the history of monarchies around the world, law enforcement was created for the primary purpose of protecting the king and advancing the royal agenda through force and intimidation. Citizens who resisted the goals of the crown were punished, often publicly, as a way of controlling the masses. The American colonists changed the structure of law enforcement, making these branches accountable to local governments. Even as commander in chief of the military, the president must answer to the other branches of government before making ultimate decisions. And the U.S. military cannot be used against its citizens by the federal government to enforce domestic policies.

Japan and Germany operate under governmental structures similar to that of the United States.

In May 1945, Nazi Germany surrendered after the long and destructive Second World War. The victorious American, British, French, and Soviet allies each occupied a region in Germany. Germany split into two countries, the Federal Republic of Germany (FRG) and the German Democratic Republic (GDR) controlled by the Soviet Union. In 1947, as cold-war tensions grew with the Soviet Union, the United States initiated the multibillion-dollar Marshall Plan, officially the European Recovery Program, to rebuild the democracies of Western Europe. The Marshall Plan included the American, British, and French occupation zones of Germany. Americans gave $12 billion ($100 billion 2018 USD) to West Germany and took the lead in transforming the country from a dictatorship to a democracy. This led to the establishment of a federal government structure similar to that of the United States, with 16 states, termed Bundesländer.

The Americans oversaw the first local elections in 1946, which were followed by the first national elections in the combined American, British, and French zones in 1949. The 1949 elections formed the Federal Republic of Germany (West Germany). But West Germany did not regain full sovereignty from the occupiers until 1955, ten years after the occupation began.

Germany is classified as a parliamentary and federal democracy with a bicameral legislature. The chancellor is the head executive. Working with a group of advisory ministers, the chancellor has the power to make certain decisions with the consent of the parliament, termed Bundestag. These representatives are proportionately elected by the German people every four years to create and pass laws. The other half of the parliament is made up of the Bundesrat, which represents the interests of the individual states. Members of the parliament elect the federal president, a mostly ceremonial post with a term of five years. The country consistently ranks among the top five wealthiest countries in the world, and its citizens are prosperous. Its economy is considered one of the strongest among all European nations, and the country places second among the world's largest exporters of goods. Its educational system also stands out, offering older students free technical and vocational training that meets the specific needs of the nation's workforce. Strong legislative measures and livable wages protect workers. Family and leisure time is promoted, adding to the high standard of living that most Germans enjoy.

During the same period in Japan, the most important reform carried out by the American occupation was the establishment of a new constitution to replace the 1889 Meiji Constitution. The final constitution, which was submitted to the Japanese government by General MacArthur on February 13, 1946, protected people's civil liberties and contained Japanese approval to retain the emperor, though he was stripped of all power. Before Japan's defeat, Emperor Hirohito was officially regarded as Japan's absolute ruler and a quasi-divine figure.

Though Japan is classified as a monarchy, the emperor's role is only symbolic. The constitution states that he is a symbol of the government, serving ceremonial duties, such as presiding over ceremonies and conferring specific honors at the discretion of the National Diet, which is the legislative branch of the nation's federal government. The National Diet consists of the House of Representatives and the House of Councilors. These elected officials work independently to enact the decisions of the executive branch, which is headed by the prime minister, who performs duties with the assistance of a cabinet, much like the president of the United States. The constitution of Japan also ensures a separate law-enforcement arm by creating a judiciary that is separate from other branches of government.

Japan is ranked as one of the wealthiest nations in the world. Though the islands are crowded, most of the residents live relatively well, ranked 11th highest in the 2010 United Nations Quality of Life Index. Its school system also consistently ranks at the top of the global list, with a strong emphasis on technology and finance.[74]

The United States, Germany, and Japan are three excellent examples of countries where a government of the people and by the people works for the people's best interests. The world's population is poor and suffering because most government leaders do not run their nations with this structure. The legacies of governing structures developed by dictators and monarchs remain, and their effects are still felt by the majority of people around the world. Even when the citizens of these nations decide to revolt and fight for their rights, the lasting results are rarely in the interests of the people. The American Revolution (1765–1783) is a rare example of a citizen revolt that produced real, sustained improvements for the people, thanks to the common goal of preventing the concentration of power and keeping the power of the government in the hands of the people.

Note that in these three nations—the United States, Germany, and Japan—the culture, continent, language, religion, and race are all different, but the structure of government based on the balance of power has created three of the most successful economies of the world. Notably, 77 among the top 100 consumer brands in the world came from these three nations—61 of them from the United States, ten from Germany, and six from Japan.[75] The top five brands in order of brand value are Apple, Google, Coca-Cola, IBM, and Microsoft.

Unfortunately, governing structure, which should be considered the most fundamental requirement for prosperity, gets the least attention. I believe most people, including leaders themselves, lack an understanding of how a government structure designed to command and control the population benefits the rulers and not the needs of the people.

Summary

A new form of government emerged when the people of the United States of America revolted against British rule and created a structure that keeps a check on concentration of power. It is designed to protect the inalienable rights of each individual—"Life, Liberty and the pursuit of Happiness." The American Revolution led to similar rebellions, starting in France and continuing into the twentieth and twenty-first centuries, as recently as the Arab Spring of 2011 that lit a spark of revolt in oppressed parts of the world. People observe the American example, which, in spite of its imperfections, has undeniably created remarkable wealth and prosperity.

THE REAL ISSUE: CORRUPTION

5

"The opposite of poverty is not wealth, it is justice."

—Bryan Stevens

What Is Corruption?

Corruption is misuse of governmental power for illegitimate
private advantage. When governments are corrupt, it results in a lack
of justice. Corruption takes place at multiple levels. Petty corruption is
categorized as government officials soliciting bribes for access to public
amenities such as admission to schools, obtaining business licenses, or
the services of the police. The second tier of corruption is the illegal actions of high-ranking government officials to misuse public and private
resources and distort laws to their gain. The highest level of corruption
is where national policy makers manipulate policies and the rule of law
to maintain their level of power and increase their individual wealth.

It's important to understand that corruption is never limited to benefiting only the highest-level officials. It exists at all levels of government.
Leaders' corrupt acts create an environment that permeates all areas of
the government, enabling officials at every level to gain financial benefit
at the expense of the public good. It may seem like a mild problem when
a low-level government clerk can get away with taking a small bribe.
In reality, though, the consequences of corruption are far-reaching, a
vicious circle that affects the whole society. Even small business owners

are forced to participate in the system of corruption, charging higher prices to poor consumers in order to pay bribes to officials. These factors create a kleptocratic government that takes resources and wealth away from the many and places it in the firm grasp of the ruling few. These leaders then devise new extractive political policies to maintain the cycle and facilitate its growth for higher personal profit, repeating the vicious circle. Corrupt rulers in such countries realize that in the absence of justice and accountability, money is the dominant power and to continue to stay in power, they need to continually accumulate wealth.

The prevalence of systematic fraud is an essential aspect of failing nations. The have-nots, who make up the majority of the population, live under oppressive conditions caused by lack of justice. Consider the Mafia and the organizational framework it uses to carry out crimes. The offenses range from trivial, like petty theft, to grave, like assault and murder. Each of these crimes, no matter how small, is carried out under an organized system, where the gang leaders receive benefit from the actions of lower-level members in exchange for protection from law enforcement and from other criminals. It's a system that benefits all members, not just those at the top. Corruption results in similar behavior from government officials. Lower-ranking officials either choose or are forced to support their bosses in channeling bribes up the chain of command. This environment, built on an appetite for illegal activities, enables most officials to pursue their own nefarious financial schemes.

When we make judgments about the success or failure of a nation's governing body, we approach it from the perspective of what we expect a government to do for its people. As rational thinkers, we expect a government to serve the people by formulating rules and legislation that benefit and protect its citizens. We expect the government to engage in activities that create wealth for the majority of its people and the nation as a whole. We expect the government to provide basic necessities for its people or at least make it possible for the people to satisfy their fundamental needs. We expect the government to operate within the boundaries of law and ensure that every citizen also follows the law of the land or faces legal consequences. As logical and pragmatic as these expectations are, they would lead us down the wrong road when analyzing the activities of a corrupt government. These presumptions lead us to the conclusion that corrupt governments are failing in their goals. But as explained below, this is an incorrect interpretation.

Corrupt governments are fully capable of meeting their objectives and providing for their intended beneficiaries. The goal of a kleptocratic body is not to serve the needs of the people. These leaders are not in place to make policies that benefit the citizens or build wealth for the nation. They are not even in power to maintain the rule of law. The sole objective of a corrupt government is to maintain the corruption. More specifically, corrupt leaders' goals are to extract as many resources and financial gains as possible from the nation for their own benefit and to share those gains with the officials who support them. The leaders are like Mafia bosses running a vertically integrated enterprise. They oversee a large group of individuals who view the government as a means of personal gain. To secure a position within this organization, lower-level officials provide money up the chain of command to higher-level officers and ruling politicians. What do they expect in exchange? Just like the Mafia model, they expect protection from retribution and unspoken permission to continue fraudulently extracting resources from the nation and its weakest citizens.

This Mafia-type structure helps establish the longevity of corruption, even when new leaders come into power and pledge to end fraud and theft within the government. An example is the election of Afghan president Hamid Karzai, who publicly asserted his intention to fight the corruption that has run rampant within the Afghan government for generations, but who retained two corrupt vice presidents, Karim Khalili and Marshal Muhammad Qasim Fahim. Both have been openly accused of committing the same corruptions that Karzai claimed to resist.[76] Without prohibition from his administration, the system of corruption continues.

I believe that kleptocratic behavior is driven by the inheritance of past government structures implemented by colonial powers or by kings and dictators. It is not a system designed by the current leaders. Instead, it is rooted in the history of these nations, almost like a game with rules that were created many generations ago. This game, which forms the structure of the government, is designed to benefit people in power. Since the government is structured to benefit the powerful, staying in power requires sharing wealth with other individuals in the government. Due to lawlessness and lack of structural checks on wrongdoing, this structure manifests as corruption. Just like in the Mafia, everyone in the government gets a share, and it becomes a perpetual system of extracting wealth from the people. I contend that this is why kleptocracies persist, regardless of who leads the country. Within these structures—under the rules of the game—corrupt leadership automatically emerges, and a person who does not play by the rules of the kleptocracy has limited opportunity to rise to the top. The rules of the game are like the air we breathe: it governs our lives, but we do not see it.

Even in countries with some level of judicial safeguards, property crimes go mostly unpunished because they are considered less dangerous than personal crimes. Property crimes are defined as offenses where the goal is to take money or property, but there is no force or threat of force against the victim. Embezzlement, tax fraud, and forgery are typical examples of property crimes. In contrast, personal crimes are defined as offenses that cause physical, emotional, and/or psychological harm to the victim. Rape, assault, and murder fall under the classification of personal crimes. The relative insignificance attributed to property crimes is one of the reasons that corruption is allowed to thrive in failing nations. However, it is a fallacy to presume that property crimes do not cause physical, mental, or psychological harm to their victims, especially those who live in a society where bribes and coercion virtually control every aspect of life.

Indicators of Corruption—Paltry Tax Collection

For any nation to prosper, taxation is the grease necessary to run the economy. Per the Brookings Institute, "There is a strong correlation between prosperity and tax compliance."[77] A straightforward indicator of poor compared to prosperous nations is meager tax revenue as a fraction of the GDP. Again, corruption is used as a mechanism to circumvent payment of taxes. Level of corruption is inversely correlated to the amount of taxes collected. As reported by the World Bank, wealthier countries receive about 33% of their GDP from taxes, while nations with lower incomes receive less than 12% from taxes. While there is no standard level of tax collection, the amount taxed should at least be sufficient to cover the necessary infrastructure and basic needs of a country. Taxes play the most significant role in running a country, and a lack of tax revenue reduces economic activity and public services.

While poverty is one of the reasons why poor nations do not collect adequate taxes, avoidance of and noncompliance with tax laws is a more significant issue. Those with higher incomes, who are required to pay taxes, do not pay them due to their ability to evade tax laws. They can accomplish this through corrupt tax collectors, most of whom are there to collect bribes instead of taxes. The tax collectors do not have a choice because they have to share their collected bribes with their superiors or risk their jobs. Tax avoidance also becomes possible when citizens refuse to report their income, which is a common practice among business owners in corrupt nations. In some countries, when tax collectors attempt to complete collections, they are met with violence and life-threatening resistance. Somalia is considered one of the most dangerous countries in the world for tax collectors. Between 2012 and 2014, nearly a fifth of the country's tax collectors were killed.[78] Armed guards are now used to protect these government officials, but an extensive deficiency in tax collection remains.

Recognizing the role of taxation in successfully governing a country, the United Nations is working to establish strategies to increase taxation among poorer nations. Global economists believe that higher tax revenue not only improves infrastructure and services to the people but also leads to increased private investment, creating new jobs and opportunities for all citizens. Multinational and foreign businesses resist investing in countries without adequate infrastructure, educational opportunities, and medical facilities. Therefore, nations without essential public services experience lower private and foreign investment, which reduces jobs and financial opportunities for the citizens.

The other major impediment to adequate tax collection within poorer nations is the theft of public money. It is estimated that over a trillion dollars are stolen every year from poorer countries due to corruption. A report by the antipoverty organization ONE identified trillions of dollars illegally diverted from some of the world's poorest nations.[79] The country's leaders, in cooperation with financial criminals and other corrupt leaders around the world, use embezzlement and money laundering schemes to set up fake companies in other locales, like London, Delaware, and Hong Kong. If this money were retained within the developing nations, taxation could bring in almost $20 billion in revenue, benefiting millions of struggling people each year. According to the study, this is enough money to educate 10 million sub-Saharan African children annually. It could also provide more than 16 million vaccines against deadly diseases and give over a million HIV/AIDS patients the medications they need to survive.

The effects of corruption also impact tax collection. Many otherwise law-abiding citizens are less willing to pay their taxes when they believe the money is being misused by their government. Since they are unwilling to fund the behavior of corrupt politicians, the prevalent corruption in their country justifies their decision to withhold money from the government. Even some of my relatives, people whom I consider to have high moral values, do not pay taxes. They justify it by saying, "Why should I pay money to this corrupt government?"

Some countries have implemented policies that promote the theft of public funds through elaborate money laundering schemes. India utilizes a system called participatory notes, or P-notes, which is an offshore derivative instrument used to convert black money into white securities, allowing anonymous investments in Indian stocks.[80] Dr. Subramanian Swamy gave a detailed explanation of how this works.[81] A government official steals several million rupees from India. He takes the Indian rupees and moves the money to Switzerland via the "hawala" channel (explained in the next paragraph). The money is held in a Swiss bank, where it can be kept in secret due to the country's banking laws. To launder the money, or make it appear legitimate, the politician purchases a P-note security from such banks as Goldman Sachs or Morgan Stanley. P-notes can be sold freely to another investor. P-note investors are not required to register with the Securities and Exchange Board of India, the government entity that regulates investments within the country. The P-note is then used to purchase Indian stocks. Once the shares increase in value, they are sold for rupees, as laundered money. The anonymous nature of the participatory notes makes it extremely difficult to prove that these profits originated from stolen money. While this practice has occurred regularly throughout India's contemporary history, the Securities and Exchange Board of India currently claims that it has almost entirely stopped the use of P-notes.[82]

Now, let's return to hawala, which is another significant way of hiding illegally obtained money that enables tax fraud.[83] Often called the underground banking system, hawala allows for the transfer of money without any actual movement of the money from one party to another. For example, if I wanted to transfer $500 to a family member in another country, I would give the funds to a hawala dealer, along with the family member's name, city of residence, and a secure password. The dealer then contacts another hawala dealer in my family member's country and instructs him to give her the money as long as she knows the password. The second dealer contacts my family member and gives her the money. The $500 that I gave the first hawala dealer is not transferred to the second hawala dealer before the transaction is complete. Instead, the system is based on trust, honor, and personal relationships. Hawala is an ancient practice originating in South Asia. It is still used today in poor nations around the world. Money is transferred across borders without any official record keeping. Since transactions are off the record, there are no official estimates, but hawala is considered a significant contributor to money laundering, estimated to exceed $1.5 trillion per year.[84] While this may seem like an honorable way to conduct business, it breeds corruption due to the lack of documentation. Hawala dealers keep very informal receipt logs and settle debts among one another with cash. This absence of record keeping allows for the virtually anonymous transfer of illegally obtained money. Money launderers, including terrorists, can easily move money between countries while avoiding banks or government regulations. Corrupt politicians and business leaders use hawala to avoid paying taxes on their earnings.

Indicators of Corruption—Leaders Becoming Wealthy

Estimates of their wealth are not easily verifiable, but there is overwhelming evidence that most rulers of corrupt nations become extremely wealthy. For example, corrupt leaders of the following countries gained a high net worth after becoming leaders.

Examples of Estimated Net Wealth of Corrupt Leaders

Country	Leader	Net Worth
Russia	Vladimir Putin	$200 Billion[85]
Tunisia	Zine al Abidine Ben Ali	$37 Billion[86]
Pakistan	Asif Ali Zardari	$1.8 Billion[87]
Syria	Bashar al-Assad	$1.5 Billion[88]
Pakistan	Nawaz Sharif	$1.4 Billion[89]

Let's take a look at Pakistan, my country by birth. The two wealthiest people who live in Pakistan are the last two prime ministers, Asif Ali Zardari (worth $1.8 billion) and Nawaz Sharif (worth $1.4 billion).[90] Both accumulated great wealth while in power. Zardari was known as Mr. Ten Percent because he took 10% of every deal needing approval by the government. He is alleged to have siphoned approximately $2 billion into a Swiss bank account, using government contract kickbacks and other methods of misappropriating public funds. Sharif was disqualified in 2017 due to corruption allegations exposed in Panama leaks. The Pakistani Supreme Court, backed by the military, carried out his dismissal as a result of protests by Imran Khan, the opposition leader at the time.[91] The Supreme Court ruled unanimously that Sharif should be disqualified after an investigative panel determined he could not account for his vast wealth.

During his ten years in office as president of Afghanistan (2004 to 2014), Hamid Karzai received tens of millions of dollars from multiple sources, including the United States CIA.[92] The cash payments were meant to secure influence for the American government but were instead used to increase Karzai's wealth, along with that of numerous other government officials. In 2017, he was named one of the highest-paid politicians in the world by *People with Money* magazine.[93] Taking into consideration factors like upfront pay, residuals, and endorsements, the magazine estimated Karzai's net worth at $245 million.

There are many methods of corruption employed by rulers to get rich. One common method is to receive kickbacks by awarding domestic megaprojects to foreign companies. For example, copper mines in Zambia were sold to the Swiss with complete disregard for the environmental hazards impacting the local population. In other instances, rulers take kickbacks for awarding vast military and public works contracts. According to the *New York Times*, Dassault Aviation, a French military contractor, paid Asif Zardari $200 million in 1995 for a $4 billion jet fighter deal. Benazir Bhutto and her husband, Asif Zardari, are suspected of obtaining over $1.5 billion in illegal profits through kickbacks on government transactions and the selling of state-owned lands.[94]

In early 2004, the German anticorruption NGO (nongovernmental organization) Transparency International released a list of some of the most self-enriching national leaders in modern history.[95] One of the most notable figures was former Indonesian president Suharto, who is estimated to have misappropriated between $15 and $35 billion. Coming to power in the 1960s as part of a political coup, Suharto ruled the country for more than 30 years. He presented himself as the father of the Indonesian people and brought a notable amount of economic success to the country through oil production. Though he claimed to embrace some principles of democracy, his regime always kept a tight rein on any outspoken opposition. Through increased foreign trade and infrastructural development, he was able to raise the standard of living for many within his country. However, not everyone was a supporter of Suharto, and many members of the opposition accused him of stealing billions of dollars from Indonesia. He began filling his government cabinet with family members and cronies in the business community, ensuring that his political desires would prevail over any opposing views. His opponents referred to his rule as "KKN," which stood for corruption, collusion, and nepotism. He placed state-run monopolies under the direction of family members, who returned the favor with million-dollar donations to Suharto's "yayasans." These charitable organizations were publicly tasked with building much-needed schools and hospitals, but instead the funds were used by Suharto at his personal discretion. Suharto further ensured his financial well-being by creating a bureaucratic infrastructure that was virtually impossible for business owners to traverse without the assistance of a Suharto family member. In return for this assistance, the business owner had to provide the family member with a prominent position within the organization or an equity stake in the business. The examples of Suharto's corrupt influence over the government are numerous, from valuable state contracts for family members to unlimited borrowing from the country's central bank with no repayment obligations.

In 1997, the drastic devaluation of the Thai baht triggered a region-wide economic downturn and Indonesians were hit especially hard. Amid widespread dissatisfaction and protests, Suharto resigned from office in 1997, only two months after he had won a controversial reelection. He was charged with corruption in 2000, facing allegations of over $500 billion in embezzled funds. Judges ruled that he was unfit to stand trial due to an unexplained "brain disease."

Kosovo is also governed by a kleptocratic regime, and according to reports, many of Kosovo's political leaders have managed to create extremely wealthy lifestyles, with some having a net worth of more than several million euros.[96] In 2012, the European Union External Action Service reported information about illegal payments between the Kosovan Ministry of Internal Affairs and an Austrian state printing company contracted to print Kosovan passports. According to the report, these payments totaled more than 1.4 million euros.[97] Another reported incident involved a former transport minister and current deputy president of the ruling Democratic Party who, along with six other suspects, was arrested on charges of organized crime and the embezzlement of at least 2 million euros.[98]

Examples of corrupt leaders are legion: PLO chairman Yasser Arafat has been accused of misappropriating his country's money, to the sum of $1 to $10 billion. Chinese prime minister Wen Jiabao retired from office, leaving his close relatives in control of more than $2.7 billion in assets.[99]

But any discussion about financial corruption by a national leader must include Russian president Vladimir Putin, who is allegedly worth an estimated $200 billion, an amount that many analysts believe was illegally obtained through government programs that he has implemented during his time in power. Putin's early experience laid the groundwork for his corrupt endeavors as president. He spent years working in Russia's security agencies, including the KGB, and was later named director of the FSB, the security organization that followed the KGB. He was first elected Russia's president in 2000 and reelected in 2004. Term limits kept him from running again in 2008, but his reign continued after Dmitry Medvedev was elected president and named Putin prime minister. Putin orchestrated the extension of the presidential term from four to six years and was reelected to the presidency in 2011.

Publicly, Putin claims to oppose corruption and vows to provide stiffer penalties for related offenses, but these public declarations are a far cry from the reality of what happens within his administration. For example, a highly publicized effort to arrest organized crime heads reportedly ended with the president secretly allowing many of the accused to walk away. He was then charged with orchestrating alliances between organized crime leaders and high-ranking government officials. Putin uses these connections to steer government contracts toward individuals he can control and away from those who voice opposition. He is also accused of holding secret investments in several state-run industries, including oil and natural gas companies, creating a continuous stream of hidden wealth for himself and his cronies. While the United States imposed sanctions on various government officials within the Kremlin, Russia steadily avoided making any direct accusations against Putin. Finally, the U.S. levied sanctions against Putin and his political allies in 2014, pointing to the president's dubious investments in the energy industry.[100] The evidence is clear. Putin is the richest individual in the world, with a worth—dubiously gained—that rivals entire countries. Yet Putin vehemently denies these claims, placing his own estimate of wealth at around $100,000.

Indicators of Corruption—Unequal Wealth Accumulation

In corrupt nations, it is not only the political leaders who control the vast majority of the nation's wealth. One percent of the wealthiest individuals in the world own 40% of the world's wealth. To be fair, even in nations where adequate resources are available to care for all citizens, there are very few individuals controlling a vast majority of the country's wealth. This probably comes as little surprise. But when analyzed for corrupt nations, you recognize a glaringly obvious disparity in the distribution of wealth among citizens.

Decades of regulations designed to enhance the power and prosperity of political leaders create a situation where the majority of wealth is concentrated in the hands of a few elite. Morocco provides an excellent example where the difference between the lifestyles of ordinary citizens and the elite can be characterized as the difference between a shantytown and a palace. While the majority of the country's citizens live in poor conditions, members of a super-rich ruling class live in decadence. Each day, ordinary people are forced to view the ostentatious lifestyles of the elite. Meanwhile, the majority of people live in abject poverty, with not even electricity for basic everyday needs. While the majority of the nation's citizens live in slums, the elite live in lavish neighborhoods lined with villas and luxury vehicles. The clean, expansive streets offer beauty salons, fitness gyms, and grocers selling the most sought-after goods. Guard dogs keep watch over the neighborhoods, ensuring that most of the country's citizens are kept outside.

According to a report in *Al-Monitor*, an online media reporting site on the Middle East, the elite of Morocco can be divided into two basic groups. The first comes from old money, the descendants of ministers, ambassadors, and governors. Their families used their political clout to build levels of wealth that have persisted for generations. The second group is the "nouveau riche" or new rich. These individuals have been able to profit from their personal contacts and positions within the government. A survey conducted by South African market researchers concluded that the number of Moroccan citizens with a net worth of more than a million dollars doubled between 2000 and 2015.[101] However, the level of poverty and unemployment within the country experienced no positive change during the same period. These numbers characterize a nation where wealth significantly grows for a few citizens while the majority of residents remain destitute. *Forbes* magazine recently reported that, within this struggling economy where millions of people live in poverty, one individual increased his income by $600 million in a single year.[102] But Morocco is not alone in its system of income inequality. Extreme concentration of wealth is a common characteristic among corrupt nations.

In Liberia, there are generally only two classifications of wealth, the extremely rich and the extremely poor. According to a report by the African Development Bank Group, less than 5% of the nation's population can be characterized as middle class.[103] More than 80% of the population lives on less than $1.90 per day. Only about five percent of the population is formally employed, and of those who are fortunate enough to have jobs, 80% don't have a regular income. Within Liberia, citizens with college degrees live in meager apartments, where they are forced to share a bathroom with up to 100 other residents. At the other end of the spectrum lies the top 20% of the population, who own about 45% of the country's total wealth. Liberian senators are compensated at more than $12,000 per month, and that does not include substantial allowances for lavish housing, along with a long list of other perks.[104] The total cost of running the legislative body of this incredibly impoverished nation equals more than 10% of the country's total revenue.

China is on a steady path of economic growth, mostly due to a vast increase in exports. Yet this advancement in the country's wealth has not reached the nation's poorest residents, as income inequality reached its most extensive gap in history. One percent of the population controls more than a third of the country's total wealth, while a quarter of the entire population shares a meager one percent of the wealth.

Guatemala is consistently ranked as one of the poorest countries in Central America.[105] Almost 60% of the citizens live in poverty, including more than 68% of the country's children under the age of five. The majority of the poor population is indigenous and lives in the countryside, essentially left behind by their government without any infrastructure or public assistance. The country's malnutrition rate is one of the worst in the world; entire families go without adequate nutrition. The same goes for the literacy rate, which is substantially lower than the average in Latin America. Within the poverty belt of the Northern and Northwestern regions, the average child attends school for only 3.5 years, and that number is even lower for girls. But not every Guatemalan citizen lives in abject poverty. One percent of the population lives very well, controlling about 65% of the nation's total wealth, while five percent of the population controls about 85% of it. The rich live in secluded communities, where the cost of the least expensive homes are 70 times the country's average yearly income.[106] They live in white stucco mansions with easy access to grocery stores, parks, nightclubs, and shopping boutiques. These private enclaves allow the super-rich to live away from the poverty and crime that stifles the rest of the country. Iron gates keep out the majority of Guatemalans and serve as a stark reminder that while they live in poverty, the smallest percentage of the population basks in abundance.

Impact of Corruption on Economies

Corruption is a mechanism to enable privileged people to extract wealth from ordinary people. It permeates even at the lowest levels. In *Thieves of State: Why Corruption Threatens Global Security*, Sarah Chayes describes how shocked she was to learn that even the poor maids in Kenya have to pay for job placement.[107] Corruption is an invisible tax collected by anyone who can get away with it.

Corruption destroys trust between two people engaged in a business transaction. I can have a legally binding contract, but if I don't have legal safeguards and the ability to enforce them, I cannot ensure legitimate business with another party. In this scenario, the two sides engaged in business would use illegal methods to obtain revenge if a contract is broken. For example, in Pakistan, businessmen affiliate themselves with thugs within political parties or the police by regularly paying them. This is called "bhata." similar to extortion by Mafia for protection, it is a subscription fee that is paid by business owners to stay in business and obtain protection. It is similar to having ties to the Mafia to operate an illegal business such as distributing and selling drugs. The significant distinction is that the corrupt practice becomes the norm for every type of business. It works as a tax on business, yet the poor consumers pay for it. In addition, it increases barriers to new businesses and precludes free-market competition. New competition can be wiped out. For example, if I own a bakery, I may force out new competition in my territory by seeking help from my bhata recipients.

Impact of Corruption on Citizens' Daily Lives

When you live under a corrupt government, simple everyday tasks become challenging even insurmountable for most people. Those of us residing in the U.S. carry on with our daily lives without consideration of whom we will need to bribe or influence to fulfill our needs. When we see a doctor, we may worry about the cost of the visit, but we do not have the added stress of finding money to bribe the doctor. We can enroll our children in school without worrying about bribing school administrators. We live in the unappreciated luxury of a nation where the rule of law prevents rampant corruption.

According to Transparency International, more than one in five people around the world have been forced to pay a bribe for general healthcare.[108] Sadly, this is only the tip of global healthcare corruption. Countless other individuals are denied necessary assistance because of fraudulent prescription drug practices. In Kosovo, two commonly used cancer medications were replaced with an obscure, more expensive option across the nation. This one change caused treatment costs to increase from about $10,000 to more than $1.2 million, effectively pricing the majority of citizens out of adequate care while extracting astounding amounts of money from more affluent residents. A man in Morocco attempted to obtain an emergency procedure for his young daughter.[109] After racing to the medical facility, he was told that the necessary brain scan would not be available for months, leaving the child in danger of permanent brain damage. He was also told that the testing could only be obtained with a payment of $60 in addition to the standard cost of treatment. To secure medical treatment for his daughter, this man would have to pay more than a third of his total monthly income, making a heartbreaking choice between his only daughter's health and his entire family's well-being. This is a decision that many people around the world are frequently forced to make.

A recent Transparency International survey,[110] outlined in the table below, shows that in Pakistan 75% of those surveyed paid bribes to the police, 68% paid bribes for courts and legal services, and 61% paid bribes for utility services. India is worse than Pakistan in bribes paid to public schools and hospitals. These results highlight that corruption is an everyday incidence in unethical countries.

Have you paid a bribe to any of these six public services in the past 12 months?

Country	Public Schools	Hospital	ID Document	Utilities Services	Police	Courts
Australia	4%	2%	1%	0%	1%	3%
South Korea	5%	3%	1%	1%	3%	6%
Japan	0%	0%	0%	0%	0%	Not Asked
China	29%	18%	16%	Not Asked	20%	20%
India	58%	59%	59%	53%	55%	45%
Pakistan	9%	11%	38%	61%	75%	68%

Countless individuals around the world are also compelled to make this decision when trying to secure basic schooling for their children, since corruption within a government also extends to its educational system. In countries where public education is included in the national budget, the available funds become a significant target for fraudulent activities.[111] The results are widespread and place an unthinkable burden on families in these countries. For example, Kosovo's school admissions are sold to the highest bidder. If a family is unable to pay the bribe, its children are denied the fundamental right of education. When funds are stolen from education budgets, children are the ones who suffer most. Educators often sell textbooks and government-purchased supplies to private parties. They also sell student grades, negatively skewing testing results and educational statistics. Teachers and administrators gain their positions through bribes or family connections, leaving the vital job of educating youth in the hands of underqualified individuals. Educational corruption results in generations of uneducated or undereducated children.

Even more essential than education is our daily need for adequate food. Many of us, when our families need to eat, go to a store and purchase what is needed. This simple task becomes much more difficult in a corrupt society. In India, a food program was instituted to help combat the malnutrition and hunger that affects more than 40% of the nation's children.[112] With the investment of an additional 200 billion rupees, free rations were to be supplied to more than 800 million needy people. Yet corrupt officials sold the rationed goods on the black market for much higher profits. There are even reports of selling rations back to government procurement offices.

In China, experts blame corruption for the prevalence of food-borne illnesses.[113] Rotten fruit is made to look fresh with bleaching agents and harmful chemicals. Reports of baby formula mixed with melamine reached national headlines, while meats are reportedly treated with banned steroids. In 2011, the *Chinese Journal of Food Hygiene* stated that more than 94 million Chinese people become ill and more than 8,500 die each year from food-borne illness. Even after passage of the Food Safety Law, failure to implement regulations combatting corrupt deals between government officials and food producers have kept Chinese citizens at the mercy of an inadequate and potentially deadly food supply.

These problems are not limited to China. The television show *Mazaak Raat* airs in Lahore, Pakistan. The show provides a satirical view of realities its viewers face. Guest speaker Mohsin Bhatti discussed how fish at the famous Muzang fish restaurants is stored in filthy conditions, infested with bugs and insects, and even in the toilet.[114] The United States National Institutes of Health states that dangerous pathogens are frequently found in foods sold in Pakistan.[115] The lack of official supervision over food production and merchants adds to the prevalence of food-borne illnesses. These problems reportedly extend to most foods, including milk, grains, and even nuts, where studies have found high levels of mold and metal contamination.

Securing employment is another apparently straightforward process often frustrated by corruption. In a corrupt society, level of education or experience is usually of little consequence. Even if you are the most qualified applicant for a position, you are not likely to get the job without an inside connection. For government positions, corrupt officials hire family members instead of qualified candidates or choose applicants who will pay them a bribe. These leaders know that corruption is essential to extracting wealth, and they want to ensure that members of their workforce are willing participants in the process. Within the private sector, employers often choose workers who have some personal or financial connection with important government agents. As explained by Chayes in *Thieves of State*, the Moroccan revolution was largely led by highly educated, underemployed citizens. These individuals had earned PhDs but routinely lost employment opportunities to unqualified family members of political officials. Further adding to their frustration, they were forced to live in impoverished shantytowns while elites awarded themselves lavish palaces and extravagant vehicles.

Corruption limits people's ability to live a normal life. I will share a few firsthand experiences with corruption in Pakistan. At 18 years of age, I needed to obtain a passport. What should have been a simple process quickly turned into an example of institutional corruption when the person providing the form told me I could bypass the queue by paying him 100 rupees under the table. Another personal example, as I noted in chapter one, was my experience, also at the age of 18, of trying to obtain a driver's license. I learned that because officials were not interested in helping an ordinary citizen, they would give me the runaround. After waiting in line for the entire day, I decided it was not worth it for me to obtain a driver's license and I would just drive illegally. Again, these might seem like minor stresses, but when young people see that they are unable to exercise their rights and follow the law in a reasonable way, breaking the law becomes an everyday practice.

These are simple examples, but similar incidents routinely impact citizens in dealing with their governments. In Kenya, it is estimated that the average citizen is forced to pay 16 bribes each month to meet their daily needs.[116] While the majority of these payments are small, bribes valued at more than $700 make up about 41% of all payments made to various political officials. For people who do not have money or connections with high-level government officials, rightful access to services is usurped every day. Those unfamiliar with these types of corrupt environments may be shocked to hear that it is a common practice to brag about one's ability to break the law and get away with it. By knowing someone higher up in the government, some individuals can get away with most illegal activities. In sum, corruption impedes the efforts of average citizens to fulfill their daily basic needs and responsibilities.

Impact of Corruption on Foreign Investment

For developing and financially disadvantaged nations, foreign investment is vitally important to the growth of the economy. Most international corporations are wary of investing in a country lacking the rule of law and protection of property rights. During the 1980s, investment in developing countries by developed nations rose dramatically through efforts to create a more globalized economy. Along with these expanded efforts came stricter regulation of fraudulent investment activities, such as penalties exacted through the U.S. Foreign Corrupt Practices Act.[117] Yet even with increased monitoring and more serious penalties, concerns about corruption have largely halted investment. Law and order in a nation attracts investors, while the existence of uncontrolled corruption does the exact opposite by:

► increasing the cost of doing business,

► creating uncertainty about the ongoing cost of corruption and coping with unethical officials,

► encouraging fraudulent activities among intermediaries who work for investors within the country,

► and, in some cases, implicating investors in unwarranted criminal charges if they don't comply with the demands of corrupt government officials.

Corrupt practices are estimated to add more than 15% on average to the total cost of foreign investment projects. They also create uncertainty for the investors about the country's business environment and the expected rate of return. When faced with these unanswered questions, investors are less likely to make investments in these countries, which is extremely unfortunate because these are the countries that are most in need of investment. Some studies assert that a decrease in corruption from the level found in Azerbaijan to that prevailing in Estonia is associated with an increase in the probability of investment from 4 to 19%.[118]

A corrupt government is similar to a drug-dealing ring. There are unwritten rules established between the people involved in the ring, both the sellers and the buyers. Outsiders are not allowed to join the group unless a ring member vouches for them or they have something of particular value for the leader of the drug cartel. Corruption in government works in virtually the same way. Unwritten rules govern the behavior of involved individuals, and outsiders are restricted from entering; when they do, they are required to support the extraction game.

In addition to local interests benefiting from corruption, international supporters uphold the ruling party and perpetuate the continuous atrocities of kleptocracy. In Tunisia, real estate is a booming business and investors compete to control the waterfront properties that wealthy European tourists rent to enjoy sunny and warm weather. Though these coveted lands are plentiful within the country, only a handful of families own the vast majority of this real estate. These landowners make deals with foreign investors to build resorts, which would seem to grow the nation's tourism industry and thus strengthen the economy of the country as a whole. In reality, the people of Tunisia are separated from the economic advantages. Foreign investors bring in Europeans to staff the higher-paying positions at the hotels and resorts, thwarting employment opportunities for the locals. Most food and supplies are imported, again preventing economic opportunities for local businesses. Tunisian citizens are not even allowed to visit the beaches of most of these resorts. In Tunisia, the tourism industry is a closed system benefiting the ruling class and foreign investors.

Impact of Corruption on Entrepreneurs

When ordinary citizens are unable to pursue their dreams because they don't have access to the same opportunities as the rich and powerful, their inspiration and creative spirit suffocate.

The finance ministry is one of the leading tools for fraud in Tunisia. This corruption hits entrepreneurs especially hard. Instead of using random systems for tax audits, assessors target specific entrepreneurs, usually based on what value the business could provide the government. Tax liability is openly manipulated at the whim of the ruling class. For example, a business owner may be granted a reprieve from tax payments. However, the assessors keep track of these favors and use them to collect future bribes. If the owner ever refuses to comply with the orders of the officials, the tax debt is reinstated with exorbitant penalties due immediately.

The public water authority controls water supply for local farmers looking to grow their businesses. Officials use this power to influence the growers' prices. If they want to pay a lower price for crops, they stop the supply of water to the land, forcing the growers to meet their pricing demands or lose their farms. Corrupt party leaders reward chosen entrepreneurs with government loans, along with seed and fertilizer subsidies. These decisions are usually based on which businesses are financially supporting the party leaders or promising future return of favors. When infractions are documented, the government often holds punishment over the heads of business owners to enforce obedience.

In 2005, Chayes made the challenging decision to launch an entrepreneurial venture, providing economic opportunities in Kandahar, Afghanistan. She launched a business named the Argon Cooperative with the goal of creating soap from local natural resources. A pillar of persistence, Chayes spent nine months making weekly trips to the local Department of Agriculture, attempting to register her co-op. Every trip was met with disappointment as she was told that the director was away or the necessary forms were unavailable. When she attempted to make the co-op's first deposit into the national bank, she again faced a setback. The bank clerk demanded a bribe in order to open an account. Adamantly resolved to conduct business properly, Chayes confronted the teller and demanded a receipt for the payment. Her first request was met with indignation and resistance. After involving the bank manager, the clerk became extremely irate and demanded she return the next day for a receipt. She refused and proceeded to sit on the man's desk in protest. Another clerk eventually produced a receipt.

Chayes felt victorious in her refusal to give in to the corrupt system. However, when she left the bank, she encountered an Afghani man who was not as successful in his business endeavors. He had reluctantly paid the bribe that was demanded of him, but he still received incomplete service and felt that he was on the hook to pay more. It was a glaring example of the privilege she held as an American foreigner beside the deplorable conditions experienced by Afghani entrepreneurs. The level of corruption ordinary citizens face in these unjust nations is often enough to quash their dreams, destroying their business ventures and depriving the country of the benefit of their services and potential employment opportunities for others.

Impact of Corruption on Business

While large corporations tend to receive the lion's share of attention, it's actually small, locally owned businesses that are the cornerstone of a thriving national economy. They generate employment and cultivate feelings of pride within the community. But running a business in a country where corruption runs rampant is exceedingly challenging. Businesses are unable to transact efficiently while dealing with the maze of red tape designed to extract bribes. Imagine that you own a local food market. Every aspect of your business is vulnerable to the whims of self-serving officials and their fraudulent behaviors. Securing a location for your business may require bribes to government inspectors. Putting inventory on your shelves may require bribes to transportation officials or taxation officers. Enjoying the most basic protections may require bribes to local law-enforcement agents. Other officials might require continuous monthly payments in exchange for permission to stay in business. Every step of the way involves pressure from people looking for personal gain. Very few business owners can afford the high price of doing business, leaving only politically or financially powerful individuals to run the nation's businesses. The whole process results in an anticompetitive business environment in which only a few succeed and those who are successful block new participants.

In Uzbekistan, one group of brave businessmen stood up to the establishment and created a coalition of business owners committed to resisting corruption. This group comprised furniture factories, construction companies, bakeries, and transportation businesses. Thousands of poor Uzbekistan residents found employment within this group and were paid considerably higher salaries, thanks to the minimum wage established among the group. These workers also enjoyed sick leave, healthcare assistance, and free meals. Each owner contributed 10% of their profits, and the funds were used to finance charitable acts, like sporting events for local children or payment for an employee's medical expenses. The group created a sense of community unheard of within the kleptocracy of Uzbekistan. They proudly operated outside the nation's banking system, which effectively shielded them from governmental control.

Government officials felt threatened by the success of the group, especially when it began to grow significantly, attracting new entrepreneurs and workers. Instead of recognizing the benefits of these efforts, officials saw the group as a threat to their long-established system of corruption. Just by conducting business, it brought the morality of the government into question, which was a recipe for punishment under the country's ruling clan. The government labeled the group as militant extremists, accusing them of trying to overthrow the government and create a Muslim nation. The leaders were formally charged with conspiracy, thrown into jail, and subjected to a long, drawn-out trial biased in favor of the government. This exemplifies how, in a corrupt society, attempts to create a new employment model and conduct moral business are thwarted by the government and might even be dangerous.

Business owners are not the only victims of a corrupt economy. Owners who do stay in business must pass on those costs to someone, and that someone is the everyday consumer who needs the products or services offered. As a result, consumers are forced to pay substantially more for all products, adding to a cycle of poverty and struggle.

Impact of Corruption on Resource Utilization

Many of the world's poorest countries are rich in natural resources, which would seem to equate to greater economic stability. Instead, rampant fraud due to corruption leads to the misuse of these valuable resources. When used correctly, natural resources can have a positive impact on a nation's wealth, but unfortunately, corrupt leaders abuse them for personal gain. Instead of generating national income through taxation and sale of mineral rights, officials sell off valuable assets to corrupt business leaders in exchange for kickbacks. To ensure the continuous fleecing of resources, these leaders implement anticompetitive policies that create monopolies and drive up costs for residents. As a result, poor consumers are forced to pay more for their nation's resources.

They are essentially made to buy back resources that were stolen from them at inflated prices. Imagine that you owned a collection of valuable coins and a government official stole them from you. Then another government official offers to sell you back the coins for an extremely high price. A nation's resources belong to its people, and only proper use of these resources builds up a country's collective wealth and helps provide for its citizens.

Let's revisit the issue of Tunisian tourism. The beaches and waterfront properties are resources that should be used to benefit the country as a whole and strengthen its economy. Instead, the corrupt business practices discussed earlier maintain a system where the only beneficiaries of these valuable resources are a small group of elites.

Impact of Corruption on the Judiciary

A nation's judiciary is responsible for interpreting the country's laws and ensuring that they are followed to promote justice for all citizens. This is a vital part of any successful governing body, holding even the most powerful individuals accountable. For the judiciary to be effective, it has to be autonomous, free from the control or influence of government officials. Judicial officers are charged with making impartial decisions, independent from personal motives. When this impartiality breaks down, the result can be devastating for the nation. When citizens of successful countries come in contact with the judicial system, they expect to be treated fairly, with the same level of consideration as any other person. They present their cases to the court and presume that the decision maker will give it fair and balanced consideration. This expectation is what makes the judiciary work. It is the reason why citizens in rule-of-law countries overwhelmingly accept the decisions of the court and comply with their orders.

You would be hard pressed to find these same expectations among the citizens of a corrupt nation. These citizens tend to see the judiciary as an arm of the ruling elite, working at their discretion to hand down decisions that benefit them. Average citizens know that fairness is unlikely, especially when the interests of the powerful are at stake. They also know that enough money or influence goes a long way in determining the outcome of a case. In a report by Transparency International, the majority of Pakistani households reported encountering corruption while participating in the judicial process.[119] This isn't a chance occurrence or occasional problem; it is the norm, affecting the majority of the population. That makes it an institutionalized system of corruption. Indicators of judicial corruption:

▶ A court clerk accepts a bribe to fast-track a case past numerous other backlogged cases. Or the reverse, where a court clerk delays a case, sometimes for so long that the other party gives up.

▶ Judges accept bribes to rule for one client, regardless of the law.

▶ Judges are pressured by government officials to rule in favor of a particular side.

▶ Politicians appoint unqualified family members and friends to judicial positions.

▶ Prosecutors accept bribes to drop certain cases or bring unsubstantiated charges against individuals.

▶ Witnesses accept bribes to change their testimony or are intimidated into not testifying.

▶ Opposing attorneys accept bribes to withhold evidence or disclose confidential information.

As you can see, there are numerous opportunities for corruption to occur among members of the judiciary. A 2011 Transparency International report listed the judiciary as the most corrupt institution in Pakistan, equal only to the police.[120]

Impact of Corruption on Law Enforcement

Law enforcement goes hand in hand with the judiciary. While the goal of the judiciary is to interpret the law correctly, the purpose of law enforcement is to enforce the law. In successful countries, citizens call on law-enforcement agents to protect them from individuals who seek to harm them or impede their individual rights. Law-enforcement officers are expected to investigate the situation and take appropriate action. This duty extends to all citizens, regardless of their economic or political standing within the country. In the United States, if a high-ranking congressman is caught embezzling funds, he is arrested and subjected to a judicial process just like any other citizen. If he is sentenced to prison, law enforcement must respect the decision of the court and oversee his incarceration to ensure that he pays his debt to society.

This is not the case in corrupt countries. Police corruption in Mexico has reached epidemic proportions. Local police forces work in collusion with drug cartels to further their illegal activities and protect their financial interests. The news is filled with stories of police-sanctioned abductions and kidnappings.[121] Federal agents have been tortured and murdered at the hands of local officers, while women routinely report being raped and sexually assaulted. A survey by the National Institute of Statistics and Geography revealed that 63% of Mexican citizens have no trust in their local police.[122] In addition, 66% of respondents view their local law-enforcement agencies as corrupt. But the problem reaches higher than the local level. State police also face numerous allegations of kidnapping and working in collusion with drug cartels. At the federal level, agents are accused of killing civilians with no respect for the judicial process. There are also allegations that various divisions within the federal police commonly block one another from investigating certain matters. Between 2012 and 2013, the Mexican federal police received 1,400 human rights violation complaints, with torture being a chief concern.

An article by the Institute for War and Peace speaks about a man in Kenya who is pulled over by the police several times a day as he drives a bus through the streets.[123] The exchange is always the same: an official demands to see his credentials, and when he hands them over, he includes about 50 shillings (60 cents) between the documents. On average, these bus drivers pay about 200 shillings per day to operate their vehicles. "Police will always find something," the bus driver states. "It's easier to pay them petty bribes to avoid intimidation and all kinds of inconceivable accusations related to traffic offenses." In a survey by Transparency International, Kenyans categorized the police as the country's most corrupt institution.[124] More than 90% of those surveyed called the department corrupt, and more than 70% reported that they or a family member had to pay a bribe to a member of the police force within the past year. Bribery and intimidation are so widespread that they are considered business as usual among most Kenyans. Samuel Kimeu, Transparency international's executive director in Kenya, explained,

> A general sense of impunity currently prevails in the public service in so far as corruption is concerned. With little political leadership on the matter, corruption has been left largely unattended... The fact that no police commissioner or inspector-general has been held to account for their failure or inability to tame the widespread corruption means there is little motivation within to deal with the problem... The public is no longer willing to report bribery experiences to the police because they do not have the confidence that the [incidents] will be acted upon.

Impact of Corruption on Law-Abiding Nations

The U.S. Foreign Corrupt Practices Act (FCPA) penalizes U.S. corporations for paying bribes to do business in foreign countries. Not having the option to pay bribes constrains U.S.-based businesses from commercial ventures in most third-world countries.

Corrupt countries are not free markets where anyone can show up and compete to sell a better solution. Competition creates better products and services, resulting in higher value to consumers. Since the majority of the world lives in countries where corruption stifles competition, opportunities for entrepreneurs to openly compete are limited. Only the large multinational corporations are able to sell to these corrupt countries because of their connections and ability to influence government officials. This constrains small U.S. entrepreneurs, reducing their growth opportunities.

Summary

Every dollar that a corrupt government takes from the wealth of a nation is a dollar that is not used to feed the hungry, clothe the poor, care
for the sick, or protect the innocent. To view this from a humanitarian
perspective, consider these statistics:

► World hunger organizations estimate that a mere $1.50 is
  enough to provide a week's worth of school lunches to a
  hungry child.

► It costs about $4.00 to provide 20 years of safe and clean
  water to one person.

The money that is being stolen from these nations is, in some cases,
enough to end the appalling levels of poverty within the country. But
even these disturbing examples do not adequately address the impact
that corruption has on the world. Putting the ethical issues aside, the
global economy just cannot afford the level of corruption that currently exists around the world. The World Bank estimates that corruption
costs the global economy more than a trillion dollars.[125] That is an incredible number to wrap our head around, so let's take a minute to consider how much a trillion dollars is worth.

► One trillion dollars would allow you to spend $54 million a
  day for 50 years.

► The United Nations has calculated that it would cost $30
  billion to eradicate world hunger for a year.[126] With one trillion dollars, hunger across the globe could easily be wiped
  out.

► One trillion dollars could build 125,000 water wells in
  countries where citizens have no access to clean water.[127]

► With one trillion dollars, more than 25 million vaccines
  could be made available to vulnerable children around the
  world, today as well as for future generations.[128]

According to the World Bank, this trillion dollars in corruption includes reported bribery and theft within governments, among business industries, and by citizens to procure public services that should be provided free of charge. Even more disturbing is the fact that poor reporting and inadequate measurement tools make this a conservative estimate. The actual cost of global corruption, especially including the cost in lost opportunity, is many times greater than a trillion dollars.

Corruption permeates the poorest nations of the world, with misuse of government power embedded from centuries of colonial and monarchical rule. Political structures created for command and control of people and resources reward the most corrupt players. These rulers are incredibly wealthy compared to the citizens because "money requires power and power requires money." Justice is the opposite of poverty, and corrupt governments stifle the potential contributions of billions of human beings, impacting all of us across the globe.

WHY CORRUPTION OCCURS

6

---

*"One of the biggest curses from which India is suffering—
I do not say that other countries are free from it, but
I think our condition is much worse—is bribery and
corruption. That really is a poison."*

—Muhammad Ali Jinnah

To understand fully the fundamental reasons for corruption, it is essential to consider how the macroenvironment impacts human behavior. Through real-world examples, I will discuss how the environmental influence that I call the *invisible force* can sway us to be law-abiding or to act unlawfully.

How Environment Affects Behavior

"Tell me how I am going to be measured, and I will tell you how I will behave." The professor opened with this quote on the first session of my Managerial Accounting course at the University of Minnesota. While she offered it to introduce a discussion about organizations and accounting, my mind fixated on its ramifications on human behavior.

Let's first discuss this accounting principle from a business perspective. Later I will expand on how it impacts overall human behavior.

Within a business organization, leaders often use performance metrics to reward employees. Performance metrics affect how employees think they are being measured and consequently rewarded. For example, if an employee knows that her performance on a specific task is being evaluated, she will likely work harder to excel at that particular task. Of course, the workplace represents only one slice of a person's daily life. Unlike the workplace, where people go for part of their day, the societal environment influences each moment of their existence. People can leave work or decide to change jobs, but unless you move to another country, you can't escape the societal norms that unconsciously influence your behavior.

Even though most of us fail to realize it, we all live by the environmental rules that surround us. Adam Smith was an eighteenth-century economist and philosopher. His invisible hand theory describes an unobservable market force that helps the supply and demand of goods in a free market reach automatic equilibrium.[129] While I agree with his theory in regard to the pricing of goods through equilibrium, I don't agree that the extension of this theory to the pursuit of self-interest would miraculously result in a well-functioning society. I believe the theory of the pursuit of self-interest resulting in a prosperous society is only valid when people are free to do good and only good.

Our lives are fundamentally structured by the environments we live in. Humans require an equilibrium to operate. For example, when we drive a car, we drive according to the situation around us, such as other cars, weather, traffic, the road conditions, and the state of our car. To travel safely to our destination, drivers must coexist in equilibrium. Accidents occur when this equilibrium is violated. I believe it is this autonomous power of our subconscious brain that relentlessly evaluates our environment and guides us to drive safely. We take this powerful subconscious function for granted, just like the air we breathe. Since I am unaware of a name for it, I like to call it the *invisible force* that leads us to equilibrium.

Let's look at another variation of the driving example. In most countries, people follow traffic signs and regulations while driving a car, but more importantly, we also drive according to how other people are driving around us. Traffic laws may mandate that we are not supposed to cross into the oncoming traffic lane. But if it is necessary to avoid a collision, we swerve into the oncoming traffic lane. Another example is the posted speed limit. Even though the legal speed limit is evident, most people do not follow the speed limit as long as they can get away with it. As soon as a police car shows up, everyone slows down to drive at the speed limit. The point is that we live not by the clearly specified and known rules and laws, but the subconscious *invisible force.*

As human beings, the *invisible force* helps us to proceed in our best interests and act according to our environment. The same concept applies to the pursuit of our goals, such as how we earn a living and what we do for pleasure. No matter how badly we may want to assert our independence, our behavior is influenced by our environment. Growing up in Pakistan, I used to play cricket with neighborhood kids. Cricket is a favorite sport, there and I never even considered playing anything different. Now that I live in the United States, I play tennis like the majority of people I live and work with. My environment has changed my behavior and my preferences.

The choice of whether we react positively or negatively to an opportunity is also tied to our environment. If an individual lives in a society that rewards good deeds, they pursue good deeds. However, if that same person lives in a society where crime and corruption are rewarded, the may not only participate in unlawful activities, but also not even recognize the opportunity to pursue good deeds. I am not suggesting that everybody who lives in the same environment is going to behave exactly the same way. We do have personal biases and the ability to control our actions. However, the daily pressures of living within a corrupt society lead most people to take advantage of the benefits and comforts that come with participating in the corruption. Meanwhile, the fruitless struggle to do the right thing makes honest citizens feel disgusted and become depressed.

In addition to the macroenvironment, there are microenvironments around each human being. We are influenced by our families, friends, colleagues, extended families, religious institutions, and so on. However, in this book, I would like to focus on the macroenvironment of a country. Each individual's environment is formed by what and who are around them, but it all ultimately connects to the environment of the country as a whole, i.e., the macroenvironment. The macro environment refers to the larger society and influences the microenvironment of all people living within that society.

How do the leaders of a nation impact the macroenvironment? The leaders set the direction that affects everyone in the country. If they act corruptly, the majority of the country is affected and influenced by their actions. As previously stated, corrupt leaders intend to extract the wealth out of a nation, leaving the ordinary people poor. A core issue of this book is the impact of acute governmental corruption, with vertical channels in place to manage the flow of money from the bottom to the top. To survive in this environment, most people feel forced to become part of the corrupt process. The most unfortunate consequence is that corruption becomes so ingrained in the everyday lives of these citizens that just like air, or like what I am calling the *invisible force*, it is not recognized, and everybody blindly behaves in service of the corrupt environment.

Numerous theories explain the variations of people's behavior within an unjust society. Moral relativism, a school of thought dating back to ancient philosophy, is a theory that people shape their morality and judgment based on their circumstances.[130] It opines that there is no single standard for what is moral and just. Instead, individuals develop their standards based on their environment. Though it was first discussed among ancient philosophers, moral relativism made a strong reappearance during the early twentieth century as Western social scientists sought to debunk the widespread belief that European morals and values were superior to those held by residents of Eastern countries. During a 1947 United Nations debate on human rights, the American Anthropological Association announced that "moral values are relative to cultures and there is no way of showing that the values of one culture are better than those of another."[131] If we were to accept the legitimacy of moral relativism, we would explain that the residents of unjust societies act in irrational ways because they do not recognize the immorality of their actions. They are born into an environment where actions that are deemed improper in a just society are taken by the majority of the population in their unjust one. They grow up seeing corruption all around them, and it shapes the development of their internal moral compass to the point where they don't view it as a crime. Instead, they view it as an acceptable way of life. Therefore, they have no hesitation about acting in ways that unjustly affect others.

The debate over moral relativism is a lively one. I strongly disagree with the argument that moral values are based on culture. A person traveling to the United States from another country behaves differently upon arriving. Let's take as an example an individual flying from Pakistan to Chicago. While at the Islamabad airport, he would not follow the queue just because that's what people are doing around him. However, once he arrives in Chicago, he waits in lines and follows the queue. If a person's moral values were based on their culture, their actions would not change due to a change in their environment.

Another widely accepted reason for immoral behavior within an unjust society can be explained by the "When in Rome" factor. The phrase "When in Rome, do as the Romans do" dates back to 387 A.D., when Saint Augustine visited Milan and discovered that the church there did not fast on Sundays. Upon asking Saint Ambrose how to proceed, the response was to follow the customs of the local church. "When in Rome" is a depiction of the *invisible force* of the environment on people. People living in a corrupt society become accustomed to the immoral actions that govern their daily lives. They are aware of the unlawful actions, but the *invisible force* drives them forward with the "When in Rome" factor. The *invisible force* subliminally compels them to accept and act within the environmental norms.

A personal example is that whenever I go to Pakistan, I drive exactly like the other drivers around me without giving it a second thought. I believe my subconscious mind knows that if I don't drive the same way as those around me, I will not be able to survive. Even citizens who desire to live lawful lives get caught up in immoral activities as they strive to care for themselves and their families. People living in corrupt countries must pay bribes to meet many of their daily needs. From obtaining a loan or permit to filing a police report, these citizens spend a significant percentage of their meager incomes to pay necessary bribes.[132] They don't do this because they want to participate in a corrupt society; they do it because it is the way that their society functions.

Across the globe, millions of individuals live their lives under corrupt government leaders. Unfortunately, the actions of these leaders have far-reaching effects throughout these nations, trickling down to all levels of government and affecting private businesses and the majority of citizens. One reason this occurs is that most people follow their leaders, even when their leaders act immorally. Why do people act in this way? One explanation is the theory of political obligation, where people feel obligated to follow the actions of their leaders. Historically, this stems from the claims of leaders as divinely chosen—using religion for political persuasion. Leaders would present themselves as chosen by a divine or supernatural power, asserting that they had been selected to lead because they were superior to the people they rule. Believing these claims, subjects often placed their rulers on a level above themselves and pledged undying loyalty to them. When leaders acted in an immoral manner, they would provide a religious justification for their behavior, often stating that the divine power caused their actions. Needing to feel closer to their leaders, citizens would begin mimicking the actions of their rulers in the misguided belief that following in the leader's footsteps would make them closer to this divine status and, by extension, closer to God.

Thomas Hobbes was a sixteenth-century English philosopher and is regarded as one of the founders of modern political philosophy. In a theory similar to *invisible force*, he argued that citizens agree to give up some of their autonomy and abide by the rules of a governing body to live in what is perceived as an orderly society. This is called the social contract theory.[133] Hobbes lived during the English Civil War. The underlying basis of his theory is that self-interest intrinsically motivates all human action. We act according to what adds value to our lives. We also have an innate ability to efficiently pursue our wants and desires. Therefore, to live in a society that meets our fundamental interests, we give up some of our power and autonomy. It is essentially an unwritten agreement we enter into with our government. Even if citizens are acutely aware of the corruption that saturates their government, they "Do in Rome as the Romans do."

Humans also have a need to feel successful in their personal and business lives. Leadership naturally involves power over other individuals, so when citizens wish to exhibit success, they look to their leaders as examples. If they observe lawlessness, they tend to mimic it. In corrupt societies, the ability to break laws and get away with it is seen as a symbol of higher social status. It means that you are connected to influential people through your job, your family, or your acquaintances. Others within the community observe your social status and treat you with greater respect, as someone who can get things done and potentially help them with their needs. They see you as an individual in a privileged position; though it may sound ridiculous, your ability to break the law is considered an achievement.

Recent Examples of Human Behavior Driven by Environment

In 1982, Dr. James Q. Wilson, an American political scientist, and Dr. George L. Kelling, an American criminologist, introduced the broken windows theory.[134] It asserts that a safer, more lawful community, absent of serious crime, stems from a system of "zero tolerance" for petty crimes such as broken windows and graffiti. Though such small offenses may seem harmless, they serve as environmental triggers and signal that it is okay to commit more serious crimes. The broken windows theory gained significant attention from law-enforcement agencies across the country, including New York City, where violent crime was rampant in the early 1990s. The city's train system was notoriously dangerous for travelers. The police department implemented a quality-of-life initiative, which included a policy of cleaning graffiti from the trains each night. This was done to remove the assumption that it is permissible to commit crimes. Only two years after implementation, the crime rate had reportedly dropped within the city, with a 40% decrease in felony crimes and a 50% reduction in homicide rates.

In support of their theory, Wilson and Kelling point to an experiment conducted by Stanford University. Using the inherent struggle that exists between prisoners and guards, the study sought to examine how individuals react to perceived power. The study involved 24 college-aged participants. Half of them were assigned as guards within a simulated prison, and the other half were assigned as prisoners.[135] The prisoner volunteers were put through numerous simulations meant to degrade them and enforce the oppressive nature of prison.[136] The guards were allowed to make up their own rules, virtually given complete freedom to invent a system for maintaining order among the prisoners.[137] The result was extensive aggression from guards and rebellion from prisoners.[138] Prisoners began to exhibit self-endangering behaviors just a couple of days into the study. Many of the guards behaved in an unexpectedly aggressive manner. They exhibited hostility toward the prisoners, often arbitrarily punishing them with excessive penalties. Participant behaviors were so alarming that researchers halted the study prematurely, after only six days.

The New York City blackout of 1977 offers an additional example of environmental impact on individual behavior. On July 13, 1977, the power went out in New York City for 25 hours. With no lights, the city experienced numerous incidents of severe crime, including the looting of more than 1,600 stores.[139] More than 1,000 fires were set, including 14 multiple-alarm incidents. By the time electricity was restored, 3,776 people had been arrested and over $300 million in damage had been done. The same people who lawfully went about their daily lives turned to criminal activity when the conditions of their environment changed. A herd mentality took over, in which the wrongful actions of others became normalized and therefore acceptable to individuals who would otherwise never act in such a destructive manner.

You can witness this type of behavior, though not equally severe, on a crowded crosswalk. If one person crosses the street when the pedestrian light says not to, others will follow. Again, these are otherwise lawful people reacting to the *invisible force* of their environment.

The key question is, "How can we expect people living with injustice to behave justly?" The way we live mostly depends on the way we feel about our lives and ourselves. We act based on our thoughts, and our thoughts drive our feelings. Compare a person who is free to an individual who is imprisoned. The basic needs of the person in prison are met. They can eat, sleep, and breathe. However, their feelings about life are going to be different from those of a free individual. They will feel hopeless and depressed. Instead of truly living and enjoying life, they deal every day with the frustration of missing out on the free world. Meanwhile, the free individual can wake up with a plan for the day, set goals, and enjoy being alive. While this is an extreme example, it accurately portrays the pain of living in an oppressed society. Even if people's basic needs are met (and most people's are not), they are not afforded the luxury of enjoying life. Instead, they are bogged down in meeting their basic needs for survival. To further understand the effects of our individual needs, let's review Maslow's hierarchy of human needs.

Maslow's Hierarchy of Human Needs

In his 1943 paper "A Theory of Human Motivation," Abraham Maslow offered a psychological theory describing the order of human needs. The following illustration demonstrates Maslow's theory.

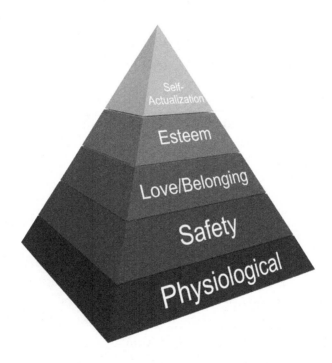

Physiological: The hierarchy of needs begins with the physiological necessities of life. These are the basic physical requirements for survival, including food, air, water, and shelter.

Safety: The second level entails safety. This includes physical security, feeling safe from the threat of hurt and harm. It also includes fiscal safety, which comes from reliable employment and the ability to amass a level of wealth to ensure financial security.

Love/Belonging: Once an individual has adequately fulfilled physiological necessities and a sense of safety, they can spend more time and energy on the level of love and belonging. Within this level, individuals develop their ability to build and maintain significant relationships. This is vital for individuals to thrive and succeed in life.

Esteem: The next level involves esteem. To reach their full potential, humans must feel respected and have a sense of self-worth. Without this stage, individuals can experience depression, feelings of inferiority, and a lack of necessary self-confidence. When individuals feel weak and helpless, they cannot reach their full potential.

Self-Actualization: The top level of Maslow's hierarchy is self-actualization, where individuals can focus on reaching their full potential. This is the level where people can develop their optimal individual achievement as well as their contribution to the larger world.

Maslow's theory is vital to understanding the plight of individuals living their lives in a kleptocracy. While these needs are presented as separate levels, they actually overlap and change throughout an individual's life. We all have to deal with each of these needs on a daily basis. Every day, we spend some of our time and energy meeting our physiological needs, promoting our safety, maintaining our relationships, strengthening our self-esteem, and moving toward self-actualization. These needs are part of everyone's daily life, no matter where you live in the world. The differences arise in how much time and energy we are required—or able—to spend on each of these areas. For example, the average person living in a prosperous country has reasonable access to such everyday necessities as food and housing. They also live in a society where their safety and security are not in constant jeopardy. Therefore, these levels of the hierarchy do not require a large percent of their time and efforts. However, the average individual living in a corrupt nation must work hard each day to meet their physiological and safety needs. They must spend so much time on these needs that there is little opportunity to think about the higher levels in the hierarchy.

The following graphic further illustrates the time spent by the majority of citizens living in corrupt vs. just nations.

Time Spent

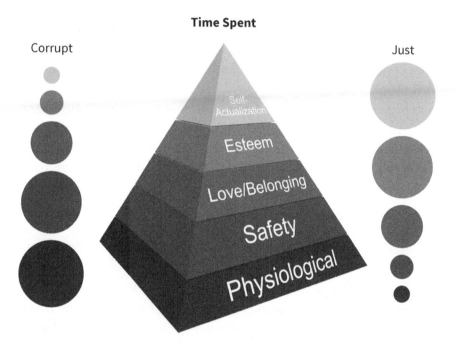

For the majority of individuals living in a corrupt and unjust country, daily time and effort are dedicated to meeting their physiological and safety needs. People living in just and prosperous nations spend fewer hours meeting their basic needs each day, enabling them to spend more time on the higher levels of the hierarchy.

The bottom line is, if you are living in a society where your basic needs are not being met, it becomes virtually impossible to achieve your full potential. If people are stuck obtaining their basic human necessities, they are not going to be able to pursue self-actualization. For example, the majority of people in Pakistan must spend a lot of time meeting their basic needs. They face electrical outages due to load shedding, shortages of natural gas used for cooking and heating, long queues for purchasing compressed natural gas, long waits and run arounds at government offices for basic services, water shortages, food shortages, etc. They also have to worry about the security of their family members due to a lack of protection from thugs and thieves provided by the police.

The majority of people in the world are stuck on the first and second level of Maslow's hierarchy of needs—they are struggling to survive. They live with an ever-present feeling of disgust that most residents in a just society cannot even imagine. The *Merriam-Webster Dictionary* defines oppression as "an unjust or cruel exercise of authority or power." In his book *Pedagogy of the Oppressed*, Paulo Freire explains that oppression prevents people from acting in a fully human manner.[140] Instead of being treated as valuable human beings, they are treated as objects, used solely for the benefit of the oppressor. When you live in a society that treats you as an object, you tend to ignore your basic moral compass.

Why Corruption Occurs

Widespread corruption can only take place in a government that allows the exercise of unchecked power with no consequences for illegal acts. A system of checks and balances ensures the distribution of power to prevent power from falling into the hands of one or a few. In corrupt countries, the absence of checks and balances enables corruption to thrive by allowing government officials to act without fear of consequences. Over the long run, systemic corruption influences the environment so profoundly that the majority of people do not even realize their actions are perpetuating the process.

A main impetus for corruption is the cooperation of law enforcement with lawbreakers. Most crimes and wrongdoings are first encountered by law enforcement—the police. When laws are enforced unconditionally, with equal consequences for all citizens, efforts to bypass them decrease.

In corrupt countries, law-enforcement officials routinely pick and choose when and how they will enforce the laws on a citizen. They base their assessment on self-benefit, the directions of their superiors, and the power status of wrongdoers, including their ability to pay bribes.

When a crime is reported to the police, the fundamental question is whether it is in the best interest of the police officer to enforce the law. In nations where corruption dictates law enforcement, police officers are better off in most situations not punishing the perpetrator. If police officers do enforce the law, they most likely will not get any reward or recognition for it. In reality, even if police officers want to do their jobs, in most cases they get punished for it. For example, a police officer in Islamabad, Pakistan, told me that the minute they arrest a person for a crime, their phone starts ringing with calls from powerful politicians and higher officials, such as government ministers, demanding the criminal's release because he is connected to them. If police officers do not act according to these edicts, they can be fired or, more frequently, transferred to a remote location where the quality of life for them and their families would be miserable. This is a typical example of a country where the central government controls the police force. The ruler of the country has the authority to hire or fire any person who does not obey orders. Therefore, laws are rarely enforced to punish the powerful.

You may be surprised to learn that many corrupt nations maintain so-called independent agencies that are supposedly established to address and punish corrupt government officials. These so-called anticorruption institutions are rarely successful in meeting their stated goals for a few reasons. First, they seldom have any real intention of ending corruption. Leaders create these agencies to pay lip service to the problem, bolstering their public image of being tough on fighting corruption. Pressure from international human rights organizations, requirements from investors, and demands regarding loans from other countries are some of the factors that lead officials to form these agencies. Secondly, these agencies lack independent authority to enforce anticorruption laws or punish wrongdoers within the government. Their powers are meager, and their attempts at real change can even cause the anticorruption office's employees to lose their jobs and face criminal charges. In most cases, these agencies are used by the politicians in power to subdue their political opposition.

For example, Uganda is notorious for rampant corruption. The majority of citizens live without basic necessities. In 1988, Ugandan officials created the Inspectorate of Governance. They called it an independent institution responsible for "eliminating corruption, and abuse of authority and public office."[141] Though this entity is supposed to be independent of the government, the Ugandan president appoints (with Parliament's approval) the inspector general of government (IGG), who heads it. The president also has the power to remove the IGG if government officials determine that the individual is incompetent or unable to perform the duties of the position. Do you see the problem? Corrupt government officials can appoint and fire the very people who are supposed to investigate their actions and hold them accountable. A report by Human Rights Watch discusses the failures of Uganda's Inspectorate of Governance to enforce anticorruption laws effectively.[142] It asserts that, while the office has been able to prosecute some lower-level government officials successfully, efforts to prosecute and punish high-level officials most often fail.

This problem is not unique to Uganda. Anticorruption institutions in other corrupt nations experience similar failures, mostly stemming from the confluence of two barriers. First, since these institutions are created for lip service, they are not given the resources needed to carry out their missions. Second, consistent failure to address corruption creates a nationwide environment in which citizens routinely avoid reporting crimes and seeking assistance from law enforcement. Most individuals do not expect law enforcement to protect them because they are unable to afford the bribes that are demanded to secure the services of the police officers.

Ms. Zar Aslam is an acquaintance of mine who narrowly escaped kidnapping in a rickshaw when she was a student in Lahore, Pakistan. Such incidents of sexual assault are widespread in Pakistan and often go unpunished due to law enforcement's unwillingness to hold accusers accountable.[143] To protect other women from harassment by male rickshaw drivers, Aslam and her friends from Pakistan living in the U.S. started the Pink Rickshaw service in Lahore to provide taxi services provided by female drivers to women passengers. Getting the business launched was extremely challenging, as her team had to make several attempts to get appointments with government officials for required approvals.[144] When the rickshaws were finally purchased, the team discovered after multiple mechanical failures that they had been falsely sold reconditioned vehicles, even though they had paid for new ones.[145] The seller had over-hauled, repainted, and sold the rickshaws as new. When these women tried to get help from the police, the officers started harassing them. They refused to register a first information report (FIR) unless the women paid them a bribe. The report was reportedly not registered for more than three months after the initial complaint. Aslam believed that the police officers deliberately delayed the registration of their case to protect the cheaters. The police later claimed that the accused had fled abroad and not much could be done. The numerous challenges brought on by the corrupt environment of Pakistan caused the Pink Rickshaw organization to struggle during the first year of operation.

Law-enforcement misconduct is a widespread problem in corrupt nations. An article in the *Criminal Justice Degrees Guide* lists the ten most corrupt law-enforcement agencies in the world.[146] Haiti sits at the top of the list, followed by Mexico and Kenya. Iraq and Afghanistan are also in-cluded on the list, along with Sudan and Russia. Sources list lack of over-sight and accountability as major factors in the high levels of corruption. Many agents choose to routinely supplement their incomes by demand-ing bribes from innocent citizens and accepting bribes from criminals.

Haitian police officials have been accused of engaging in notori-ous corruption for decades. In 1994, the Haitian National Police De-partment was formed with the goal of establishing a new agency to alleviate the corruption that ran rampant in the former military-style law-enforcement agency. However, allegations of corruption continued. Members of the National Police Department were accused of partici-pating in drug trafficking and elaborate kidnapping plots. Human rights experts accused police officials of using excessive force against citizens, and politically motivated killings occurred regularly. In 2010, the peo-ple of Haiti were hit by a devastating earthquake that killed more than 200,000 people and left millions without shelter. Even through the re-construction of the severe destruction, stories of corruption continued. As is common practice after such natural disasters, international aid and assistance poured into the country in the form of food supplies, medical equipment, and temporary shelters. According to an article in the *Daily Caller*, there was no government structure in place to register aid vehicles when they first entered the country to provide assistance.[147]

However, shortly after their arrival, Haitian police began ticketing and impounding the vehicles, mostly holding them ransom in exchange for excessive bribes. The aid organizations were told to either pay half of each vehicle's worth or hire Haitian police officers for a fee of $100 per day, even though their standard wage was only $7 per day.

After the police, the second tier of law enforcement is run by the courts. In an unjust country, corruption limits the effectiveness of the judiciary. If a crime does make it to the court system, the actions of the judiciary are again driven by money and power. Even when political officials present the judiciary as an impartial and neutral entity, the reality is that the government plays a substantial role in handing out its idea of "justice." Judges are appointed based on their relationship to government leaders. Once their family members and friends are in judicial positions, officials use these connections to influence the outcome of cases. A judge may be ordered to dismiss an action or rule in favor of a particular party, regardless of the evidence. In 1986, Mikhail Gorbachev publicly called for independence within the Russian judiciary in an attempt to present the country as a fair and just nation.[148] In 1991, the judicial branch of the national government was created by official decree. It was proclaimed as independent from the legislature and state power. In the years to follow, Boris Yeltsin and Vladimir Putin made additional reforms that seemed to support the judiciary's independence. An internal oversight board was created to promote the self-regulation of judicial members. Funding decisions were removed from the Ministry of Justice to further distance the judiciary from the influence of the state. It appeared that real changes were being made to establish an independent and trustworthy judicial system to adequately serve Russian citizens. But, as is the norm in corrupt nations, what the leaders presented to the world was vastly different from what was occurring.

These rulers make accusations of corruption within organizations where the leadership is not aligned with their fraudulent personal goals. Under the false claim of cleaning up the organization, they remove uncooperative leaders and replace them with people who will follow their commands, allowing them to act in any way they choose no matter how illegal or corrupt. In Russia, none of these so-called judicial reforms resulted in improvements to the judicial process. In 2005, the International Bar Association stated concerns over the dismissal of many Russian judges who refused to conform to demands made by government officials. Several surveys have also found a wide public perception of judicial corruption. A Transparency International survey found that 78% of respondents do not expect to find justice in the courts. These results are tied to prevalent use of bribery in the courts. This example shows that having additional rules, regulations, anticorruption committees, or layers of government without independent structural checks does not reduce corruption. The INDEM Foundation researched and quantified the cost of obtaining justice in the Russian courts. They estimated the cost at $358.00, which is often paid to judges who decide cases in favor of the "highest bidder."[149] These payments are especially troubling when you consider that the average Russian only earns about $1,400 a month. The need to pay more than 25% of one's monthly salary to prevail in a court case is disturbing. In a corrupt nation, certain people routinely get away with their crimes, first with the collusion of law enforcement and second with the assistance of a corrupt judiciary.

When people are faced with corrupt law enforcement, they understandably rely on relationship-based structures to obtain protection from criminals. They develop relationships with influential members of the government, both formally and informally, and depend on them for protection of their interests and needs. It's very similar to the structure of gangs or the Mafia, except the leaders are politicians, military, law-enforcement officers, government bureaucrats, or landlords. Citizens who are poor or lack connections with the powerful elite become vulnerable to wrongdoers who take advantage of unprotected people.

This type of environment creates unwritten rules that connected people use to get away with unlawful activities. Typically, one influencer does a favor for another influencer—an illegal act is performed with the expectation of either a bribe or a future return of an unlawful favor. For example, government officials may overlook enforcement of building codes for a landlord as long as the landlord reduces their rent. It is a crime that goes unnoticed yet results in unsafe or substandard housing. Who you know is more important than what you know.

For those who do not know the right people or are unable to purchase law-enforcement support, obtaining basic necessities is difficult and survival is a challenge. Gary Haugen spoke about this in his TED Talk presentation, "The Hidden Reason for Poverty the World Needs to Address Now."[150] He talked about a young girl named Griselda from Guatemala who was raped in broad daylight by men from her community. This girl and her family could not afford to buy the help of law enforcement, leaving her unable to live her life safely. She cannot even go to school due to the constant threat from her abusers. In fact, she rarely leaves her home at all for fear of another attack. While there are laws in place to protect Griselda and thousands of other girls like her, there are no systems in place to enforce them. Her gifts and potential will likely never be realized due to her inability to thrive under a system void of police protection for people who cannot afford it.

Remember that living in an unjust society essentially forces people to behave unjustly, conforming to the macroenvironment and the circumstances that I call the *invisible force*. As Haugen also points out, in Karachi, Pakistan, there is a 50% shortfall in the supply of water versus the actual demand. Since the demand cannot be met, most residents have installed water pumps that suck water out of the public utility water supply. This is an illegal activity, and it limits the amount of water that neighbors can access. However, since going without water is not an option, people are left with a choice to either participate in the criminal activity of installing a water pump to get their share of water or buying water from a water tanker. The issue is compounded because in most cases the water trucks are also getting water illegally. The well-known "water tanker Mafia" illegally punctures pipelines and siphons off water to sell at inflated rates on the black market. "In many places, such as Korangi, people end up having to buy the water that was intended for their homes," says journalist Taha Anis.[151] Frustrated by the scarcity and poor quality of the water, almost three-quarters of Karachi residents do not pay their water bills, according to the Karachi Water and Sewerage Board. Do the residents of Karachi have a choice not to participate in this illegal system of obtaining water? My answer is no.

Once a person gets into corrupted behavior patterns, there is no end to it. Those impacted by injustice behave in frustration, and their reactions may not be moral. Just imagine people living in a society where they *never* feel that they have justice. We shouldn't expect that such people would rise above their exasperation and act honestly. In principle, I do not want to give bribes. Yet one time I arrived at the Islamabad airport with two laptops, one for work and one for personal use. The customs officer at the airport told me that I was not allowed to bring two laptops without paying import duty. Even though I was not planning on selling them in Pakistan and planned to take them back to the U.S., they forced me to pay them a bribe to get out of the situation. They have made this into an art form. I asked the customs officer how much I would have to pay and he said about $100. The porter helping me said, "They are trying to hassle you for money, just offer him ten dollars." I took his advice; the customs officer agreed and told me to drop off the bribe with the person sitting in the import duty collections window. So, multiple people are teamed up to collect bribes in a wholly organized fashion. This is just another example of vertically integrated kleptocracy.

Given the chance, human beings take advantage of beneficial opportunities as an innate survival instinct. Presented with the option to steal money without consequences, most humans are going to push the limits and steal. In an environment where the entire law-enforcement apparatus, from police officers to the judiciary, is a support system for corruption, people have no motivation to do what is right, especially when they may even be punished for following the laws. Looking out for their own benefit, the majority of the population becomes part of the game. If the president or the prime minister gets a cut of the public projects, then everyone all the way to the bottom looks for their piece of the action. The whole country becomes a command-and-control operation where the rulers control all activities for their benefit and use everyone in between to control the people. Over time, it becomes part of how people behave within that environment.

Summary

Corruption happens when a country's laws are not enforced. Laws are not enforced because a few people have too much power. A famous saying dating back more than one hundred years explains it: "Power tends to corrupt, and absolute power corrupts absolutely."[152] Corruption takes place when the police and the judiciary are not independent and when a country is not governed by distinct branches of government maintaining checks on one another.

ENVIRONMENT FOR PROSPERITY

7

"Growth is never by mere chance;
it is the result of forces working together."

—James Cash Penney

Thus far, we have discussed the core causes of corruption and that
something needs to be done for all of us to benefit from the potential
contributions of every human. In this chapter, we will look at the need
of individuals to be able to live up to their highest potential. We have
to recognize that the prosperity of a nation is an aggregate of the contributions of each citizen. Lifting all humans to the maximum of their
abilities results in prosperity for the entire country.

Equal Rights for Every Citizen

To maximize the wealth of a nation, we have to maximize the well-being
of each and every individual. Again, people act in ways that make sense
to them. Their decisions are driven by what is in their heads, and what
is in their heads is driven by their experiences and feelings at that particular moment, the ***invisible force***. Our microenvironment drives our
experiences and our thoughts. I like to refer to the microenvironment
as our bubble. As human beings, we live within our bubble, which is a
mental framework driven by what is around us. For a nation to prosper,

the focus has to be on what provides each person with the best feeling of life within their bubble.

Remember, there is an order to every human being's needs, from the physiological necessities of food and water to the psychological needs of love and self-actualization. We all work to fulfill each one of these needs on a daily basis. Unfortunately, the majority of people in this world are forced to spend most of their time trying to survive from one day to the next. They live in a state of physical and psychological persecution that individuals living in a just society cannot even imagine.

Tim Jackins of International Re-evaluation Counseling Communities explains the effects of living in an oppressive society in the following way:

> One of the things that an oppressive society plasters on us all is that "this is the way it is, and it will not change." Every society perpetuates the illusion that it is the last and greatest thing possible. . . Part of oppression is to make us feel hopeless about what happens in society. We're told that the inequities and the oppression will always exist: "This is the way society is, and you are small and meaningless, and there is nothing you can do about it." And alone—small, meaningless, and alone.[153]

When you live your entire life within an unjust system, you never have the opportunity to experience an environment where you are encouraged and helped to thrive and meet your full potential. Living in a just environment does not guarantee success, but it does provide greater opportunities to succeed. Our feelings drive our thinking. As discussed earlier in this book, everyone has an innate desire to be treated fairly and equally. Living in a just environment enhances feelings of positivity, which translate into positive thinking and the desire to pursue opportunities that lead to self-actualization. Not every citizen in a just environment will be able to achieve complete self-actualization, but just knowing that it's a viable possibility makes them more fulfilled and satisfied. By comparison, people living in an unjust environment do not experience the same feelings of satisfaction. Instead, their brains conform to the corrupt environment. Without even thinking about it, they rightly believe they do not have equal opportunities. It becomes part of their being—their *invisible force*—limiting their desire to live up to their potential.

As a simple example, let's compare a person with $100 in the bank to an individual who has $10 million in the bank. Both people will sleep in a bed and have three meals a day, but what goes on inside their minds will differ. The person with the $10 million is going to be dreaming of bigger and better things versus a person with only $100. The millionaire feels they have more opportunities and choices, which makes them strive for more. The person with $100 is focused on meeting basic needs. Our feelings are driven by what we believe we can do. It's all about the feelings and emotions that drive us to pursue opportunities.

Based on Maslow's hierarchy of needs, people stuck in the first stage, trying to meet the basic physiological needs for food, clean water, and shelter, are going to experience an inferior feeling of life and a frustrated and weak state of mind. On the other hand, people who are at the top of this hierarchy and can achieve internal and external respect, and finally self-actualization by reaching full potential, are going to be far more optimistic.

This observation is affirmed by Gleb Tsipursky, cofounder of Intentional Insights. In his article "Autopilot vs. Intentional System: The Rider and the Elephant," Tsipursky states, "Intuitively, our mind feels like a cohesive whole. We perceive ourselves as intentional and rational thinkers. Yet cognitive science research shows that in reality, the intentional part of our mind is like a little rider on top of a huge elephant of emotions and intuitions."[154] He explains that the majority of our behavior is driven by our subconscious, which he describes as our "autopilot system." We humans have a false sense of our capabilities and overestimate what we control.

In the grand scheme of things, we are not a whole lot more capable than other animal species. For example, we think we are in charge of our destiny, but in reality, we live in our bubble—our microenvironment. Again, our bubble is shaped by the experiences provided by our environment. For example, we may kill a fly without realizing that the same can happen to us pulling out of our driveway and getting hit by a truck. The point I want to make is that, similar to a fly, we have very little control over our environment, even though we think we are in control.

Similar to all living things, our core need is survival within our environment. To examine the impact of environment, consider the ecosystem. The ecosystem is an integration driven by the adaptation of living and nonliving things.[155] The living creatures, defined as biotic, balance their existence with everything around them, including the nonliving things called the abiotic. For example, plants and animals that live in a desert environment must be able to adapt to survive the challenges of excessive heat and lack of water.

For a simple plant organism, environment may be defined as the condition of the soil, temperature, availability of air and water, and access to sunlight. For a human being, our abiotic environment consists of physical resources such as safe housing and availability of food and clean water. The microbiotic environment includes relationships with people—family members, friends, and coworkers. The macrobiotic environment is our belief in the fairness of our government and confidence in law-enforcement agents and the judiciary to protect us. Just like any other species, we must conform in order to survive. Just as a seed falls from a tree and fights for its survival by adapting for access to soil and sunlight, we go through life adapting to our abiotic and biotic environments.

This process of adaptation starts at birth. From childhood, individuals have an innate sense of what is fair. You must have heard an unhappy child declare that something isn't fair. Even as children, we quickly recognize when we are not being treated fairly, and each unjust incident makes us feel angry, frustrated, and helpless. In a corrupt nation, citizens consistently experience these feelings as they are systemically mistreated by individuals with power. As explained in earlier chapters, even simple, everyday tasks are subject to the frustrations of unequal treatment. Many things are taken for granted in developed countries, such as obtaining a driver's license or a business permit. However, in most poor countries, only the wealthy or connected can secure these necessities without bribing officials. When the harsh reality of inequality is a consistent part of your life from the day you are born, you subconsciously accept that equality is not available to you. This mistreatment causes frustration because it goes against our core sense of justice.

Most individuals living in such an environment are frustrated but have a difficult time identifying the cause of their frustration. There are two reasons for this disconnect. First, these individuals may themselves begin acting corruptly. Intrinsically, they take on the characteristics of people around them as well as the corrupt leaders of the country. These individuals do what they deem necessary for survival within their corrupt society. The second reason is a lack of belief that they can achieve success. These individuals are born into a society where their efforts will not be rewarded unless they are members of wealthy families or the powerful elite. Survival instincts inspire some to take advantage of corrupt practices; others refuse to be part of the injustice and become depressed, demotivated, and disengaged.

The injustice these individuals face in their lives is based on inequality within their nations. Equality means that all are treated equally, with equal access to justice and opportunity. A just macroenvironment impacts our microenvironments and our feelings about our lives. The important point to note is that living in an unjust society impacts our thoughts and feelings. Life is defined by what is in our heads. Our actions are driven by our minds, but as a highly efficient system designed for survival, our brain continuously and subconsciously senses our environment and updates our thoughts and feelings. When equality is present, it creates possibilities. Even if the outcomes are uncertain, people are more likely to pursue a better life if they believe equal opportunity for success exists.

In a nation that values equality, individuals believe in the possibility of success, even if they come from meager beginnings. They can use education, knowledge, creativity, and personal drive to obtain a better place in life. Now I am not suggesting that individuals in less-corrupt nations never experience inequality, but legislative attempts to control such unfairness create the feeling of equal opportunity. By denying equality to specific groups based on income, race, religion, gender, or geographic location, we dehumanize them. We are essentially telling them that they are not worthy of equal treatment. This inequality creates the belief in some people's inferiority, which leads to a system of superiority, which leads to systematic supremacism: Those who are part of the superior social class dominate, control, and subjugate those who are not.

Results drive almost everything we do. We want to be healthy, so we exercise and eat nutritiously. We want to earn a higher income, so we work hard and acquire more education. The potential for a reward motivates workers to produce better because they feel they are working toward something that can prove beneficial to them.[156] In a just society, the potential for living a life that adequately represents your efforts and talents is the reward. Individuals work toward the possibility of a good life because they know it is a genuine possibility. But in an unjust society, effort and talent go unrewarded, and the citizens of these nations are aware of this painful fact. When placed in a position where the reward is based on how much money you have and who you know, we lose the incentive to work toward an unattainable outcome. We have an innate drive to conform to our bubble, and we play by its rules. If the rewards are not based on hard work, we don't work hard.

Inequality goes hand in hand with injustice. A society where systematic inequality is allowed to run rampant also supports systematic injustice. People are not only mistreated in their everyday lives but also also face prejudice within the criminal justice system, whether they are an accused offender or an accusing victim. The most damaging aspect of injustice is the effect it has on the hearts, minds, and souls of its victims.

Recall your own experience. Have you ever felt cheated? Maybe someone cheated you in a game, or you felt that you were cheated out of a grade or job opportunity. It's a disgusting feeling and one that may have a lasting impact. You know that wrong has been done. You also know that you have been negatively affected by that wrong, but you are powerless to fix it.

For people to have a positive feeling in life, they need to live in an environment they believe is just and equal. Again, these are the rules that define our bubble. Corruption means that the wealthy and powerful will benefit from illegal use of their status. Corruption kills our inner drive and puts a country in a vicious cycle where the majority of people become apathetic, losing their drive to succeed. As a result, people who have an opportunity to migrate often move to prosperous nations and contribute their talents to these countries instead of their home country.

Bryan Stevenson is the executive director of the Equal Justice Initiative in Montgomery, Alabama, and a professor of law at the New York

University Law School. He gave a TED Talk where he made a statement I find incredibly thoughtful and accurate: "The opposite of poverty is not wealth, it is justice."[157] I strongly agree with this idea as it pertains to our current global situation. Nations are not failing due to a lack of wealth. They are failing due to a lack of justice. When systems of justice and equality are implemented and enforced, the people and economy of a nation will flourish.

In a just and equal environment that supports individual motivation, the country moves in a virtuous cycle. As I stated at the beginning of this book, I dream of an environment that enables all people to have freedom, but only the freedom to do good. Again, we conform to our environment; if we believe that the only road to success is doing good, we become motivated to do good. I believe that when we live in an environment that allows for only good, doing good makes us feel better and we become better human beings. We are motivated and happy because by nature that's how we are programmed and our actions are aligned with our consciences.

Scientific studies have proven that people feel better when they do good.[158] Unfortunately, an environment that does not reward virtuous acts invites people to perform unlawful and unethical acts for survival. Once they get away with doing wrong and have achieved some financial success, they get caught up in this vicious cycle of wrongdoing. For a person who commits a crime due to hunger or the need to feed their family, it becomes very difficult to get out of the life of crime and work at a regular job. Similarly, consider government officials in poor countries like Pakistan. Once they have compromised their conscience and performed a corrupt deed, they continue on that path. When they gain some wealth, which is considered success, it becomes almost impossible for them to stop. Success is addictive. They can't escape because, just like being part of the Mafia, everyone around them is part of the same game of corruption. Their actions may continue to bother their conscience, but after a while it becomes second nature to continue the game.

Yet at what cost? A friend of mine left Pakistan and emigrated to Canada midcareer. When asked why he left his home, he replied, "I can't continue to live a life of corruption." All humans have an innate need to do good. We just need to provide an environment that rewards doing good. Even the people who have amassed wealth due to corruption live in fear of losing that money and their lifestyle. For that reason, they keep their money in offshore bank accounts and hire guards to protect them. I believe they would sleep better in an environment where they feel secure due to a just legal system and law enforcement in place to protect everyone. I'm not asking for something that has never been done before. The purpose of this book is for people to understand what has caused some nations to thrive and what people living in nations that are poor and struggling need to copy. For a just system that does not allow people to do wrong, the following requirements must be observed.

Requirements for a Just System

Rule of Law

A similar thread runs through the historical and cultural fabric of corrupt nations: the elite are above the law. In a society where groups of people are allowed to operate outside the reach of the law, the laws become futile. The purpose of having laws is to regulate the actions of people within a society. They are meant to protect the masses and enforce the rights of each individual. When a person breaks the law, it often negatively impacts the life of another individual. Ideally, the perpetrator should be punished to deter it from happening again. But what if the person who broke the law faces no consequence? What if that person is allowed to change the law to decriminalize their actions and walk away without any accountability? This is the reality in countries where the elite transcend the law. They are allowed to act in a way that manipulates the laws as well as the people. This leads to the corruption that we see occurring across the globe today.

As previously stated, the problem does not stem from a lack of laws. It stems from a failure to enforce the laws. Any legal action requires evidence, and if law enforcement is corrupt, who is going to produce the evidence necessary for a conviction? In situations where law enforcement does do its job and produces proper evidence, a corrupt judiciary can still prevent justice. The judge may refuse to give a sentence, significantly delay judgment, or choose to declare a mistrial or define the alleged crime as politically motivated. This allows the perpetrator to get away with this crime and continue illegal activities. Within a corrupt legal system, any person who tries to enforce the law against a powerful person risks facing punishment by some law-enforcement agent, even via false allegations. In this type of broken system, anybody with the power and money to push law enforcement around can potentially get away with a crime.

For example, in July 2016, members of the Pakistani army were deployed to rescue the kidnapped son of Chief Justice Sajjad Ali Shah, who serves in Karachi.[159] According to reports, the kidnapping stemmed from Shah's failure to fulfill a deal he made over a verdict. Since he had allegedly been paid for his cooperation, the culprits kidnapped his son to force the unjust verdict. Other theories allege that it was done as a bargaining chip to negotiate future verdicts. But even if there was no deal being played out in this case, violent situations like this frequently occur within corrupt nations as a method of forcing a decision or action.

To gain a greater understanding of the impact of living in a society where the elite are above the law, it is useful to examine the connection between corruption and crime. As I indicated previously, evolution has influenced human nature to push boundaries. Just like the child who sneaks a cookie from the cookie jar, we are genetically programmed to challenge the limits placed upon us. When this impulse is used in a positive manner, our instincts lead us to invent better methods of productivity. However, when used in a negative manner, this instinct leads us to place our own desires over the common good, acting with disregard for the interests of our society as a whole. Corruption is the result of people breaking the constraints of law within their societies. In countries where gaps exist between laws and law enforcement, systematic corruption persists.

Human behavior is driven by a choice between risk and reward. Risk is measured by a person's situation. If I am a millionaire, I will not attempt to steal $100 because the reward is very small compared to the risk it causes me. However, if I'm destitute and hungry, with not much to lose in life, the risk I face by stealing $100 is far less significant. A person with no hope of succeeding in their society will resort to crime or even to suicide because they believe they have nothing to lose. Another important consideration of risk and reward is the probability of getting caught and facing punishment. If that same millionaire believes there is no chance of getting caught, their perception of the situation may change; the reward of $100 becomes worth the low risk. Even in countries where blatant crimes are punished, people still push the boundaries by attempting to improperly influence the decisions of others. For example, a corrupt American lobbyist might use a U.S. senator to facilitate a defense contract award. There are laws against this type of behavior, but the low risk of getting caught in comparison to the potentially lucrative reward encourages it. While it may prove difficult to control the level of reward that comes with committing a corrupt act, we do have the ability to create systems where there is a high risk for committing a crime. Most of the world's unjust nations are failing because they do not have systems in place that create a high level of risk for criminal acts, at least not equally for all citizens.

Corruption and disrespect for the law is not relegated to governmental and financial elite. Ordinary citizens can also see themselves as above the law. They live in a corrupt society, where every day they observe the actions of corrupt law-enforcement agents and dishonorable judicial systems that bend to the will of anyone with money. This continuous exposure can cultivate the audacity to act outside the law, with no fear of retribution. They don't have the resources to buy themselves out of trouble, but they do feel confident knowing that the government is not going to protect their victim or seek justice for certain groups of people. For example, a woman is raped every 20 seconds in India. This appalling statistic is actually even more disturbing because experts believe this number is drastically underrepresented and most of these incidents never result in an arrest, let alone a conviction. Living in this environment has created gangs of men who unapologetically rape women and girls.

The tragic rape and killing of Jyoti Singh exemplifies this point. Singh was a young medical student who was returning home from a movie with her male friend. They unknowingly boarded an off-duty bus and quickly became alarmed when it deviated from the expected path. Jyoti's male companion was brutally beaten and eventually knocked unconscious by the six men who were already on board. They then turned their brutality on Singh, beating and raping her repeatedly. The two were then thrown from the moving bus. Singh sustained serious injuries to her genitals, uterus, and abdomen. She went through numerous surgeries, some even involving the removal of her damaged intestines. She died 13 days after the attack. Though the suspects were arrested relatively quickly, the incident ignited protests over the government's failure to protect women from the unchecked violence they face every day. Demonstrations took place across the country, with women and men clashing with law-enforcement agents. Internationally, protesters marched at Indian embassies, demanding justice for Singh.

Ultimately, one of the suspects was found hanging in his cell. One juvenile suspect (though his actual age was in question throughout the trial) served three years. The trial of the remaining adult offenders was a continuous slap in the face of Indian women. Defense attorneys repeatedly placed blame on the victim, questioning her integrity and respectfulness. The four men were found guilty and sentenced to death by hanging, but subsequent appeals have prolonged the judicial process and none have thus far been put to death. In response to protests, several Indian states announced plans to pass legislation aimed at preventing and better prosecuting such violent acts. Years after Singh's murder, the frequency of rape remains high and has even increased in some cities. This is especially alarming because officials continue to estimate that 99% of rapes occurring within India go unreported.[160] In addition, one of the convicted assailants spoke with the filmmaker of the documentary *India's Daughter*. In the interview, he blamed the victim, exemplifying the level of entitlement and disregard for the law that continues to prevail. As long as this type of above-the-law thinking is allowed to continue, all the legislation in the world will prove ineffective at protecting Indian women.

For laws to work, they must be enforced equally all members of society. Otherwise, residents begin transcending the laws because of their wealth, their political power, or simply their courage. In a lawless society, human behavior automatically adjusts to the environment, and many people living in these countries consider breaking the law a normal part of life. The frequency of rape in India is an extreme example of how some people will continually break the law as long as they know they can get away with it. Corruption continues because the individuals controlling the system are benefiting from it in the short run. But in the long run, everyone would be better off living in rightful societies without the constant threat that someone will damage their well-being.

Checks and Balances—Distributed Power

The only proven method of promoting the rule of law is implementing a system of checks and balances. Many people equate democracy with the right to vote. However, what is essential for prosperity to thrive is distributed power rather than unchecked concentrated power. When checks and balances are in place, each branch of government is regulated by other branches to ensure that no individual or group obtains unilateral power to compromise individual rights. Though the United States is far from perfect in its prevention of government corruption, its constitution and the distributed government are a compelling example of how checks and balances can work.

American President Franklin D. Roosevelt was elected during the height of the Great Depression and served the longest presidential tenure in U.S. history: 12 years from March 1933 to April 1945. Even though he is regarded as a defining figure in American history, his presidency faced numerous challenges that exemplify the system of checks and balances in the U.S. Roosevelt ushered in a comprehensive plan named the New Deal, which was a collection of policies and regulations aimed at improving the financial condition of the nation and its citizens. One of his policies, the National Industry Recovery Act, was met with considerable opposition. The legislation sought to strengthen workers' rights, regulate working conditions, and limit industrial competition. The act was challenged in court, and the Supreme Court unanimously found parts of it unconstitutional. Roosevelt then introduced additional legislation, the National Labor Relations Act, with the same goal of strengthening workers' rights to form unions and protect against unjust employers. This also faced opposition in the federal courts, but Roosevelt acted to prevent the Supreme Court from striking down the regulation. He appealed to the American public with assertions that the

United States Constitution did not expressly endow the court with the power to challenge legislation, and he accused the court of acting in a legislative capacity rather than as a judicial body. Roosevelt further claimed that the court was overworked and proposed legislation for mandatory retirement of all judges at the age of 70, which would essentially allow him to pack the court with six new judges. When the bill was sent to the Senate, legislators overwhelmingly voted to remove any language about constraining the Supreme Court. Ultimately, Roosevelt's National Labor Relations plan was ruled constitutional by the Supreme Court, but his efforts to bypass the court and arbitrarily change the laws of the nation for his agenda were shut down by the legislature. The system of checks and balances, which is designed to keep even government elite within the law, prevailed in the end.

Just Tax Collection and Distribution

Tax revenue is the money collected from a nation's citizens through taxation. These collections can have a variety of sources, including income, goods, services, and property ownership. In a prosperous country, these funds are used to provide services to citizens. Adequate taxation strengthens a nation's economy and promotes effective governance. It is the job of a country's government to work toward social justice and equal economic opportunities. These objectives cannot be met without the funds from adequate taxation.

For a nation to serve its citizens, taxes must be collected equitably and distributed justly. A simple way to identify countries where corruption is rampant is to examine tax collections and distribution. Nations can only thrive if tax revenues are collected fairly and used in a manner that benefits the entire country instead of a select few. All citizens are held accountable for paying taxes into the nation's coffers, and tax revenues are shared among the citizens. I recognize that examination of tax collection is not an apples-to-apples equation between countries, but just for the sake of comparison, let's look at the amount of taxes collected in some prosperous countries compared to developing nations. According to IRS (Internal Revenue Service), the US federal government collected about $3.5 trillion in taxes in 2018.[161] On average, this represents $21,833 for every worker in the country. In 2018, the average for OECD member countries is 25.5%.[162]

In corrupt countries, it is all about money—money is power, and power is used to extract money. So the system of taxation works quite differently. The citizens of an unjust country are disadvantaged in three ways. First, taxes are collected unjustly. The country's leaders are routinely able to avoid paying taxes, even though they are the highest earners with the most tax liability. Second, leaders spend tax revenues for personal benefit, while ignoring the needs of the masses. Third, even when revenue is officially budgeted for public services, the money often gets spent in ways that benefit leaders, with no regard for the allocated budget. The combination of these three elements creates a systematically ineffective taxation system that stops a nation from thriving.

Tax revenues are extremely important for any county, usually providing its most significant source of income. With fair taxation, the citizenry benefits from adequate schools, necessary infrastructure, and social assistance. Taxes are effectively collected when every individual is held accountable for the payment of their tax responsibilities. All citizens face civil and criminal liability if they fail to pay or cheat on their taxes. Yet in corrupt nations many people pay no taxes with impunity. For example, shockingly few Indians pay taxes. According to an article by NPR, only two percent of India's 1.23 billion citizens paid income taxes for the 2016 tax year: 37 million (3% of the population) Indians filed taxes, and just 27 million (2% of the population) paid any taxes.[163]

In fact, in most poor countries, even though the laws mandate tax payments, the vast majority of people work around these laws and face no consequences. For example, of the 319 political leaders serving within the National Assembly of Pakistan who filed tax returns in 2014, 109 paid no taxes at all.[164] For those who did pay, the amounts were meager considering the lavish lifestyles that most maintain. When corrupt leaders refuse to pay their fair share of taxes, they are essentially stealing money from their citizens. This is especially true considering the fact that most leaders of corrupt nations are considerably wealthier than the people they govern. Their failure to pay taxes, whether through an outright refusal or by tax evasion, often represents millions or even billions of dollars taken from the coffers of these countries.

The World Bank conducted a study on the effects of tax evasion on the economy of a developing nation.[165] In this study of Malawi, it was estimated that corruption robbed the economy of approximately 5% of its GDP. Even worse, tax evasion accounted for about 10% of the country's GDP. Based on these numbers, researchers concluded that, if the country accurately collected all taxes that were rightly due, the government's revenue would increase by an incredible 50%. As one Malawi Revenue official explained, "If we collected all the taxes, we will then not have to depend on foreign aid." This lost money represents revenue that could be spent to better the lives of citizens. Schools, infrastructure, and job development all suffer when countries fail to fully collect taxes.

The leaders of these countries use various methods of tax evasion. They find places to hide their earnings, so the country is unable to assess and tax them. In April 2016, documents leaked from a Panamanian law firm identified several international leaders as owners of offshore accounts used to evade tax liability within their countries.[166] Among those included in the report were associates of Russian president Vladimir Putin, Icelandic prime minister Sigmundur David Gunnlaugsson, Argentina's president Mauricio Macri, and Chinese president Xi Jinping. According to reports about the incident, these leaders and many of their family members are accused of hiding millions of dollars in assets through the use of offshore bank accounts. This exemplifies their unwillingness to pay their fair share of taxes, even if it means breaking the law. With no legal repercussions, these wealthy leaders are allowed to continuously take what lawfully belongs to the people of their country.

As I have previously explained, corruption doesn't stop with the leaders. Systematic corruption extends to all levels of society. Store owners craftily hide transactions to reduce income and avoiding paying tax. It is common knowledge within Pakistan that virtually every business owner maintains two sets of books, one set for tax records understating the amount of revenue, and the other set with actual income for internal accounting. As if this corruption were not bad enough, tax revenue is further reduced because government officials are not motivated to collect taxes. Instead, they use their positions to demand bribes. Umar Cheema, the author of a Center for Investigative Reporting study, said it best: "If politicians don't pay taxes themselves, they have lost the moral authority to impose taxes on others."[167]

In corrupt countries, people who are supposed to pay taxes are not interested in paying, and people who are supposed to collect taxes are not interested in collecting. Just imagine a nation where there is very little motivation for anybody to be generating any taxes. For example, my father ran a hotel in Islamabad. He attempted to pay appropriately assessed taxes, but the tax collector was not interested. Instead, he would sit there all day long asking for different reports. He would harass my father in hopes that of being paid a bribe to get rid of him. My father was an unusual person and stuck to his guns instead of paying bribes, but most businesses don't have the liberty to take the just course of action. Many business owners choose to pay the bribe. Though these funds represent far less revenue than the tax responsibility of the nation's leaders, this stolen revenue is nonetheless a substantial loss for the country and its people.

According to a report by Transparency International, Greece also grapples with widespread tax evasion, carried out through the actions of corrupt tax collectors: "A poor system of tax inspections, helped by the opaque tax code, allows individuals and companies to bribe inspectors and evade taxes."[168] The report estimates that citizens of Greece pay between $100 and $20,000 in bribes to evade tax collection.

The collection of property taxes is also impacted by corrupt practices. These tax liabilities are based on the value of property owned and transferred. In the U.S., property is valued by the government based on comparisons of actual sale prices. This way, the valuation is more likely to be accurate for collecting taxes. In most countries with corrupt tax practices, the only statement of valuation is derived from the sale price. To avoid paying taxes, the seller often reports a sale price that is significantly lower than what was actually received for the property, effectively stealing money from the nation.

Added to the problems of collecting taxes is the distribution of taxes. After failing to fully collect taxes from all its citizens, a corrupt nation often uses the collected revenues to financially benefit the leaders, in many cases without respect to how the money was budgeted. The hallmark of a corrupt leader is dedication to their own interests instead of their people's. Therefore, decisions about where to spend state revenues often center on what will benefit the leader and their cronies instead of what will benefit the people as a whole. An article by the International Monetary Fund[169] discusses the impact of corrupt government investments on a country's growth. Projects are not chosen for their economic value to the country as a whole. Instead, leaders select opportunities that offer them the ability to benefit from financial kickbacks and monetary bribes. They look for projects where family members and their cronies can collect payments from the government. When choosing contractors to perform the tasks of the project, they ensure that their corrupt partners receive the contracts, even if they are not adequately qualified to take on the responsibilities. To fulfill their self-serving goals, leaders also promote and select projects that can be prolonged, ultimately adding to the leader's profits. These corrupt acts significantly diminish the economic worth of an investment project for the nation as a whole and also reduce the financial growth of the economy. In addition to the financial implications of these practices, citizens end up with inadequate infrastructure. Badly constructed infrastructure requires constant repairs, which provides further opportunities for corruption and keeps the vicious cycle repeating endlessly.

Corrupt leaders often devote tax revenue to improving areas near their homes and those of their constituents, leaving other areas of the country without the benefit of tax revenue. Sudan, classified as one of the most corrupt nations in the world, provides a perfect example of this systematic inequality. Khartoum is one of the country's three main cities. It is the national capital of Sudan and home to many of the nation's leaders. An aerial view of Khartoum reveals a thriving urban area with expressways, paved roads, and buildings. As the country's major tourist destination, the city also boasts innovative architecture, historical landmarks, and luxurious hotels. A substantial percentage of public money is spent furthering large projects within this area, along with the state's other large metro areas. According to a World Bank report,[170] in 2006, the country's five biggest projects located in these metro areas accounted for more than 60% of the annual portfolio. Meanwhile, development in the rural areas of the nation remains underfunded, if funded at all. As reported in *South Sudan Poverty Profile*,[171] most of Sudan's poverty is concentrated in the rural areas. Now, this fact in and of itself is not shocking. It is typical for a nation's poor to reside mostly within rural communities. However, in Sudan and other corrupt countries, the residents of these areas are forced to deal with deplorable conditions due to the unwillingness of their leaders to distribute public funds in a fair manner. In rural areas of Sudan, residents are provided with grossly underfunded educational systems. They also have limited access to clean water, so basic sanitation needs go unmet. The lack of water also lowers agricultural productivity, resulting in fewer opportunities for income growth and an inadequate food supply. Infrastructure is nonexistent in many of these areas, along with political influence and criminal justice protections. The leaders have abandoned the needs of the country's rural areas to build up the localities surrounding their homes. They do this for multiple reasons. First, these are the areas where the wealthiest and most powerful individuals live. Leaders cater to these individuals in exchange for financial favors and political support. Second, they are seeking to improve their political standing with their constituents within these localities. The third reason goes back to the systematic goal of lining their own pockets. Development in the areas near their homes is easier to manipulate, allowing leaders to provide their family members with contracts and benefits from financial kickbacks.

You don't have to look as far as rural areas to see inequities in revenue spending. In many cases, they are prevalent within a radius of only a few blocks. While the streets and neighborhoods directly surrounding the residence of the wealthiest elite are pristine and beautifully developed, residents living a short distance away endure poor infrastructure and a lack of essential government services. The streets of wealthy neighborhoods are well maintained and free of trash, with newer businesses and convenient accommodations. Less than a mile away, roads are in poor condition and trash containers are overflowing. The leaders of these nations spend public money to ensure that they can live in the best surroundings with no regard to the conditions most citizens endure. Saudi Arabia is an excellent example of this problem. The elite live in lavish estates and palaces. Gold and jewels are used to adorn their shopping malls, where high-quality goods from around the world are sold. The streets are kept in impeccable condition, lined with palm trees and well-lit after dark. Yet, only a few blocks away, citizens live in concrete blocks, where they step outside to debris strewn about the alleyways. Slums are increasingly overcrowded, with children running around without shoes and beggars asking for handouts in the streets. It's a picture of Saudi Arabia that leaders don't want the world to see.

Tax distribution plays a crucial role in redistributing wealth.[172] Fair tax distribution is the key to providing services to the poor and disbursing necessary needs such as clean water and power. A progressive tax policy redistributes the wealth, creating higher economic activity and just allocation of resources. To distribute taxes fairly, tax collection and distribution should be handled not only at a federal level but also at the local level. Again, the point is that money is power and power should be distributed to reduce opportunities for corruption.

Money Kept within the Country

In a thriving nation, property rights are protected and enforced by law. This includes not only the money of the people within the country, but also money invested by foreigners. Corrupt leaders who have stolen funds from their own nations, such as Zardari in Pakistan, Suharto in Indonesia, and Robert Mugabe in Zambia, understand the benefits of the property rights of a country. They invest their wealth in thriving foreign countries to protect it from the next dictator. For example, wealthy Chinese often invest their money in the U.S. and other Western countries. Though the practice is characterized as the U.S. borrowing money from China, Chinese businesses and individuals are investing in the U.S. stock market, treasuries, and real estate to ensure their gains are protected against potentially corrupt future governments within their own countries.

There are countless examples of corrupt leaders extracting money and resources from their countries for personal gain. PLO chairman Yasser Arafat has been accused of misappropriating an estimated $1 to $10 billion from his country.[173] Zardari allegedly used government contract kickbacks and other tactics to siphon over $2 billion from Pakistan into a Swiss bank account.[174] In 2013, when former Chinese prime minister Wen Jiabao left office, international news sources reported that his close relatives controlled more than $2.5 billion of the country's assets.[175] Kosovo is also governed by a kleptocratic regime, mainly consisting of members of the Democratic Party of Kosovo, one of the country's largest political parties. One report on the wealth of Kosovan politicians revealed that many of these civil servants had amassed significant personal wealth, sometimes in excess of several million euros, even though they were earning relatively low incomes in their political roles.[176] The European Union Rule of Law Mission in Kosovo (EULEX) reported allegations of illegal payments amounting to 1.4 million euros made between the Kosovan Ministry of Internal Affairs and the Austrian State Printing Company, a business that had won a government contract to print Kosovan passports.[177] EULEX arrested the country's former transport minister, along with a deputy president of the ruling Democratic Party of Kosovo and six other suspects on charges of organized crime and embezzlement.

We have previously discussed the outrageous situation of Russian president Vladimir Putin. Although estimates of his personal wealth range as high as $200 billion, he claims that the estimates are false and that his net worth is approximately $100,000.[178] Regardless of the precise amount, Putin and all other kleptocratic rulers not only have amassed great wealth, but also control the economy of a country and benefit personally from every possible project that takes place there. In these countries, the government is somehow involved with any business transaction that takes place.

As an example, I mentioned to a friend, originally from Ukraine and now living in the U.S., that Putin is worth $200 billion. He responded that Putin is not only worth $200 billion, he owns the whole Russian economy. Normally we would think that a person owning $200 billion would benefit from their resources, but in this case, Putin is benefiting from the whole Russian economy.

When viewing these numbers from a distance, it is easy to miss the significance of the problem and how it affects the citizens of these failing countries. Every dollar that a corrupt government official takes from the wealth of the nation is a dollar that is not used to feed the hungry, clothe the poor, care for the sick, or protect the innocent. The money that is being stolen from these countries is in many cases enough to end the appalling levels of poverty. But when there are millions and even billions of dollars at stake in a country where individuals are placed above the law, the reward of corruption far outweighs the risk.

Increased Foreign Investment

Analysts view foreign investment as a major resource for economic development and growth. These contributions lead to the formation of a more competitive business environment and increased development.[179] International corporations invest capital that funds long-term projects and brings in financial resources that may not otherwise be available in the country. They also work to spread best practices in the areas of proper corporate governance and legalities, while introducing the host nation to new technologies and funding efforts to develop new ideas. Some of the most prosperous nations in the world have taken advantage of these benefits by welcoming foreign investment. Australian real estate and infrastructure growth is largely due to foreign investments by the United States, the United Kingdom, Japan, and China.[180]

Corruption and lack of secure property rights increase the business risk for foreign investors. Many stakeholder nations have strict laws against paying bribes, which is a requirement to do business in corrupt countries.

Efficient Use of Natural Resources

A nation's resources come in a variety of forms, including natural resources due to geography and agricultural resources cultivated through labor. However, a country's most important resource is the people. Given the right opportunities and a fair chance, individuals can produce immeasurable benefits for their countries. Any one of a nation's resources can be a strength within a just environment. But, in an unjust environment, that same resource becomes a weakness.

First, let's look at how the misuse of natural resources affects the citizens of an unjust nation. According to an article in *Slate* magazine, countries rich in valuable natural resources often grow more slowly and experience greater inequalities than countries with far fewer resources.[181] This is often referred to as the "resource curse." One of the main reasons for this is resource extraction, where foreign nations extract the country's resources and utilize them for their own economic gain. For many countries, this results from inequitable agreements with foreign companies in which the companies receive the lion's share of profits, leaving the citizens of the resource-rich nation with none of the benefits. Instead of establishing internal industries to create domestic profits, the nation's leaders focus on the quickest option to get a cut from exporting the natural resources.

For example, in Zambia, most citizens must survive on less than a dollar each day and more than 40% are undernourished. This tragedy exists in a country rich in an extremely valuable natural resource—copper. As reported by WarOnWant.org, Zambia produced $5.7 billion of copper during 2010.[182] However, mining companies only paid the government for mining about $633 million. This trend continued in 2011, when the government earned revenue from $1.3 billion worth of mining production, even though more than $7.2 billion in copper was mined. Two of the country's mining companies pay no corporate taxes or royalties at all, effectively allowing them to extract the country's resources without any compensation. Glencore is one of the world's largest mining companies, controlling more than 50% of the world's traded copper. Its holdings in Zambia include the Mopani copper mines, which consists of several underground mines. In 2013, the company reported $233 billion in revenue, which is ten times larger than the GDP of Zambia. If some of this money stayed within Zambia, it could be used for schools, infrastructure, and job creation.

Saudi Arabia is another nation rich in natural resources but poor in economic opportunities for its citizens. Its massive oil reserves have created an extremely wealthy elite, who live in palaces and own properties around the world. However, only a few kilometers from their luxurious estates lie extreme poverty and constant struggle. The income inequality within Saudi Arabia is alarming; how can a nation so rich have citizens that are so poor? Saudi Aramco is the country's national oil company. It pays no royalties and, partly due to the exploitation of foreign labor, its exploration costs are extremely low. This state-owned company has an estimated market value between $2 and $10 trillion, and is considered to be the largest oil company in the world.[183] But the company's exact numbers are elusive due to the secretive manner in which the company is run. While there is no concrete evidence of corruption within the company, it is quite evident that the profits of this state-owned company are not being used to equally benefit all citizens.

"Feudalism" is a term rarely used to describe modern social and political systems. Originating in medieval times, this social structure centered on a land-ownership system where the crown granted vast properties to members of the nobility in exchange for military service. Landlords allowed peasants to live on the land in exchange for their loyalty and service. The hierarchal nature of this social structure permitted landowners to control and manipulate the peasants, very similar to a system of slavery.

The land-ownership structure of Pakistan perpetuates the feudal system, with a relatively small number of landowners maintaining control over the majority of the population. As reported by the Pakistan Institute of Labor Education and Research, only five percent of the country's agricultural households own and manage more than 66% of the nation's total farmland.[184] These landowners control thousands of acres of land, where poor people are forced to live and work under their strict oversight. Landlords control virtually every aspect of their lives, including how much water is distributed and whether a school will be built on the land to educate the children. Through debt bondage, many of these people are effectively enslaved, forced to work for little or no compensation while paying unreasonably high rents for ill-kept housing. Their well-being relies on the whim of the landlord, who can choose to evict them at any time without justification or any legal process.

Feudalism has no place within a just society. Pakistan's system of modern slavery dramatically minimizes the value of the country's land and its potential use. Countries such as South Korea, Japan, and India have maintained feudal systems within the last century, but state-led land reforms worked to dismantle this social structure.[185] In the 1950s, Indian legislation began placing limits on amounts of landholding. As a result, many former tenants were able to become landowners by purchasing newly released land parcels directly from the state.

Many scholars regard land reforms in South Korea as an example of successful transition from a feudal system. After World War II, feudal lands were handed over to the tenants for very little compensation.[186] More than half of all land changed ownership. The immediate result was an 80% decrease in income for the top four percent of the population. Conversely, the bottom 80% of the population experienced an average 20 to 30% increase in their incomes. The South Korean government then used subsidies and credits to assist new landowners with their agricultural efforts. Though the current system is far from perfect and some injustices are still present, the overall effect of land reform was an eventual 50% increase in rural incomes, along with a more equal and just rural society. This exemplifies how the productive use of land ownership benefits the nation as a whole.

Outcomes of a Just Environment

Individuals thrive in a society that protects their rights. Due to injustice, resources of a corrupt nation are not utilized productively. Public projects and jobs are given not to the most qualified, but to the most influential or the person that pays the highest bribe. Corruption creates barriers that prevent people from creating value; economy stalls and poverty prevails.

On the other hand, justice and equal opportunity promote business development and competition. Citizens thrive in nations where competition is allowed because it drives the economy to grow and develop, improving the country's entire environment by facilitating creative destruction. "Creative destruction" is an economic term that refers to the process of replacing obsolete technologies with innovative ones. As industry and business evolve, opportunities follow. Citizens are free to explore their creative talents, invent new technologies, and implement fresh solutions.

In centralized economies such as China, the government rather than the private sector drives most of the economic activity. Creative destruction rarely occurs because government-owned enterprises have no domestic competition, so there is minimal incentive to innovate. However, throughout the last decade, the Chinese government has increasingly implemented privatization policies to support innovation among small-business entrepreneurs. In 2013, 11.3 million new companies registered in China, with 95% of them representing privately owned small businesses.[187] Yet, despite what looks like movement in the right direction, the Chinese government continuously misses one crucial aspect of creative destruction: the elimination of outdated enterprises. Though new businesses are developing within the country, there is still an abundance of state-owned companies that are allowed to continue operating in a substandard manner. Creative destruction only works when the growth of innovation and removal of the outdated co-occur. Since that is not happening in China, many economic experts believe that the economic growth of the last two decades is unlikely to last. I share this skepticism, based on events that took place in Soviet Russia, where the Communist party took resources from the country's agricultural sector and reallocated them to the industrial sector. Russia experienced significant growth following these economic policy changes. However, prosperous democracies do not have corrupt protection against competition; ultimately, the Russian industrial revolution busted because of lack of creative destruction.

People as Valuable Resources

In a just nation, people are seen and treated as valuable resources. Their minds and abilities are cultivated and they are encouraged to prosper through education, training, and employment opportunities. In an unjust nation, people are undervalued as resources in one of two ways: workers are subject to mistreatment or their labor is exported to other countries. Labor is one of the largest exports of poor countries. In these countries, people essentially become commodities, traded as cheap labor instead of being leveraged as a resource for domestic development.

Prosperous nations have trouble filling lower-paying and high-tech jobs in growth industries from within their populations. As a result, businesses look outside their countries for foreign labor. In search of better opportunities, workers leave their countries for work in developed nations. But a migrating worker is not just about a physical body; the nation also loses that person's skill, creativity, and earning potential. "Brain drain" is a term that refers to the migration of educated and skilled workers out of developing nations. The medical field is especially affected by this trend. As reported by the U.S. National Institute of Health (NIH), "Trained health professionals are needed in every part of the world. However, better standards of living and quality of life, higher salaries, access to advanced technology, and more stable political conditions in the developed countries attract talent from less-developed areas."[188]

To further understand this point, let's consider the achievements of immigrants in the United States. Residing in a just environment with equal opportunity has helped many immigrants flourish and achieve extraordinary prosperity. Some of the most profitable and iconic businesses in the world owe their success to immigrants who escaped oppressive regimes. A report by Business Insider found that more than a third of the top American tech businesses were founded by first- or second-generation immigrants, many of them formerly from nations fraught with corruption.[189] At the age of eight, the family of Jerry Yang immigrated to the United States from Taiwan. A graduate of Stanford University, he founded the Internet phenomenon Yahoo! and accumulated a net worth of more than a billion dollars. Eduardo Saverin, a Brazilian immigrant, is the cofounder of Facebook. At just 34 years old, he has an estimated net worth topping $7 billion.

Immigration is a boon for value creation and innovation in the United States. The 25 top tech companies in the United States were founded by first- and second-generation immigrants.[190] Again, an environment that supports the efforts of all citizens enables everyone to contribute to the society. The following table lists the value created by immigrants in the U.S.:

50% of Most Highly Valued Private Tech Companies Founded by First-Generation Immigrants (May 2017)

Company	Immigrant Founder	Country of Origin	Market Value ($B)
Uber	Garrett Camp	Canada	$68
Palantir	Peter Thiel	Germany	$20
WeWork	Adam Neumann	Israel	$17
SpaceX	Elon Musk	South Africa	$12
Stripe	John Collison, Patrick Collison	Ireland	$9
Slack	Stewart Butterfield, Serguei Mourachov, Cal Henderson	Canada/Russia/UK	$4
Credit Karma	Kenneth Lin	China	$4
Tanium	David Hindawi	Iraq	$4
Instacart	Apoorva Mehta	India	$3
Wish (ContextLogic)	Peter Szulczewski, Danny Zhang	Canada	$3
Moderna Therapeutics	Noubar Afeyan, Derrick Rossi	Armenia/Canada	$3
Bloom Energy	K.R. Sridhar	India	$3
Oscar Health	Mario Schlosser	Germany	$3
Hourzz	Adi Tatarko, Alon Cohen	Israel	$2
Avant	Al Goldstein, John Sun, Paul Zhang	Uzbekistan/China/China	$2
Zenefits	Laks Srini	India	$2
ZocDoc	Oliver Kharraz	Germany	$2
AppNexus	Mike Nolet	Holland	$2
Sprinklr	Ragy Thomas	India	$2
The Honest Company	Brian Lee	South Korea	$2
Zoox	Tim Kentley-Klay	Australia	$2
Jawbone	Alexander Asseily	UK	$2
JetSmarter	Sergey Petrossov	Russia	$2
Quanergy	Louay Eldada, Tianyue Yu	Lebanon/China	$2
Mu Sigma	Dhiraj Rajaram	India	$2
Razer	Min-Liang Tan	Singapore	$2

(continued)

Company	Immigrant Founder	Country of Origin	Market Value ($B)
Unity Technologies	David Helgason	Iceland	$2
FanDuel	Nigel Eccles, Tom Griffiths, Lesley Eccles	UK	$1
Medallia	Borge Hald	Norway	$1
Apttus	Kirk Krappe	UK	$1
Robinhood	Baiju Bhatt, Vlad Tenev	India/ Bulgaria	$1
Rubrik	Bipul Sinha	India	$1
Infinidat	Moshe Yanai	Israel	$1
Warby Parker	Dave Gilboa	Sweden	$1
Actifio	Ash Ashutosh	India	$1
Anaplan	Guy Haddleton, Michael Gould	New Zealand/ UK	$1
Gusto	Tomer London	Israel	$1
Proteus Digital Health	Andrew Thompson	UK	$1
AppDirect	Daniel Saks, Nicolas Desmarais	Canada	$1
Carbon3D	Alex Ermoshkin	Russia	$1
CloudFlare	Michelle Zatlyn	Canada	$1
Compass	Ori Allon	Israel	$1
Eventbrite	Renaud Visage	France	$1
Evernote	Stepan Pachikov, Phil Libin	Azerbaijan/ Russia	$1
Offerup	Arena Van Veelen	Netherlands	$1
Tango	Uri Raz, Eric Setton	Israel/France	$1
Udacity	Sebastian Thrun	Germany	$1
Zscaler	Jay Caudhry	India	$1
Zoom Video	Eric Yuan	China	$1
ForeScout	Noga Alon, Hezy Yeshurun, Oded Comay, Doron Skikmoni	Israel	$1

Even for first-generation immigrants born outside the United States, the environment has enabled them to create about 50% of the most highly valued private tech companies:

60% of the Top 25 USA Highest-Valued Tech Companies Founded by First or Second Generation Americans, 2016 (Ranked by Market Capitalization)

Rank	Company	MktCap ($MM)	Last Twelve-Month Revenue ($MM)	Employees	1st- or 2nd- Gen Immigrant Founder/ Cofounder	Generation
1	Apple	$800,898	$220,457	116,000	Steve Jobs	2nd Gen, Syria
2	Alphabet/Google	$679,533	$94,765	73,992	Sergey Brin	1st Gen, Russia
3	Microsoft	$540,127	$87,247	114,000	—	—
4	Amazon	$475,958	$142,573	341,400	Jeff Bezos	2nd Gen, Cuba
5	Facebook	$440,900	$30,288	18,770	Eduardo Saverin	1st Gen, Brazil
6	Oracle	$186,230	$37,429	136,000	Larry Ellison/Bob Miner	2nd Gen, Russia/2nd Gen, Iran
7	Intel	$170,748	$60,481	106,000	—	—
8	Cisco	$157,502	$48,510	73,390	—	—
9	IBM	$143,264	$79,390	380,300	Herman Hollerith	2nd Gen, Germany
10	Priceline	$91,597	$11,014	20,500	—	—
11	Qualcomm	$84,982	$23,243	30,500	Andrew Viterbi	1st Gen, Italy
12	NVIDIA	$84,395	$7,542	10,299	Jensen Huang	1st Gen, Taiwan

(continued)

Rank	Company	MktCap ($MM)	Last Twelve-Month Revenue ($MM)	Employees	First- or Second- Gen Immigrant Founder/ Cofounder	Generation
13	Texas Instruments	$80,822	$13,764	29,865	Cecil Green/J. Erik Jonsson	1st Gen, UK/2nd Gen, Sweden
14	Adobe Systems	$70,193	$6,153	15,706	—	—
15	Netflix	$70,007	$9,150	3,300	—	—
16	Salesforce	$64,611	$8,863	25,000	—	—
17	PayPal	$61,492	$11,273	18,100	Max Levchin/Luke Nosek/ Peter Thiel/Elon Musk/	1st Gen, Ukraine/1st Gen, Poland/1st-Gen, Germany/1st Gen, South Africa
18	Applied Materials	$48,896	$12,942	15,600	—	—
19	Yahoo!	$48,570	$5,409	8,500	Jerry Yang	1st Gen, Taiwan
20	Automatic Data Processing	$45,345	$12,213	57,000	Henry Taub	2nd Gen Poland
21	Activision Blizzard	$43,923	$6,879	9,400	—	—
22	VMware	$39,538	$7,093	18,905	Edouard Bugnion	1st Gen, Switzerland
23	Cognizant Technology	$39,339	$13,831	261,200	Franciso D'souza/Kumar Mahadava	1st Gen, India/1st Gen, Sri-Lanka
24	eBay	$37,774	$9,059	12,600	Pierre Omidyar	1st Gen, France
25	Intuit	$35,501	$5,089	7,900	—	—

Here are some additional examples of people from the developing nations of India and Pakistan who have contributed to the U.S.:

▶ Gurbaksh Chahal was born in Punjab, India. At the age of four, he moved with his family to the United States. After dropping out of high school at the age of 16, he started a company called Click Agent and sold it for $40 million within two years. Yahoo purchased his next endeavor for more than $300 million.

▶ Vinod Dham, "the father of Pentium"—the CPU chip most-used in personal computers by Intel Corporation—was born in Pune, India. He relocated to America after refusing to pay a bribe to Indian officials for an education grant. He finished his education at the University of Cincinnati and went to work at Intel. Dham is partially responsible for the invention of the company's first memory flash chip. He also went on to serve as CEO for Silicon Spice, which eventually sold for $1.2 billion.

▶ Shahid Kahn is of Pakistani descent. He immigrated to the United States and completed his education at the University of Illinois while working as a dishwasher. He went on to own one of the largest companies in the United States, along with the National Football League's Jacksonville Jaguars. With an estimated worth of more than $6.8 billion, he has earned the distinction of America's wealthiest individual of Pakistani origin.

▶ Michael Chowdry was born in a Muslim family in Pakistan. He moved to the United States and graduated from the University of Minnesota in 1978 with a degree in agricultural aviation. Since he loved to fly, he flew crop dusters to pay for college tuition. After graduation, he became a broker, buying and selling landing rights at airports. Unfortunately, he died in 2001 while flying. Aviation businesses he founded such as Atlas Air are worth over $1.4 billion.

▶ Indra Nooyi began her life in a country where the rights
of women are constantly crushed. Born in Madras, India,
Nooyi immigrated to the United States for the purpose of
finishing graduate school. She went on to shape the Pepsi
brand as CEO of PepsiCo.

▶ Satya Nadella, the CEO of Microsoft, was born in India.
Upon graduating from the Manipal Institute of Technology,
he immigrated to the United States, where he earned a master's of computer science and an MBA. He began his role as
CEO of Microsoft in 2014.

▶ Sundar Pichai was named CEO of Google in 2015. A native of Tamil Nadu, India, he moved to America in order
to further his education at Stanford University. He began
his career at Google in 2004 and was eventually named as
the company's product chief. Among his many accomplishments, he led the efforts that turned Google Chrome into
the most popular web browser worldwide.

▶ Shantanu Narayen is an Indian-born professional who
served as president and chief operating officer of Adobe
before being named as the company's CEO is 2007. The son
of a schoolteacher and plastics worker, he holds an MBA
from the University of California, Berkeley and a master's
of computer science from Bowling Green State University.

Success is not limited to the super wealthy. Immigrant achievement
can be seen at all levels of society, from many countries, and among
many racial groups. Among black immigrants in the United States, the
Pew Research Center shows that in 2013, the median annual income
was $43,800.[191] Many of the black immigrants are from impoverished
and failing countries, such as Haiti, Nigeria, and Ethiopia. However,
when placed in an environment where efforts and talents are allowed
to flourish, many reach levels of significant financial success. According
to a BMO Harris Private Banking survey, 24% of Canadians with liquid assets of $1 million or more classified themselves as immigrants,
while another 24% classified themselves as first-generation Canadians,

meaning they had at least one parent born outside the country.[192] Another proof of immigrant success in a prosperous and just society is the winning of Nobel Prizes. Each year, the foundation awards prizes in physics, chemistry, physiology or medicine, literature, and peace to the most innovative scientists, researchers, writers, and peace-builders in our world. In 2016, six Americans received Nobel Prizes in the areas of chemistry, physics, and economics. All six of these award recipients are immigrants.

This exodus of highly capable workers from poor nations hurts these countries in several ways. First, it wastes the educational investment that these professionals obtained from their home country. Education is an investment in the future of a nation. By limiting opportunities and failing to create an attractive environment for working and living, these nations are missing out on the benefits of their investment. Second, it leaves the people of these countries without the adequate know-how to build and prosper. Doctors, educators, and business leaders are essential to the prosperity of any society. When unjust countries essentially push their most talented citizens out the door, they are also pushing out one of their most valuable resources.

People flourish in a nation where they are treated respectfully as workers. In many unjust countries, some workers are treated as slave labor. They work in horrific conditions for meager pay. These workers routinely face physical and sexual abuses with no legal recourse. Some nations have been exposed globally due to their level of human rights violations. The United Arab Emirates has experienced substantial growth over the last few decades, leading to a construction boom. To meet labor demands, the country's businesses have brought in migrant workers, mostly from South Asia.[193] UN investigations uncovered the deplorable conditions these workers are forced to endure. Many work for less than $125 per month and are forced to live in substandard housing. Employers forbid them from forming unions or advocating for their rights. It is a common practice for employers to retain workers' passports to prevent them from leaving the country.

Migrant workers in Saudi Arabia are also forced to endure substandard conditions, with slavery-like practices rooted in gender, racial, and religious discrimination.[194] Unlike the UAE, where most migrant workers perform construction-related tasks, migrant workers in Saudi Arabia perform various service jobs. Many of the men work as delivery drivers, custodians, trash collectors, butchers, barbers, and plumbers. Women serve as childcare providers, bakers, seamstresses, and beauty technicians. These jobs require skill and knowledge, yet these people are treated with disrespect and outright cruelty. Many times their wages are withheld, and they are left with no money to purchase food or other necessities. They are often forced to work twelve-hour days and sometimes all night without compensation. Women are routinely assaulted and raped by their Arab employers, who face no legal punishment. They are often kept behind locked gates with no individual freedoms. When accused of criminal activity, these workers are subjected to secretive trials with no real due process. Human Rights Watch has received numerous reports of workers beheaded as a result of these unjust legal proceedings. Clearly such horrifying conditions create an environment where people are physically and mentally kept from flourishing.

Public and Private Partnerships

Once a country has implemented structural checks and balances to minimize corruption, the government can boost the economy by creating public and private partnerships. Here are some examples of these partnerships working for the benefit of citizens of the United States.

Scientific Research

The Internet is an integral part of daily life in the United States, and the government played a role in creating and developing it into what it has become today. The U.S. Department of Defense funded the first workable prototype of the Internet in the 1960s.[195] To expand access to the Internet, several state and federal programs subsidize the cost of Internet services to make them more affordable for low-income people. For example, a federal program called Lifeline offers discounted Internet access for individuals and families enrolled in government housing or food programs.[196]

Almost 90% of the American population goes online for various reasons, including work, shopping, and entertainment.[197] This widespread access to the Internet significantly affects the country's economy. Online shopping has created an environment where individuals across the country can buy and sell from one another quickly and easily. Some entrepreneurs have built entire companies around online commerce. Internet access has also expanded educational opportunities for U.S. residents, with one in four higher-education students taking courses online.[198] The Internet allows these students to fit classes into their schedules, so they can earn a degree while still in the workforce or taking care of a family. Higher degrees equal higher wages and taxation, which benefit the country's economy as a whole.

The U.S. Department of Defense helped to develop the technology behind Global Positioning Systems (GPS). As the navy searched for ways to track submarines traveling underwater, it experimented with navigation using satellites.[199] By 1973, the agency had created a fully functional navigational system. Today, GPS is owned and operated by the U.S. government to assist with national defense, homeland security, and military operational needs. However, it is also used by private organizations and citizens for numerous reasons that benefit the economy. Instead of using maps and written routes, millions rely on GPS to give them real-time directions for getting from one location to another. People use the service to quickly locate everything from their children and pets to their cars. In the business world, GPS has transformed the transportation industry as well as package-delivery services. It has also become a valuable resource for public transportation, which helps get individuals to and from jobs, schools, and other activities that boost the national economy.

The NIH (National Institute of health in the US) conducts research on curing illnesses and promoting the health of American citizens as well as individuals across the globe. It is the largest biomedical research organization in the world and also operates the world's largest clinical research hospital.[200] The scientific breakthroughs and technologies developed by the NIH have been credited with helping to extend the lifespan of individuals born in the United States, reducing the death rate from heart disease, and improving treatment and prevention of HIV/ AIDS. The NIH grants billions of dollars to private researchers, including institutions, universities, and small businesses. These monetary investments drive innovations in public health, which benefit society as a whole. From an economic perspective, these investments create jobs and expand industries, such as pharmaceuticals, biomedicine, and medical equipment.

Policy Restraints on Harmful Private Enterprise

Tobacco is a major industry in America, with revenues in the billions of dollars. The U.S. Centers for Disease Control (CDC) estimates that nearly 40 million people use cigarettes in the United States, which has created a serious health crisis within the country.[201] Even nonsmokers feel the effects of cigarettes, with about 25% exposed to secondhand smoke in their homes or workplaces, or in public spaces. According to the CDC, almost 15 million children aged three to eleven are exposed to secondhand smoke each year. This exposure, along with widespread use, has created a public health crisis with almost 500,000 Americans dying from cigarette-related illnesses annually. However, even with the incredible amount of suffering and death attributed to the tobacco industry, the revenues of large tobacco companies consistently grew. It wasn't until the U.S. government began speaking out about the risks of smoking that these companies were forced to start taking some responsibility for the dangers inherent in their products.

In 1964, the country's chief public health officer warned about the link between cigarettes, cancer, and lung disease.[202] During the 1990s, tobacco companies were pressured to pay out billions of dollars in order to compensate governments for the tremendous costs of caring for people with cigarette-related illnesses. State and city governments started passing laws to ban smoking in enclosed public places, including work environments, restaurants, and recreational facilities. These governments also used high cigarette taxes to discourage people from buying them. Numerous studies suggest that these government tactics have been effective at decreasing the number of smokers and related deaths.[203] Smoking rates in the U.S. decline each year. The CDC reports that in 2005, 21 in every 100 adults smoked cigarettes. That statistic decreased to about 15 in every 100 adults in 2015. These numbers demonstrate how government action against the powerful tobacco industry benefited the public as a whole. Though nonprofit and medical organizations have always made efforts to prevent people from smoking, none had enough power and resources to stand up to the special interests of the billion-dollar tobacco industry. It took the strength and influence of the United States government to make a real difference and hold these companies accountable. By investing in efforts to inform citizens and creating laws to protect everyone from the dangers of smoking, the U.S. government has been able to save lives.

Large-Scale Public Service Projects

The U.S. Interstate Highway System is often referred to as one of the greatest public works projects in history. It began in 1965 to promote quick and safe travel between the nation's states.[204] A cooperative effort between the federal and state governments, the $129 billion project now covers more than 48,000 miles. Ninety percent of the costs were covered by the federal government.

The impact of the interstate system has been tremendous for American citizens. Roadway construction on the interstate highway system has provided hundreds of thousands of jobs, for workers ranging from engineers to manual laborers. It has also expanded opportunities for individuals who cross state lines for employment purposes. Private companies have financially benefited from the ability to offer goods and services to customers in other states, while their customers benefit from the timely movement of these goods across the interstate roadways. Interstates also drive commercial and residential development in the areas where drivers access highways. Entire cities have developed around interstate exits, capitalizing on recreational and business travelers. All Americans have benefited in one way or another from their government's willingness to invest money and resources into the U.S. Interstate System.

Summary

As discussed in prior chapters, people contribute and thrive when they feel positive. People think and act positively when they live in a just society. Justice must be served equally to all people and not just a subset of the population. As Martin Luther King Jr. said, "Injustice anywhere is a threat to justice everywhere. We are caught in an inescapable network of mutuality, tied in a single garment of destiny. Whatever affects one directly, affects all indirectly."

People or parties in majority do not have more rights than minorities. A true democracy is a mechanism to protect the rights of all individuals, creating checks and balances within a distributed government so that no one person can harm another person and be able to get away with it. People flourish in countries where people are free, but only free to do good. Once a government becomes for the people, of the people, and by the people, it can start providing the best possible opportunities for individuals to prosper by investing in projects for the public good.

SUCCESSFUL DEMOCRATIC STRUCTURE

8

"Injustice anywhere is a threat to justice everywhere."

—Dr. Martin Luther King Jr.

A true democracy is not limited to fair elections; it must also create a structure to enforce checks and balances on government organizations. The primary goal of the democratic structure is to provide every citizen with equal protection under the law. This structure is not something that carries out the will of the people only at the time of elections. Rather, it is a control system that continuously regulates the actions of government servants to fulfill the requirements of the constitution. As stated earlier, the environment drives behavior and must be defined by enforced rules and checks, not what is merely written on a piece of paper.

As stated previously, I believe the U.S. government provides the most successful governmental structure to safeguard individual rights while providing the freedom to do good, but only to do good. Yet, although the American structure is the best one to protect human rights, it is not perfect. While I understand that many people around the world hate the U.S., I ask those people to understand what makes the U.S. strong. Even if you consider the U.S. an enemy, there is room to learn from it. Acknowledging that the U.S. government is not perfect, Chapter 9 will highlight opportunities for improvement in the U.S. system of government.

Structure to Protect Individual Rights

The fundamental purpose of a government should be to serve every individual by protecting their rights. When we create an environment where every person is protected with justice and equality, they have the opportunity to live up to their fullest potential. The prosperity of a nation is the aggregate of the wealth of individuals. The democratic structure works not only at the macro but also at the micro level, from the day-to-day practice of serving every individual. The macro level is important, but the structure collapses if it fails to provide the micro-level safeguards for every person.

I cannot express enough that when people feel good, they are more likely to do good—for themselves and for the society as a whole. A successful government promotes positive feelings among its population by protecting individual rights and providing equal justice under the law. The U.S. Declaration of Independence states, "We hold these truths to be self-evident that all men are created equal, that they are endowed by their Creator with certain unalienable rights that among these are life, liberty, and the pursuit of happiness. To secure these rights, governments are instituted among them, deriving their just powers from the consent of the governed." Thomas Jefferson wrote these words in 1776, but they continue to hold true today. These words recognize the right of all people to be free and empowered to pursue their individual happiness. They also recognize the true role of a democratic government, which is to serve the people rather than the rulers. The protection of individual rights is still as applicable today as it was at the time of the 1787 Philadelphia Convention: "This emanates from the fundamental postulate that individual rights and liberty are more important than national independence: indeed, they are the purpose of independence."

The United States Constitution is the key to the protection of individual rights in America. This is especially true for the first ten amendments to the document, referred to as the Bill of Rights. Historically, the Bill of Rights was added to the Constitution for the express purpose of protecting individuals from an overpowering government and ensuring that individuals were given the freedom to exercise their rights. For example, the First Amendment protects the individual's right to speak freely about whatever subject they choose. In corrupt nations, speaking out against a government official can result in severe punishment. Under the Bill of Rights, the government is prohibited from making any laws that restrict the free speech of the American people, so individuals feel free and empowered to speak their minds. The First Amendment also protects the right to practice the religion of your choice or no religion at all. It prohibits the government from establishing a national religion or requiring citizens to practice a particular religion. This is the opposite of preferential treatment given to the followers of the religion of the majority or the ruling class.

The Fourth, Fifth, Sixth, and Eighth Amendments also provide excellent examples of how the Bill of Rights protects individual freedoms. The rights contained in these sections pertain to criminal procedures, particularly what law enforcement and court officials can and cannot do when they come in contact with individuals.

- ▶ Fourth Amendment—The Fourth Amendment establishes the right of individuals not to be subjected to unlawful and unreasonable searches or arrest. It requires that law enforcement have probable cause before searching your home or your belongings. Probable cause is defined as having a reasonable suspicion that the person either committed a crime or has evidence of a crime in their belongings. The Fourth Amendment protects against corrupt law-enforcement officers who may try to arrest people for unjust reasons or enter a person's home to search without good cause. When arrests and searches are made, officers must appear before a member of the judiciary to present the probable cause and ask that an arrest or search warrant be granted.

▶ Fifth Amendment—The Fifth Amendment guarantees an individual's right to a grand jury to safeguard against frivolous trials. The grand jury comprises citizens of the local community who review the evidence against the accused and determine whether there is sufficient evidence to support the filed charges and proceed to a trial. The grand jury protects individuals from corrupt police officers who may try to jail individuals without adequate cause or evidence. The Fifth Amendment also prohibits double jeopardy, which is trying a person more than once for the same crime. For instance, a man is accused of stealing clothing from a store. He is arrested and goes to trial, where he is found not guilty. Under the Fifth Amendment, law enforcement and the courts cannot bring back the exact same charges, hoping to get a guilty verdict in a new trial.

▶ Sixth Amendment—This amendment guarantees a speedy trial, along with the rights to an attorney and an impartial jury, and the right to confront witnesses. It is meant to protect the rights of the accused during the judicial procedure. Specifically, it guards against an innocent person sitting in jail for an excessive amount of time while awaiting trial. It also ensures that every individual is provided with an attorney for adequate representation within a court of law. Additionally, this amendment requires accusers to testify in court in the presence of the accused, which allows the accused an opportunity to question and confront the accusers. Lastly, the Sixth Amendment guarantees an impartial jury of citizens from the accused's community. Jury service notices are sent out to registered voters within an area. Those individuals report on a specific date to serve. Attorneys from both sides ask potential jurors questions and dismiss those they feel are unable to serve impartially. The remaining individuals listen to the evidence presented at trial and decide the outcome of the case.

▶ Eighth Amendment—This amendment prohibits excessive bail. In the United States, an arrested individual can post a specified amount of money in order to be released until their scheduled court appearance. This is called bail, and it is meant to secure the appearance of the accused in court. A member of the judiciary sets the bail amount based on various factors, including the severity of the crime and the potential public threat posed by the accused. Under the Eighth Amendment, the court is prohibited from setting unreasonably high bail amounts. For example, if a person with little income is arrested for stealing food, it would be unreasonable to set that person's bail at $1 million. First, the amount does not fit the severity of the offense. Second, it is impossible for the accused to pay such an exorbitant amount. The Eighth Amendment guards against corrupt judicial officers who may try to keep an individual incarcerated for unjust reasons.

Each of the amendments in the Bill of Rights is meant to protect the liberties and rights of the people from unjust actions of the government. Even hundreds of years later, they continue to embody the goals of men like Jefferson as they set out to create a just government structure. It is also clear from Jefferson's words that he believed the main purpose of political leaders should be to serve the people of the country, not themselves. Serving in any public or government office should not be used as a moneymaking opportunity. Rather, it should be an opportunity to serve the country and work in the best interest of all its citizens.

If the system of government is structured in a way that does not allow for corrupt moneymaking opportunities, people who are not interested in serving the public are not likely to run for public offices. The structure of the government defines the rules of the game. It is not what is written but what can be enforced. What is enforced is governed by a structure of checks and balances where the power is distributed to the people. Power is distributed to the people because they have elected officers to multiple independently operating branches of government, which keep in check the other branches of the government; no one branch is able to ignore the power of another branch. One of the fundamental features of the U.S. government is that anyone elected to any office by the people cannot be fired by any other governing body, including the president of the United States. There are provisions to remove someone from office, but those provisions require approval by multiple publicly elected bodies.

Another umbrella requirement is the distribution of power across multiple segments of population. A successful structure requires that people are elected by local segments of the population to serve their communities and power is not concentrated in the capital of the country.

The fundamental question is who has the power: is it the rulers or is it the public? The elected leaders are meant to be public servants. Yet, in poor nations, the people serve the rulers. I'm proposing that the public needs to have the power to keep in check the leaders they have elected to serve them.

Leaders Are Public Servants

Public service is a commitment to serve without the desire for monetary gain. True public servants seek office because they want to serve others, even when there are more lucrative private options available. Former U.S. president Barack Obama is a perfect example. Upon graduating with honors from Harvard Law School, he had the opportunity to work in some of the most prestigious and lucrative legal firms in the world. In the 1990s, it was not uncommon for law-firm associates from Ivy League schools to earn a starting salary of $80,000 annually, with large salary increases for each year of employment. These large salaries often came with excellent benefits and other bonuses that could lead to multimillions of dollars. Had Obama chosen a career path in corporate law, he could have earned even more. The top attorney at Marathon Oil Company earns more than $3 million per year.[205] Verizon's top attorney earns $4.5 million. Simon Property Group pays its top attorney $6.8 million annually, and Qualcomm pays its top lawyer almost $10 million per year.

Obama could have easily chosen a career path leading him on the road to great wealth, but instead he chose to pursue a career in public service, consistently serving neighborhood improvement and community economic programs. He served on the Illinois Voter Project, which worked to increase minority voter turnout. Obama later decided to take a position with civil rights law firm Miner, Barnhill & Galland, where he could fight for the protection of civil liberties. Shortly after that, he launched his first political campaign for a seat in the Illinois state legislature, where the average salary in 2011 was $76,000.[206] This was a natural extension of his desire to serve the public and help people live better lives. It is that type of commitment that promotes honest and principled leadership.

In countries with successful democratic structures, the top leadership offices are rarely filled by the nation's wealthiest individuals. Instead, the leaders have a net worth that, even if higher than the average citizen, is attainable and reasonable for the economy of their nation. Even Donald Trump, who is unusually rich compared to prior U.S. presidents—indeed, he's presumed to be richest president in the history of the United States—ranks at 156 on the *Forbes* list of the wealthiest people in America.[207] Compare his wealth to Pakistan's prime ministers Sharif and Zardari, who are listed as the second and fourth-wealthiest people of Pakistan.[208]

Let's revisit a table we presented a few chapters back to examine this point. The United States is home to more than 10 million citizens with a net worth topping a million dollars.[209] A count of Canadian millionaires lingers around one million,[210] and the number of millionaires in the United Kingdom tops 700,000.[211] When citizens of these nations look to their leaders, they see levels of economic success that they can aspire to achieve. This is wildly different from the experience of a citizen in a corrupt nation, where leaders have amassed a net worth that is inconceivable for 99.99% of the country's population. There are only about 2,300 billionaires in the entire world,[212] and the number of them in national leadership positions of corrupt nations is disturbing. A Russian citizen, with an average wealth of $11,000, cannot aspire to the estimated $200 billion net worth of Putin.[213]

Net Worth of Top Official Compared to Average Citizens

Country	Net Worth of Top Official	Average Net Worth of Citizens
United States	$3.1 billion	$301,000
Canada	$2 million	$248,300
United Kingdom	$2.5 million	$320,400
Russia	$40 billion–$200 billion	$11,000
North Korea	$5 billion	$1,300 (per capita income)
Sudan	$1 billion	$960 (average annual income)
Kazakhstan	$1 billion	$1,958 (per capita income)

Note that the prior three presidents of the United States were worth an average of $7.8 million at the time of their election to the office. President Bill Clinton had a modest net worth of $400,000.[214] President George W. Bush had an estimated net worth of about $20 million, mostly gained through inheritance and investments.[215] President Obama had a net worth of approximately $3 million.[216]

While many corrupt rulers are wealthy before taking office, they take advantage of their power and use it to further line their pockets with assets that rightly belong to the citizens of the nation. In countries without checks and balances, *wealth leads to power, and staying in power requires wealth*. For example, Transparency International lists former president of Indonesia Suharto as the most corrupt leader in history.[217] During his time in office, he allegedly stole more than $15 billion from his country. Ferdinand Marcos of the Philippines ranks second on the list, allegedly stealing more than $10 billion while in office as the number of his citizens living in poverty doubled.

Compare this to Obama and his vice president, Joe Biden, the two most powerful individuals in the world during the Obama administration, who are far less wealthy than the kleptocratic leaders of developing nations. Even with his importance as U.S. vice president, Biden struggled with the expense of a medical emergency. As reported by American news sources, Biden's son died from cancer. The expense of caring for him during his illness took a heavy toll on the family's finances, and Biden planned to sell his home to assist his son. Obama offered to provide Biden with the necessary money to prevent him from selling his home. Another example of Biden living like an ordinary citizen is that he rode the Amtrak train from his home in Delaware to Washington, DC, for work approximately 8,200 round trips. Obama and Biden were not poor by any stretch of the imagination, but Biden still dealt with the type of financial problems that many average citizens face.

A successful democratic structure regulates its leaders and puts laws in place to prevent the use of the office to amass personal wealth. Under United States law, most federal officials are prohibited from holding any assets that may conflict with their duty to uphold the interests of the American public. This may include earning any additional income while serving in office if it creates a conflict of interest. For example, the U.S. Constitution contains the Emoluments Clause, which states that "no person holding any Office of Profit or Trust under them, shall, without the Consent of the Congress, accept of any present, Emolument, Office, or Title, of any kind whatever, from any King, Prince, or foreign State."[218] This clause was added to the Constitution in an effort to prevent the corruption of government leaders via monetary gifts from other leaders.

In the tradition of true public service, most American presidents have voluntarily placed their financial assets into a blind trust. This means they turn over control of their assets to another individual or company to manage while they serve as president. Canadian leaders have followed this example. Canadian prime minister Justin Trudeau voluntarily placed his assets into a blind trust after winning the country's election. These gestures, especially when not mandatory, make people less likely to question whether the leader is working on their behalf or in their own interest, which fosters trust in the president's motives even among constituents who may not agree with their policy decisions.

Selection of Political Candidates

The process by which political leaders obtain office also speaks to whether their motives are for public service or personal gain. In the United States, citizens participate in primary elections to select the party candidates. In contrast to pseudodemocracies like Pakistan, political parties do not just give the party ticket to the person who pays the most or is the party leader's crony. Selection of local, state, and national political candidates are carried out through localized elections. While local politics vary by state, many cities and counties hold primary elections to select candidates to represent each political party. For example, five candidates representing a single political party may want to run for the position of state senate. The state will hold primary elections to select the candidate to represent each party. This type of democratic structure fosters citizen participation, even at the smallest local level. Citizens feel connected to the process not just by voting in the final election, but also by choosing the most appropriate candidates for the party.

The system of choosing American presidential candidates illustrates this point. It was developed to curtail corruption in the nomination process and return power to the people. Unlike most countries of the world, U.S. party leaders cannot unilaterally choose the party candidate. Instead, the process starts with a large pool of contenders. These individuals are elected by the voters in the primary elections. American citizens accept this election-based nomination as a decision made by the people and not by corrupt party bosses. Candidate selection by local citizens not only contributes to the legitimacy of the candidate but also fosters feelings of equality among the people.

Localized Representation and Citizen Involvement in Local Government

Localized elections are also used to choose leaders of smaller geographic territories. In the United States, the lowest form of government is the local government within each state. This may consist of regions, counties, or cities. Governments of smaller communities, even if part of a big city, can respond to the interests and needs of each member more effectively. For example, in Minnesota, the largest metro area is Minneapolis–Saint Paul. Called the Twin Cities, this metro has a population of 2.5 million. To serve individual citizens effectively, this area is divided into 250 local cities, each with their own independent police departments and government structures, led by a mayor and group of elected political representatives. The average population of a city in the Twin Cities metro is 10,000 people. Because of the smaller population numbers, these 10,000 people have a lot of direct influence on their local government, including their local police.

Larger cities may be further divided to meet the needs of smaller groups. For example, Saint Paul has a population of 304,000. This locality is further divided into seventeen smaller geographic districts to foster citizen participation throughout the city. The district council structure encourages citizens to participate in their government. It includes a citywide communication network, a point of contact for land-use issues, and a participatory planning process. Each district council is governed by a community council of elected volunteer members.

The fundamental point of these governmental divisions is to hold public servants accountable and serve the local population by limiting the size of each group so every voice is heard. Even in a city such as Los Angeles, with more than 3.8 million residents, these goals are achieved by dividing the locality into districts and precincts representing smaller groups. Each of these localities has its own system of government, which is the lowest level of government serving the local citizen. Localities make decisions involving schools, local law enforcement, trash collection, and other services. City and county residents elect their representatives, deciding who they want to serve their localities. Therefore, small groups of people have substantial influence in determining their leaders at each level of government. Again, this shared responsibility encourages positive feelings of participation among the citizenry. They feel they have some influence over who governs them, as well as a possible recourse if the elected official does not perform appropriately.

Distributed Democracy vs. Concentrated Majority

Though on a much larger scale, the same process is used in the election of the U.S. president. Each political party organizes primary elections at the local and state levels to determine who will run as their final candidate. For the 2016 presidential election, the Republican Party started with 17 presidential candidates. For months, these candidates traveled around the country, talking to the residents of counties and cities. They met with small groups, visited businesses, and spoke at local events. To fully understand the importance of this process, it is helpful to look at the history of the primary process. Up until 1901, the political elite handpicked the presidential candidates with no input from the majority—the ordinary citizen. Primary elections were created in response to complaints about lack of public involvement in the selection of candidates. The citizens get to know the candidates during the primary campaigns, which helps them feel more involved in the decision-making process. Also, the candidates feel more committed to the citizens and the promises made to them during the primary season.

The primary elections take place at various times throughout the country. The winner of each election is awarded a certain number of delegates, who pledge their support for the candidate based on how their party voted. By the end of the 2016 Republican primary season, the public vote narrowed the number of candidates from 17 to 4. When all primary elections are complete, the candidate with the most delegates becomes the political party's official candidate for president. This is a long and extensive process, but it is a fundamental requirement for a government for the people, by the people, and of the people.

Now, let's compare this citizen-driven process in the United States to candidate selection in Pakistan and other corrupt democratic countries. Their procedure for choosing candidates is the opposite of how it is done in the U.S. For example, to become a contender for a seat in parliament in Pakistan, the candidate has to buy the seat by paying the political party a significant amount of money. According to one report, a senate seat can cost more than $9 million.[219] There is no due process for obtaining a seat to run as an MNA (Member of National Assembly) in Pakistan. It is extremely rare for a political party to have elections to choose their candidates. Most parties are formed and led by power-ful and wealthy people, enabling only the most affluent individuals to secure leadership positions. More often than not, these are individuals who have amassed their wealth from participation in corrupt practices and illegal activities. As previously pointed out, this type of environ-ment breeds corruption. Since the candidate pays a lot of money to the party, they justify the corrupt extraction of wealth as a means of collect-ing against their investment. The requirement to pay for a political seat excludes average citizens from seeking office, which promotes a discon-nect between the nation's leadership and the people they govern. When candidates can buy their seats, the will of the people becomes irrelevant. Only the rich become party candidates, and they usually win by their association to the leading political party.

The ability to purchase a political candidacy is the opposite of dem-ocratic principles. These leaders are not selected by the people to be their trusted representatives. Instead, they buy their way into leader-ship positions. I suspect that they also sense their lack of legitimacy, which is why many of them use thugs to force their agendas and vio-lently stop any opposition to their rule. It works just like a gang. These political enforcers threaten and intimidate people into agreement or submission. They collect protection bribes to shield businesses from government law enforcement and also from the thugs of the other par-ty. For example, Karachi, the largest city in Pakistan, has areas divided up between the People's Party and MQM. Each party collects funds from all the businesses for permission to continue operating their establish-ments peacefully. If a business owner refuses to pay, both owner and customers may be bullied or beaten until the payments are made or the business is forced to close. This is precisely how criminal gangs such as the Mafia operate. Since people cannot rely on the police for protection, these henchmen—who, in many cases, are actually members of the po-lice force—are able to get away with their threats of violence.

It would be unfair to blame the people for these actions; the envi-ronment and the political structure define the rules that dictate behav-ior. The blame game is futile. We need to focus on a system that allows people to do good and only to do good. Doing the right thing in a corrupt society is almost impossible for the business and political leaders of the country. Survival of the fittest is a big part of maintaining corruption, and these political enforcers are tools in the ongoing cycle of money and power. Power is the same as money, and keeping power requires money. Whoever is in power will make sure that they control and obtain the money, and whoever has money needs to have power in order to protect their money. In a corrupt nation, there is no political structure in place to protect anyone.

This cycle of money and power also rules many African countries. Nigeria has long dealt with a culture of political thugs. Rival gangs often engage in violent fighting at the expense of innocent citizens. These individuals call themselves security advisors or political allies, but their sole purpose is using violence or the threat of violence to achieve the desires of political leaders. To impeach a governor, the first lady of Bayelsa, a state in southern Nigeria, reportedly hired almost 1,000 political thugs to cause trouble among the citizens and disrupt efforts to resist the impeachment.[220] These leaders need hired henchmen to enforce their otherwise illegitimate roles as leaders.

Separation of Powers—Checks and Balances

Checks and balances are widely recognized as crucial to proper governance, whether it is the leadership of a corporation, nonprofit organization, or religious institution. Unchecked power can quickly erode into uncontrolled domination and corruption, where leaders exploit their roles for personal gain. The process of voting by itself does not create checks and balances; rather, the structure of the government creates checks and balances. To ensure the government—a structure with multiple branches—is run by the most qualified candidates, elections provide an excellent mechanism for selecting individuals to fill public service roles. However, the function of voting stops there. Structural regulation is needed to control the day-to-day operation of the government and effectively serve the needs of the people.

In failing nations, democracy is limited to the act of voting. However, in the absence of proper checks and balances, the selection of leaders by public vote has minimal benefit to the people. What matters more is a system of justice that treats everyone equally and gives everyone the chance to do good and only to do good. Also, the purpose of a democracy is not to represent the view of the majority but to protect the rights and serve the needs of every citizen equally. The rights of each citizen are defined in a constitution to ensure consistency of service to all people.

The government structure and its checks and balances should be considered safeguards that allow political leaders to pursue only actions that serve the nation. Once a government structure punishes each citizen equally for wrongdoing, and no one is above the law, it automatically encourages people to do good within the society. A true democratic structure is a system of government that cannot be changed by one person or a small group of individuals. It does not matter who becomes a government official; the system does not let them violate the basic rules that protect the rights of all. This set of rules is defined in the constitution. If the political structure pushes more and more people to do good and be more successful, the whole nation prospers. On the other hand, if the structure of the government enables kleptocracies where the powerful can rise above law-abiding people, the majority of citizens and their nation suffer.

Merely having a constitution that protects individual rights is insufficient without a structure that can ensure its enforcement. It can only take place with the distribution of power. The U.S. political structure best distributes power because it was designed to protect individual rights and freedoms.

The theory of checks and balances dates back to ancient Rome, where the Roman senate was kept in check by the veto power of the tribune. Veto power is the ability for one political branch to cancel laws made by another branch. In the Holy Roman Empire, the church checked the actions and power of the political rulers. In 1215, English rulers issued the Magna Carta, which gave English lords powers to constrain the actions of the king. More specifically, the document required the king to recognize specific legal procedures and be bound by them. It aimed to keep the king's power in check and prevent him from acting as if he were above the law. The influence of the Magna Carta is evident in many of our modern-day political systems, including the United States Constitution.

When the Constitution was written, America had newly earned freedom. As colonists, the people had fought against the British crown to gain independence and the ability to govern themselves. While many circumstances led to the American Revolutionary War, the most potent underlying factor was the autocratic rule of the king over the colonies. The crown subjected the American colonists to irrational taxation and limited their ability to develop as a nation. In response, the colonies declared their independence, becoming the United States of America. When creating their new country's constitution, the writers remained extremely concerned about the dangers of a strong leader. They feared a return to the tyrannical rule of the British crown, seeing this type of leadership as corrupt and dangerous to the well-being of the nation's citizens. Preventing tyranny was their primary focus while writing the Constitution. The colonists were so fearful of excessive leadership that their first attempt at a constitution did not include a president or even an adequate central government. Quickly recognizing the weakness of this type of political construction, they sought to create a government structure that included an appropriate federal government with sufficient limitations on power.

The United States Constitution created a federal government made up of three branches. The executive branch includes the president and bureaucratic agencies. The legislative branch is made up of Congress, and the judicial branch is the federal court system. The founders created appropriate checks and balances by giving each of these three branches its own set of independent powers and responsibilities:

- ▶ Leading the executive branch, the president is the head of state and commander of the military.

- ▶ The legislative branch makes laws. It comprises Congress, which includes the Senate and House of Representatives.

- ▶ The judiciary interprets laws and resolves legal disputes. At the federal level, the judiciary upholds the Constitution by striking down contradicting federal and state laws.

The Constitution orchestrates this separation of governmental powers. It is designed to ensure that no single branch becomes more powerful than the others. This promotes efficiency by giving each branch specific areas of concentration but also discourages corruption through accountability and oversight. The separation of powers also works against bribery by requiring the cooperation of multiple parties, with varying interests, for the advancement of policies and laws. This provides a disincentive for collusion between government officials.

The "checks" part of checks and balances gives each branch certain powers over the actions of the other branches, so governing responsibilities are shared and no one branch becomes more powerful than the others. Most of the president's other powers, such as the ability to appoint federal judges, require approval from another governmental branch. Though the president can nominate individuals to sit on the federal bench, the Senate must ultimately approve the nomination before the appointment is finalized. The same limitations exist in regard to the president's ability to negotiate foreign treaties. Senate approval is required for the ratification of treaties.

The legislative branch is also limited in its powers. When Congress creates a new law, the president has the ability to veto it. The president can also propose new legislative initiatives and call special sessions of Congress. The judicial branch has the power to challenge both of the other branches through its ability to strike down any law made by the executive or legislative branches if it is found unconstitutional. In addition, federal judges remain in their positions for life, so they are virtually free from control by the president or the Congress. Each of these checks work together toward the goal of keeping the government balanced. No single branch can gain too much control because each of the other two branches has the ability to limit the others' actions.

Checks and balances address the critical problem within corrupt nations—the propensity for the powerful to harm the people to fulfill their own interests. In a strong democratic structure, there are checks and balances in place to protect every individual from the possibility of rogue leadership. While we would like to believe that individual morality would keep leaders from taking actions that are not in the best interests of the people, history has continuously taught us that morality often fails without a strong force and the consequences to back it up.

In prosperous democratic societies, that force stems from a tradition of independent law-enforcement agencies that uphold the law instead of the personal interests of leaders. For example, the Federal Bureau of Investigation (FBI) is one of America's top federal law-enforcement agencies. It is responsible for investigating crimes and seeking appropriate punishments for offenders. Even though the FBI falls under the executive branch, it is still able to investigate possible corruption by presidents and their staff. The Department of Justice is another example of an executive agency with investigatory powers over the president. At numerous times throughout the country's history, the U.S. Congress has called on the Department of Justice to investigate matters involving the presidency. Presidential limitations also extend to the appointment of not just federal judges but also other government heads. Once the president nominates an individual for a federal post, the Senate reviews that nomination and conducts a hearing to question the nominee. The Senate can either approve the president's nominee or choose to deny the appointment.

When citizens and the larger world believe that a nation's leader improperly controls law enforcement, two things happen. First, they begin to see the leader as above the law, able to break the laws of the land without any retribution. Second, they start to lose respect for the rule of law and begin challenging it with illegal actions.

Each year the World Justice Project presents a rule-of-law index, which includes a list of countries with the top scoring law-enforcement agencies. The study considers expert data and questions citizens about their perceptions of the nation's law enforcement and how it operates. Among the areas of concern, surveys ask about constraints on government officials, protection of fundamental rights, and regulatory enforcement. Let's look at some of these individual indicators to examine how they impact law enforcement and successful democratic society.[221]

> ▶ Constraints on government officials—This indicator measures the extent to which government officials are bound by the law. It asks whether leaders are limited in their actions by regulations and legislation. It also examines whether they are held accountable for improper acts. Nongovernmental checks on power, which we will discuss later in this chapter, also fall under this category.

▶ Protection of fundamental rights—We have previously discussed how important fundamental rights are to a successful nation. This indicator measures whether the nation's law enforcement protects fundamental rights through equal enforcement of laws and due process for those accused of crimes. Due process is fair treatment within the legal system, where every accused individual is taken through the same process and given the same rights, regardless of race, gender, or rank within the government.

▶ Regulatory enforcement—Government regulations are in place to regulate the actions of individuals and organizations. The project creators measure this indicator by determining whether regulations are adequately enforced, free from improper influences, and committed to due process.

While the U.S. Congress and president make laws and regulations, they need assistance in carrying out these laws on a daily basis. Federal departments and agencies furnish that assistance and provide an additional level of checks and balances by promoting the effective spending of federal funds. These agencies are specialized to handle specific services and areas of government. Government agencies are allotted budgets by Congress. Their leaders and employees are charged with providing services to the public, while staying within budget and ensuring that federal money is spent appropriately. If these agencies act inappropriately or fail to spend their funds in a fair and equal manner, they can be held responsible by members of Congress or the public.

Here are some U.S. federal agencies:

Agency	Area of Focus
Environmental Protection Agency	Issues involving clean air, land, and water
Department of Defense	Issues related to the defense of the country
Department of Veterans Affairs	Issues related to military veterans
Department of Justice	Issues related to law enforcement
Department of Treasury	Issues related to currency, taxes, and spending

Checks and Balances in State and Local Government

While the U.S. Constitution defines the separation of powers at the federal level, one of the most unique aspects of American government is the extension of this political structure to the state and local levels of government. Within the United States, individual state governments also work under a system in which powers are separated and each branch has checks over the others. In most states, the structure almost exactly follows that of the federal government. The executive branch is headed by a governor, who serves as the state's leader. The legislative branch consists of a group of elected representatives, similar to Congress. The judicial branch includes the state's system of courts and, just as federal courts interpret federal laws, the state court interprets state laws. At the local government level, the executive branch is run by the locality's leader, often called a mayor. The legislative branch consists of a group of council members who meet regularly to make laws and handle the daily business of the locality. These cities and counties also have judiciary branches with their own courts.

Federalism

Another critical factor in the success of this system is a concept called federalism. While checks and balances create a horizontal separation of powers among branches within the same level of government, federalism creates a vertical separation of powers between the federal and state governments. The U.S. Constitution grants specific but limited powers to the federal government. The creation of money and declaration of war are two examples of actions that can only be carried out by the federal government. All powers not expressly awarded to the federal government are reserved for the states. This means the states can perform any tasks not explicitly given to the federal government in the Constitution. Some examples include providing public education and regulating certain professions, such as doctors and lawyers. Some powers, called concurrent powers, are handled by the federal and state governments simultaneously. Enforcing the law is one of them. While the federal government manages agencies such as the FBI, day-to-day law enforcement (i.e., the police force) is managed at the state and local levels.

State, county, and city law-enforcement agencies have independent hiring, supervisory, and firing practices that do not involve the governor or other state lawmakers. This ensures that law enforcement operates independently at every level, so no one is above the law regardless of their position within the government. For the individual citizen, this creates an environment where each person feels protected by the officers of the community. When crimes occur, citizens can report to law enforcement without fear of retribution and with confidence that the incident will be appropriately investigated in a fair and equitable manner. Law enforcement officials investigate the crime and bring charges against the suspect, without pressure from government officials. If an official misbehaves, there are mechanisms in place for citizens to have their complaints heard and investigated. If allegations of corruption are true, officers are punished or fired from their positions. Furthermore, if citizens lose faith in the abilities of their law-enforcement agencies, they can change leadership through the local election process.

The independence of the law-enforcement structure is replicated in the judicial system, where judges are kept independent of political leaders. State judgeships vary. While the governor appoints some judges, most states use a general election or an election by the state's legislature. Elected judges are responsible to the people they serve, so they have to follow the letter of the law instead of bending to corrupt political leaders.

At the local level, judges are chosen through appointment by the state governor or election by the people. For example, in Saint Paul, Minnesota, the governor appoints local judges. In New York City, judges are elected by the citizens of the locality. Under both of these arrangements, judges remain in their seats for a specified amount of time, free from the influence of government officials. Also, if any of these judicial officials act corruptly, they face potential sanctions or removal from their position.

Another powerful government authority is taxation. Within the United States, taxes are collected at the federal, state, county, and city levels. The federal government and most state governments collect income taxes, a percentage of personal income given to the government. Most states and localities also collect sales tax. These taxes are added to products and services purchased within the state's geographic area. Property taxes provide localities with the majority of their revenue. Residents pay taxes on the property they own, including houses, cars, and boats. A local revenue agency levies these taxes and, frequently, the head of that agency is an elected official. Again, this discourages even the appearance of corruption because the local tax-collecting entity is separate from the state's leadership. These funds are utilized to provide city-level services like the city parks, law enforcement, and libraries. Education is a significant service funded by property taxes. This revenue is distributed to schools locally, so the people of a neighborhood provide funds directly to the schools their children attend. This local taxation and spending influence the experience of citizens at the micro level. This type of structure fosters a sense of power and influence among the citizens of a locality. They trust their representatives to make decisions in the interest of the entire population instead of the government leaders or themselves.

As discussed in the last chapter, in corrupt countries, taxes are distributed to provide the most benefit to leaders and their cronies. The distributed nature of the U.S. legislature does not allow for this extreme level of corrupt behavior. For example, as localities collect property taxes, they place the funds into the collective reserve, and spending decisions are in the hands of elected legislatures. As a result, legislators are directly responsible to their constituents and make decisions that reflect that allegiance. When deciding how to spend money collected from taxes, they take into consideration the needs of all districts and collectively make decisions about what is best for the state as a whole—not just the district where the governor of the state lives.

Due Process of Law

Another indicator of a prosperous democratic society involves equal justice for the richest and poorest members of the society. In a just country, individual rights are respected and protected for all, regardless of profession, financial status, race, or gender. The United States Constitution includes a set of rights collectively called due process of law. These are procedural requirements that every law enforcement agent and every court must follow to ensure that every accused individual has an adequate opportunity to obtain justice. These due process of law requirements include the right to know the charges against you as well as the right to remain silent and not say anything that could later be used against you. One of the most widely used due process requirements is the right to an attorney for criminal matters. If an individual is unable to afford an attorney, the court appoints what is called a public defender. Public defenders provide legal representation for people who do not have the financial resources to pay a private attorney. This system works to level the playing field so wealthy Americans are not the only ones afforded legal representation in a court of law.

Another essential aspect of due process is a legal remedy called habeas corpus. This protection from unlawful imprisonment allows prisoners to challenge the legal authority to confine them. For example, a man is jailed in a state prison for a crime he did not commit. He can file a petition called a writ of habeas corpus with the court. This document asks the court to bring him before a judge to have the judge decide if he should remain in prison or be immediately released. If the judge grants the prisoner's request, a hearing is held. The prisoner presents evidence to support his claim of being held unlawfully, and the state tries to justify the incarceration by presenting its evidence. The judge then decides whether to keep the prisoner incarcerated or order their immediate release. If the court denies the writ of habeas corpus, the prisoner can file an appeal and have his request considered by a higher court.

Habeas corpus has a long history within the American legal system. It has been used since the formation of the country to prevent individuals from being imprisoned without legitimate cause. Without it, law-enforcement officials could keep people in prison indefinitely without a fair trial or any evidence to support the incarceration—a tragic scenario that plays out every day in corrupt nations where due process is not enforced and habeas corpus does not exist. This creates an environment where people live in fear of law-enforcement officers, always worried that they may be arrested and detained for no valid reason, with no legal remedy to help them secure their freedom. Living with ongoing feelings of insecurity is tragic. Under a successful democratic structure, citizens are not in constant fear of unjust incarceration. They take comfort in knowing that, if they were arrested, due process requirements would not allow the state to hold them indefinitely without proving their guilt in a court of law.

Promoting a Fair Justice System

As with state judiciaries, most local judges are elected by the people and serve until they are voted out of office. Again, this type of direct responsibility to the citizens discourages corrupt behavior. If a situation does arise where an individual feels that a judge is exhibiting bias or prejudice, the individual can request the judge's removal from the case. The process to switch judges varies by state. In some jurisdictions, the requesting party must provide proof of the alleged bias. Other states, including Minnesota and California, require no cause at all, as long as the request is made early enough in the process.

Jury trials also promote a sense of fairness and equality among citizens. At the federal, state, and local levels, citizens are entitled to be tried by a jury of their peers. This means that citizens from the community sit on a jury and decide the guilt or innocence of an accused party. This takes the judicial decision out of the hands of one specific person and puts it in the hands of multiple people. Jury trials add to the credibility and trustworthiness of the court system.

While many countries disallow the use of jury trials, many corrupt countries do utilize them. The problem arises due to the corruption engrained in the fabric of these nations. The chosen juries are usually biased toward law enforcement or government leaders. This may occur because they are being paid off or it may stem from fear. Either way, a fair and equitable trial by jury cannot succeed in a lawless and corrupt country with compromised law enforcement.

Interestingly, many American localities hand over the pursuit of fairness to their law-enforcement agencies. Cities and counties maintain their own agencies, called police or sheriff's departments. In most states, the heads of these agencies are elected by the public or the city council for a limited term. Since an elected official cannot be fired by a superior, an elected sheriff cannot be fired by the mayor for taking a stance that the mayor does not like. No one is above the law in this type of structure because officers are directly responsible to the communities they serve.

This is not the case in most corrupt countries. Not only is the police leadership not elected by the people, they are also usually controlled by a central authority such as the president or prime minister. If the people become dissatisfied with their environment and don't trust the people who are serving them, they become frustrated. Once people are frustrated, they act negatively. An example would be a soccer team where the players don't trust the coach. Instead of each player contributing to the team, frustration may surface as individual acts that are not for the team's benefit. This is why it is extremely important that the people who are serving an environment live in the same environment. Many American localities do require their law enforcement agents to live within the city or county where they serve as police officers, establishing an even stronger sense of personal responsibility for the area's safety and enforcement of the law. And the citizens feel a sense of control over the people who are supposed to serve them.

The required use of body cameras for police officers also increases their sense of responsibility. These cameras attach to the officer's uniform and record their actions. In many localities, the footage from these cameras is made available to the public in situations where the officer's conduct comes into question. If citizens are unhappy with the actions of law enforcement, they have tools in place to influence disciplinary actions against offending officers. If agency leaders fail to act appropriately, citizens have the ability to elect new ones.

In contrast, poor countries such as Afghanistan or India operate a criminal justice system where wealth and status can buy "justice." In Afghanistan, powerful government leaders and rich businessmen routinely operate illegally without retribution. Law-enforcement agents are unwilling to investigate and seek charges, while courtroom judges accept bribes in exchange for not-guilty verdicts. As an article by International Press Service points out, average Afghans are arrested and punished for violations of the law, while powerful Afghans benefit from their status and wealth.[222] The article discusses governmental efforts to eradicate the cultivation and sale of opium. While the average Afghan gets arrested and prosecuted for possessing the smallest amount of opium, the growers and distributors routinely go unpunished. In one incident, a court advocate recalls the arrest and prosecution of one man for narcotics trafficking. Though the man offered information regarding much more powerful traffickers, the courts refused to consider the information at the direction of high-level government officials.

The Indian justice system exemplifies the same types of inequities, with gender and the caste system influencing law enforcement. For example, the *Times of India* reported a situation where men from the upper caste dragged a family of lower caste into the streets and beat them to death in front of the entire village.[223] Though the horrific crime was unquestionably committed, law enforcement agents refused even to file a first incident report (FIR), the first step to seeking justice for a criminal offense. These registrations are used in India and Pakistan to record citizen complaints as well as law-enforcement observations. Officials are required to complete these forms, yet, as reported by *Dawn* of Pakistan, they routinely refuse to do so as a means of collecting bribes.[224]

In India, female accusers have a particularly hard time getting law-enforcement agents to take their accusations seriously and seeking adequate justice for their injuries. In the previous chapter, I described the horrific rape and murder of the young medical student Jyoti Singh. Unfortunately, her situation is all too common in India, where it is alleged that a woman is raped every 20 seconds. Instead of seeking an arrest, Indian law-enforcement agents often attempt to have the rapist pay the victim. These agents then expect to be paid for the favor in the future.

It's also useful to consider the cultural traditions that undermine the effectiveness of a government's duty to provide justice for all people. In India, a woman's virtue is highly respected. When she is violated, the elders of the village see it as an assault on the woman's modesty and her family's honor. In one case, a 28-year-old woman sought the arrest of her attackers for five weeks after being gang-raped. Instead of arresting the offenders, who were known to the police, they attempted to force the woman to marry one of them. The woman became so distraught that she reportedly killed herself. For a person living in a just society this may sound unbelievable, but the number of Indian women marrying their rapists is significant.

In a truly just democracy, the rights of every citizen are upheld and protected. Majority rule is a common element of democracy, but democracy does not mean that the majority can take away the rights of minorities. A successful democratic leadership ensures that the rights and interests of the minority are just as important as the desires of the majority. The purpose of democracy is to create an environment where people are empowered to do good and face punishment for doing wrong. Individual rights can be defined as personal freedom as long as no one impacts another adversely. For example, there are numerous activities that an individual can engage in within the confines of their private home. You can listen to loud music or engage in affectionate behaviors with your spouse. However, if you participate in these behaviors in public, where you are disturbing others, you can face punishment.

Democracy is a structure that uses collective decision-making and wisdom to protect the rights of ALL individuals. It creates an environment of equal opportunity. Again, a successful democracy is not about meeting the needs of the majority, but rather using the minds of the majority to protect the rights of every individual. The creation of structural checks and balances is crucial to enforcing what is written in the Constitution to protect individual rights.

While these explanations provide a useful basis for understanding the macro level of an effective democracy, I want to reiterate the vital importance of how the governance structure makes individuals feel in their everyday lives. The real determining factor behind a political system that discourages corruption is what happens at the micro level. What are people experiencing on a daily basis when trying to conduct business and handle their private affairs? This is where the rubber truly meets the road.

Other Democratic Government Structures

I am a firm believer in learning and copying the success of others. Political experts and philosophers may question my preference for the American style of representative and constitutional democracy. Constitutional democracy is defined as a government where the courts restrain the democratic will if it violates the constitution. As discussed in Chapter 4, the U.S. government is the latest successful evolution in this government structure. This structure has created exceptional growth in not only the U.S., but also Germany, Japan, and to some extent South Korea.

Parliamentary government is another democratic structure that is adopted by many prosperous nations. However, I believe this is an older structure with reduced protection of individual rights. The U.S. has the only government structure with three co-equal branches of government limiting concentration of power. For additional information on parliamentary government, please read Preston Byrne's "A Comparison of American and English Civil Liberties."[225]

This book is intended for ordinary people like me who are not political scientists and want to follow and support a simple guideline to achieve success. Philosophical debates about the best political systems mostly lead to inaction. My take is to copy what works, make it better, and act on it.

Summary

The purpose of government is to protect individual rights and the freedom to pursue happiness. This also requires government to provide public services, health services, scientific research and development, and a military to ensure safety from external threats. Written policies and even transparency by themselves do not create the checks and balances needed to equally protect individual rights.

FLAWS IN THE U.S. STRUCTURE

9

"Big corporations and the richest 1% of Americans have poured hundreds of millions of dollars into Washington, purchasing enormous political influence and drowning out the voice of average Americans."

—Robert Reich

While the United States government structure offers the best example of a system where the protection of citizens' rights advances the success of the nation as a whole, some types of corruption remain. These shortcomings should not lead anyone to reject the structure of the U.S. government as a driver of incredible economic achievement. An effective government structure can be achieved by following the design of the American model, which has a track record of unprecedented success, while recognizing and addressing many of its mistakes.

Winston Churchill is credited with characterizing democracy as the worst form of government, except for all the others. Though democracy in practice is far from perfect, it still offers the best method of achieving equality and justice for every person. The U.S. government is not perfect; it also struggles with corruption, but on a far subtler level. Politicians are not openly paying for their seats, but wealth is a significant factor in the ability to run for office and ultimately win an election. The legal system enforces laws that prohibit big businesses from buying excessive influence and support from members of Congress, yet loopholes allow for financial support of campaigns that appear to be legal on the surface but have the overall effect of corrupting lawmakers.

American presidents have historically engaged in international military actions outside the parameters of the U.S. Constitution, and private industries have unjustly benefited from the country's armed forces. These are all undeniable problems within the U.S., but they pale in comparison to the pervasive corruption that suppresses billions of people in other parts of the world. Let's take a closer look at some of these concerns and how a developing democratic structure can avoid these pitfalls.

Reducing the Influence of the Richest Individuals

One purpose of this book is to help people outside the United States understand they can improve and safeguard their political systems when they pursue a structure with checks and balances. During the Arab Spring, many people gave their lives in the name of freedom, but most people involved ultimately ended up in the same circumstances as before. If a group of people is fighting against the current ills of a problematic system with the goal of having a government of the people, by the people, and for the people, they must also fight the systemic concentration of power. The following suggestions regarding money are meant to curb the influence of a few on the entire political process through a system of checks to reduce the influence of money. Again, checks and balances are required to safeguard the interests of all individuals. Without them, a nation cannot become a true democracy.

Allegations of corruption within the American government tend to center on a common theme: the influence of money in politics, especially during elections. It's difficult to find an area of American government that is not somehow impacted by money. However, this is not the core problem. The use of money to drive influence and relay messages is not necessarily unacceptable. The issues arise with the sources of money, which should be representative of the interests of a large group of the population and not just a few individuals. It is also important to note that the influence of money in American politics does not begin to compare to the level of corruption that exists in kleptocratic nations. While wealth does impact political races in the U.S., it is not a requirement for success.

Elections exemplify how money influences politics. In 2010, the average U.S. Senate campaign cost more than $8 million.[226] The average House of Representatives campaign cost more than $1 million. Only four short years later, in 2014, those increased to more than $10 million for a Senate race and more than $1.5 million for a House race. The most expensive races cost tens of millions.

Why are these races so expensive? America is one of the largest democracies in the world, and candidates have to get their messages out to the electorate. Accomplishing this goal costs a substantial amount of money. Media access is expensive, and candidates must raise enough money to gain that access through television ads, media appearances, and Internet promotions. Also, the American campaign season is lengthy. It requires candidates to travel for months and even years to promote their candidacy, requiring substantial travel expenses and staff salaries. There is no rule that candidates must spend this amount of money, but according to the Center for Responsive Politics, the candidates who spend more win their elections 86% of the time. Therefore, if you're unable to spend large amounts, you are far less likely to win the election. This trend trickles down into state politics as well, where the most expensive governor races have cost more than $10 million. In some states, it is common for even state legislative seats to cost more than half a million dollars.

Even with the high cost of elections, the American political system is filled with politicians who are not wealthy. Unlike in kleptocracies, extreme wealth is not a requirement for winning an election in the U.S. Less-affluent individuals have the opportunity to raise the funds necessary to launch a successful campaign. Here are some examples:

▶ Bernie Sanders, who ran for the presidency in 2016, had a net worth of about $500,000, far less than his primary election opponent Hillary Clinton. He was still able to raise more than $200 million and put forth a viable campaign by getting his message out to millions of voters.[227] The average donation for his campaign was claimed to be $27. Some estimates claim that it is higher, but not significantly.

- ▶ Vice President Joe Biden also had a net worth of $500,000, yet he was able to maintain his position as a member of the U.S. Senate for more than 35 years.

- ▶ Representative Keith Ellison, former representative and now attorney general of Minnesota, had an estimated net worth of only $25,000 as of 2014,[228] which is less than the average net worth of most Americans and exemplifies the ability of an average American to obtain a national political office.

- ▶ Senator Debbie Stabenow from Michigan had an estimated net worth of $32,500. She was first elected to the Senate in 2000 and successfully campaigned for reelection in 2006 and 2012.

An ideal democratic structure promotes the inclusion of candidates from all income levels into the governing body. An assembly of extremely wealthy individuals leads citizens to view the national legislature as a millionaire's club, removed from the everyday challenges of the average citizen. This dissatisfaction manifests in lost confidence in what the government does and how well it operates in the interests of the citizenry. Under the American political system, every citizen can seek and win even the most prestigious political offices. The more important question about the use of money in elections is not the amount of money, but the source of the money. Many political intellectuals are primarily concerned with large sums of money generated from a single source. When you have an individual or single corporation donating a large amount of money, the single contributor can gain influence over the will of a large population. The funding of elections should be democratized in such a fashion that the contributions are not concentrated. Again, money is power, and a successful democracy limits the concentration of power.

If you live in a corrupt nation, the concept of public campaign funding may be difficult to understand. The public rarely funds political campaigns in kleptocracies. Citizens do not donate money or resources to help candidates get elected. Instead, candidates are wealthy enough to fund their own campaigns. If they are getting campaign contributions, it is from influential and powerful family members or business contacts who expect to have their support rewarded later through favors.

In a kleptocracy, wealth equals power, which is driven by leveraging corrupt opportunities. In Pakistan, campaign financing by the public is rare. As discussed in an article by the *International News*, an investigation of four major political parties within the country found that only one party engaged in any type of campaign financing.[229] Yet, even with campaign finance disclosure laws in place, the party consistently failed to divulge their campaign spending.

In India, public financing of campaigns does occur but it is largely done anonymously, allowing for little oversight. The Association for Democratic Reforms analyzed campaign funding from 2004 to 2005 and 2014 to 2015.[230] Researchers determined that almost 70% of all political contributions came from undisclosed donors. This level of anonymity breeds corruption. As mentioned earlier, private donors often expect significant illegal favors in exchange for financial contributions. When donations are made in secret, the public has no way of holding the politician accountable or identifying acts of campaign finance corruption.

In an ideal democracy, candidates should raise campaign funds from a vast number of donors across the nation. While I recognize the high cost of financing an election campaign in the U.S., I believe that money raised by citizen contributors is a representation of the people's will. No one is forced to contribute money, and everyone is free to support whichever campaign they choose. So the choice to financially support a campaign is also an expression of individual participation in the election process and the government as a whole.

Campaign finance is a significant issue of concern among Americans. To prevent undue influence on elected officials from their financial contributors, U.S. law places limits on how much money an individual can contribute to a candidate. There are rules to limit campaign financing by individuals and corporations, however, there are loopholes such as:

Bundling—This involves people who gather contributions from many individuals and organizations and provide the total to the campaign. Since the bundler facilitates a large sum, they gain influence on the candidates.

Lobbyists—These people become power influencers by leading fundraising efforts as treasurers for special interests.

PACs (Political Action Committees)—These come in various forms, including connected PACs, nonconnected PACs, leadership PACs, and super PACs. Basically, these are committees that pool campaign contributions to indirectly campaign for a particular candidate. There are contribution limits on PACs. Yet, according to the Center for Responsive Politics, the top 100 individual super PAC donors contribute 80% of the total raised amount.

Soft Money—Direct contributions to candidates are categorized as hard money and regulated by contribution limits. Soft money is a loophole indirectly promoting a candidate by allowing unlimited contributions such as donations for stickers, posters, and media spots for a specific hot-button cause such as a woman's right to choose abortion.

As explained by the U.S. Federal Elections Commission, the current limits on donations are as follows:[231]

- ▶ **$2,700 per election to a federal candidate or campaign committee**. This limit applies separately to each election, which includes primaries, runoffs, and general elections.

- ▶ **$5,000 per calendar year to a PAC**. PACs are independent organizations existing to support federal candidates, but they are not controlled by the candidate or the candidate's party. Some PACs are sponsored by businesses or employee unions. They tend to support candidates who support their specific goals and interests. For example, a PAC sponsored by the oil companies will support candidates who want less regulation on the oil industry. Some PACs are ideological, supporting a particular issue or initiative. An example is an environmental PAC that supports candidates who favor strict environmental restrictions on businesses. Contributions to PACs are used to fund political candidates and other election-related activities.

▶ **Unlimited contribution to a super PAC each year.** Super PACs differ from general PACs in their ability to accept unlimited contributions without restriction on their political activities. These organizations cannot give money directly to candidates or to any political committee that gives money directly to candidates. They also cannot coordinate with candidates to determine how they will spend their money. Yet the money is substantial. As of June 28, 2017, 2,394 groups organized as super PACs reported total expenditures of $1,064,770,874 in the 2016 elections.[232]

▶ **$10,000 per calendar year to a state or local party committee.** This is the amount of money that an individual can give to a political party at the state level. The limit is shared between the state and local levels of the party.

▶ **$33,900 per calendar year to a national party committee.** This limit applies separately to a party's national committee, and House and Senate campaign committees.

▶ **Unlimited use of personal funds.** President Donald Trump, the reportedly richest president in the history of the U.S.,[233] contributed about $13 million of his own money to be elected.[234]

With the goal of reducing the influence of a few on American politics, I propose the following limitations as more likely to promote a fair and just democratic system. These numbers will have to be adjusted based on purchasing power parity for other countries.

▶ **$2,500 aggregate individual contributions to all political candidates each year.** Every person should be limited to this amount on an annual basis, which prevents any individual from gaining too much political influence over an official. I can give $500 to the Congressional candidate, $1,000 to a Senate candidate, and $1,000 to a party, but not more than $2,500 in total. When candidates receive significant sums of money from a particular person or family, they may feel obligated to reward that donor with favors when in office.

▶ **Elimination of PACs and super PACs.** These political action committees were created for the sole purpose of getting around election campaign contribution limits. Individuals contribute to these organizations instead of the specific campaign. Supporters argue that this system limits the amount of influence an individual can have over any official, but that is false. PACs and super PACs work to directly influence elections. Some of these organizations work with candidates and political parties to support particular causes. Even those that are prohibited by law from working with candidates can still spend millions of dollars to get a specific candidate into office.

▶ **$20,000 limit for candidates using their funds to support their campaigns.** Campaign contribution limitations should also be extended to candidates spending their own money. For example, a presidential candidate can spend an unlimited amount of their own money in their campaign for office. I find this lack of limit dangerous. While it may appear harmless to let candidates use their own money, the problem may lie in the origin of the candidate's funds. For example, what if a candidate receives a substantial amount of personal funds from a foreign leader disguised as a real estate transaction? They can then use that money to fund their presidential campaign. Americans do not know the source of the candidate's funds because there is no requirement that they provide tax returns for review and analysis. This scenario is possible under a democratic structure where individual candidates can spend unlimited amounts of their own funds. Candidates should only be allowed to spend up to $20,000 of personal wealth to fund their campaigns.

Corporate campaign funding is a great concern. Politicians must continually think about reelection, creating a constant need for financial support, which may, unfortunately, influence their priorities and efforts. Instead of focusing on average voters with small donation amounts, a politician may choose to spend time and energy on big corporate donors who contribute more money. As these relationships develop, big business donors often expect policies and laws that work in their favor, and candidates may feel obligated to champion these interests over those of the average citizen. This is one reason corporations should not be allowed to make political contributions. Many American candidates run successful campaigns without taking any contributions from PACs or large corporations. Some of these candidates use this as a way to differentiate their campaigns. Others do this as a way to maintain their commitment to their constituents.

If big businesses have the ability to contribute money as an entity, they can pressure lawmakers into making decisions that unfairly benefit their interests. Remember that Abraham Lincoln characterized America as a government by the people and for the people. His statement applies to both wealthy and poor people—all people, regardless of race, gender, or income level, should have equal influence over the actions and decisions of the government. But Lincoln's statement does not apply to corporations as separate entities. Contributions to political campaigns should be at an individual level—just people, one person at a time, should be able to contribute.

Under current U.S. policy, corporations cannot contribute their treasury funds to a political campaign. However, corporations have created ways to get around these restrictions. As stated earlier, they can contribute to or sponsor a PAC, which have methods of influencing elections, even if they are not allowed to give money directly to a campaign. In an ideal democratic structure, corporations should not be able to contribute any money to the electoral process. They should not be able to affect the political process. I would argue that the sole reason that corporations make monetary contributions is to influence lawmakers to promote legislation that benefits the business, even if it is against what is best for the citizenry as a whole.

Citizen confidence is the most important goal of a successful democracy. Transparency instills citizens with confidence in the election system. All public officials should be required to disclose their financials when running for office. This can easily be accomplished by requiring the public disclosure of taxes and assets for every political candidate. U.S. candidates are given the option to release their financial information. In recent history, most presidential candidates have voluntarily done so. This was a major area of contention in the 2016 United States presidential election involving Hillary Clinton and Donald Trump.

Republican candidate Donald Trump repeatedly refused to release his tax returns despite numerous requests from his opponent, members of Congress, and the American public. This refusal led to widespread speculation about his financial status, including the various sources of his earnings and donations. Though Trump won the election, his income sources remained a controversial topic among his detractors and political analysts. President Trump has also been met with controversy over his decision to not create a blind trust. Instead, he created a trust run by his oldest son. It is also revocable, which means he can assume control over it at any time. Many legal scholars assert that his actions present a conflict of interest. Placing his son over the trust along with his ability to revoke it suggests that the president will continue to exert strong influence over his assets, which may influence his political decisions. This shows why it would have been better if the law expressly prohibited all presidents and vice presidents from earning any additional income while serving in office.

Members of Congress are also under no obligation to release their financial information, though most senatorial candidates routinely share their tax returns with the public. To reduce potential corruption, financial disclosure should be required and readily available to the public on the Internet. This same requirement should also extend to all donations. Candidates ought to identify all donors who support their campaigns.

Corporate giving is also problematic in regard to interest groups and lobbying. Interest groups form when individuals come together over a shared concern or cause. For example, the American Association for Retired People (AARP) is a powerful interest group that advocates for the interests of people over 50. The National Rifle Association (NRA) is another powerful interest group, fighting for less-restrictive gun ownership laws. Corporations can also form interest groups, such as the Independent Petroleum Association of America. This interest group advocates on behalf of the oil and gas industry. The goal of an interest group is to influence government officials and persuade them to vote for policies that benefit the members of the group. While many of these groups do this by communicating directly with elected officials, a process called lobbying, others use their financial resources to influence politicians. Though there are laws in place to prohibit bribes and certain lobbying practices, many of these groups have found ways around these restrictions. One way is the use of PACs and super PACs to influence elections. Interest groups and lobbyists also find loopholes in the law to fund politicians' vacations and provide financial favors. Though many of these activities are illegal, they routinely occur in an environment where available checks and balances are ineffective.

Charles and David Koch are brothers who control the second-largest privately owned company in the United States. They have used their billions of dollars to create a highly sophisticated and powerful political advocacy operation employing more than 1,200 people in 107 offices nationwide. Their goal is to collect extremely large donations and use the funds to influence politics and elections in the United States. They reportedly spent more than $800 million to assist conservative candidates with their campaigns during the 2016 election cycle. Through strategic contributions of money and resources, the Koch brothers are able to influence American policy. For example, they do not believe in climate change, so they fund scientists, organizations, and studies that oppose climate change and question global warming. They have very definite opinions on criminal justice and routinely fund candidates who support legislation that falls in line with their views. The Koch brothers have become a significant force in the American political system, sometimes garnering even more news coverage than the candidates themselves.[235]

I know of no perfect answer to limit the influence of a few rich people, but we must find more effective ways to enforce the will of the people.

Foreign Policy—Use of the Military

Many people outside the United States perceive the nation as a giant military power driven by greed and capitalistic desires. Their perspective is based on America's foreign policy and use of military might across the globe. Even though there are numerous checks and balances to ensure that individual rights are protected within the U.S., when it comes to foreign countries, the checks and balances are weak in limiting the use of military power. Military and foreign policy are coupled in the current U.S. interaction with the rest of the world. American foreign policy would require modifications to be a guiding light of an ideal democratic structure. To consider these necessary changes, we will examine the use of military forces in other countries. Then we will explore American business and trade dealings with foreign governments. Each year, the U.S. Congress votes to spend an extraordinary amount of money to fund the Department of Defense. The U.S. government separates the country's budget into three spending categories:

1. Mandatory spending—This is money the U.S. government is required by law to spend on certain programs such as Medicare and Social Security. It accounts for about 60% of the total budget.

2. Interest on debt—This is money spent to pay interest on the nation's debt.

3. Discretionary spending—This is money that Congress decides to spend each year. There are no laws in place to restrict how this money is spent. It is up to the members of Congress to decide how to spend it.

In 2015, the amount of discretionary spending in the federal budget totaled $1.1 trillion.[236] This money was divided among 12 federal agencies, but more than a third of it was used for military spending, with the Defense Department receiving $600 billion, greater than the combined total allocated to the rest of the other 11 federal agencies.

U.S. military policy should represent the will of the people to support countries that protect human rights and democratic governments. But there is a disconnect between the will of the people and the actions of the U.S. government. The military budget does not go through public debate and scrutiny.

Discretionary Spending 2015: $1.11 Trillion

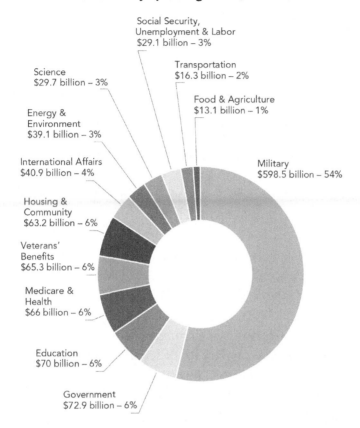

Social Security,
Unemployment & Labor
$29.1 billion – 3%

Science
$29.7 billion – 3%

Transportation
$16.3 billion – 2%

Energy &
Environment
$39.1 billion – 3%

Food & Agriculture
$13.1 billion – 1%

International Affairs
$40.9 billion – 4%

Military
$598.5 billion – 54%

Housing &
Community
$63.2 billion – 6%

Veterans'
Benefits
$65.3 billion – 6%

Medicare &
Health
$66 billion – 6%

Education
$70 billion – 6%

Government
$72.9 billion – 6%

This level of spending causes a variety of concerns, the first being the reasonableness of such a massive military budget. America needs greater public awareness and debate about the country's military spending. While the vast majority of the population argues about health insurance and the $66 billion spent on Medicare, lawmakers are quietly spending over $600 billion on the U.S. military. Military spending is justified in the name of security. But, as President Eisenhower stated, "We will bankrupt ourselves in the vain search for absolute security."

The United States spends more than any nation in the world on its military budget. Globally, the U.S. budget accounted for more than 37% of all 2015 military spending.[237] This means that the U.S. military spending budget equaled the total military budgets of China, Saudi Arabia, Russia, the United Kingdom, India, France, and Japan combined. U.S. expenditures were nearly three times higher than China, the second-highest nation with an estimated $216 billion in military spending. Russia was in third place at $84.5 billion.[238]

What justification is there for this level of spending? Are the citizens of the United States safer than the citizens of China or the United Kingdom? Congressman Ron Paul said, "War is never economically beneficial except for those in position to profit from war expenditures."

As inferred by Sarah Chase in *Thieves of State*, the United States uses its extensive military force to support corrupt leaders. Corrupt leaders use their military to suppress the rights of their populations to stay in power. Use of military force to defend corrupt leaders may provide short-term benefit but, as Chase shows, corruption caused by unjust political systems threatens global security.

Why do Sweden and Norway not need to maintain a vast military force? It is because they are not playing the game of protecting corrupt leaders across the globe. Military spending around the world is being used to sustain injustice. Instead of propagating justice, powerful corporations are using the U.S. military for the control of resources for their financial benefit. In this process, the U.S. military protects corrupt dictators. Similar to Mafia bosses, protection is provided to criminals for extraction of economic interests.

Americans believe in freedom and justice; the majority of Americans will not support a foreign policy and use of military force to propagate corruption and crime. If the will of Americans is heard, people will dictate positive and productive use of money. According to Tom Friedman's *Thank You for Being Late*, the creation of American Universities abroad has a much higher chance of reducing security threats to the U.S. than the use of military force.

The U.S. military consistently ranks first among world military powers, but when you consider which factors go into this determination, it still leaves questions regarding the effectiveness of such high levels of spending. These determinations are based solely on numbers. They say nothing about the quality of these resources or whether they result in a more effective military force. China is ranked second on the list of military spending, with a total of $84.5 billion. China's military budget is only 14% of America's defense budget. Do these numbers equate to more safety for American citizens? How many U.S. nonmilitary individuals are getting killed compared to those from China and Russia? It appears that U.S. citizens traveling abroad or even in the U.S. are more susceptible to terrorism than citizens of China, Russia, or other countries such as Japan or Germany.

This information brings up questions about why the U.S. defense budget is so high and where that money is being spent. The Defense Department's budget includes numerous expenditures, including spending on personnel compensation, missile defense, and security forces.[239] While these may sound like legitimate spending initiatives, the problem stems from the beneficiaries of these huge funds. A 2007 report by the *Washington Post* addressed the cost of America's use of private security in Iraq instead of U.S. troops.[240] It explicitly highlighted the business relationships between the U.S. government and a list of private companies, including two very controversial contractors: Blackwater and Halliburton. A government investigation found that the U.S. government was paying Blackwater and Halliburton personnel more than ten times the amount that U.S. troops would earn for the same type of services. For example, in one situation contract employees were earning an average of $600 per day. An unmarried American military sergeant, working in the same capacity, would earn only an average of $85 per day. This is only one example of the extensive, and arguably unnecessary, compensation spent on private contractors by the U.S. government.

Military leaders continuously assert that private contracting is more cost-efficient than using public resources. Yet study after study has proven that this argument is inaccurate. As stated in a commentary published by the Cato Institute, "At first glance, it sounds reasonable; after all, private contracting companies don't have to maintain standing forces, pay pensions, or provide benefits, to name just a few things that the public sector must do."[241] But, as the author points out, there has been no legitimate academic study to support this argument. "While outsourcing can be effective, doing things in-house is often easier and quicker. You avoid the expense and hassle of haggling, and retain operational reliability and control, which is especially important to the military." Even the head of Blackwater was unable to prove the cost-savings that his company allegedly provides to the United States Defense Department. When asked to support these claims before Congress, he responded, "I don't know what those numbers are, sir, but that would be a great fully burdened cost study that Congress could sponsor. They don't have to do the whole thing, just take some key nodes and really study it."

Another problem with military privatization is the lack of competition among private contractors. The production and maintenance of military equipment and adequate personnel requires a large infrastructure and an extensive budget. Few companies and organizations are equipped to handle this level of responsibility, which leaves very few alternatives. In 2011, the U.S. government spent more than $400 billion with only 100 private contractors.[242] Only 10 of those companies accounted for more than $208 billion in government contracts. As explained in the Cato article, "The market for private security services is only partially competitive, and in some cases (for example in certain areas of logistics) quasi-monopolistic." This exemplifies a significant problem for military privatization. When there are a limited number of qualified businesses to choose from, the government has less control over the cost of service. If the military wants to acquire a specific aircraft carrier, and only one company makes it, the military must pay this monopolistic company's price. This not only diminishes the cost savings but also limits the government's ability to regulate the contractor and ensure that the company is adhering to proper protocols and requirements. For example, even after a controversial 2007 shooting involving Blackwater contractors, the U.S. government was reluctant to end the company's contract.[243]

Each of these factors contributes to the unreasonable amount of defense spending undertaken by the U.S. government. You may be asking yourself how this can happen within a system of checks and balances. Unfortunately, under the American governmental system, military power is one responsibility that often falls through the cracks of checks and balances. The Constitution places military and defense decisions under the executive branch, which provides the president with extensive power over military decisions. While Congress is supposed to be consulted on certain decisions, this does not happen in practice. For example, defense budget decisions are analyzed by Congressional members and, as a group, they do have the power to deny such large funding amounts. While they may make some small reductions, they rarely institute substantial restrictions to the defense budget. One reason for this is their fear of looking unsympathetic to military personnel. When lawmakers speak against uncontrolled military spending, other lawmakers often characterize them as being soft on American security or callous toward military troops. These accusations are unsupported and false, but they work by forcing Congress members to support defense spending, even when they don't agree with it. Giving the executive branch a free pass for military spending creates a situation where the president is not making decisions that are in the best interests of the people. Instead, the beneficiaries of their decisions are multinational corporations and large defense contractors.

Even when efforts to control military spending have been implemented, defense contractors have used their substantial financial strength to influence political power. An article in *Time* magazine discussed how much money military lobbyists spent in 2015 to influence the military spending decisions of Congress.[244] Between 2011 and 2014, Congress implemented budget caps to reduce the amount of U.S. military spending. Contractors were extremely upset over these limits and reportedly sent more than 400 lobbyists to Washington, DC, for the purpose of convincing Congress members to increase military spending. In 2017, military lobbyists spent over $126 million.[245]

As we know, lobbyists are hired by businesses for the purpose of influencing government officials to act in the best interest of the corporation. They track how government officials vote and meet with them to discuss the interests of their companies. While these activities are generally not illegal, problems arise when lobbyists use money to get the legislation and decisions they want. Though there are laws in place to limit this financial influence, many corporations and industries have found ways to work around them by sponsoring trips or fundraising dinners for politicians. As reported in the *Time* article, Boeing, a $100 billion company that makes military aircraft, spent more than $13 million on lobbying in just six months.[246]

The other problem with inadequate checks and balances on military spending is the lack of oversight involved when decisions are made to engage the U.S. in military operations. The U.S. Constitution was written hundreds of years ago by forefathers who sought to safeguard the country. Under the Constitution, even though the president is the commander in chief of the military, Congress has the sole power to declare war. This is done to take such an important and costly decision out of the hands of a single person and place it in the hands of a group, which requires a majority consensus before taking the country into a war.

Unfortunately, many U.S. presidents have gotten around this requirement by involving the military in armed conflicts without formally declaring war. Even though the Constitution states that the United States would not go to war without the approval of Congress, presidents have circumvented this check by not using the term "war." Even though Congress has not officially declared war since 1941, the U.S. has been involved in numerous military campaigns. For example, in 1950, Congress discussed the declaration of war in response to the invasion of South Korea by North Korea. Yet instead of seeking congressional approval, President Harry S. Truman deployed troops in South Korea on his own. He claimed that his designation as commander in chief of the military gave him the right to act in this manner. Although Congress later approved the president's actions, this is not the constitutionally correct path for these decisions. Many presidents have followed suit since Truman, with American forces fighting in Vietnam, Afghanistan, Iraq, and Iran without formal declarations of war by Congress.

Why does this happen? Similar to the spending controversy, if Congress members refuse to support a presidential action that sends troops into combat, they are seen as soft on American security and unsupportive of American troops. Feeling the pressure of these accusations, they consistently support the president's military actions.

In 1973, Congress tried to rein in the president's power to send troops into conflict by passing the War Powers Act. This law places a few limitations on the president and the executive branch:

▶ It requires the president to consult with Congress before sending armed forces into hostile conflicts and to maintain congressional consultations as long as soldiers remain in such situations.

▶ It places reporting requirements on the president any time they introduce armed forces into hostile conflicts.

▶ It compels the president to withdraw armed forces from conflicts within 60 days unless Congress approves ongoing military action or Congress is physically unable to convene due to an armed attack on the United States.

These guidelines are concrete, and they became law over the objection of President Richard Nixon. However, every president since 1973 has ignored the War Powers Act and continued to send troops into armed conflicts without congressional approval.

In a successful democracy, this disregard for checks and balances should not be allowed. The rules are in place to control the powers of the government and to protect all citizens. I propose there should be further checks to ensure that no military spending or involvement can take place outside the U.S. without the approval of both houses of Congress.

Foreign Policy—Business Dealings

The Foreign Corrupt Practices Act (FCPA) was enacted in 1977 to combat corruption between private U.S. businesses and foreign governments. It has two general provisions. The first prohibits corporations and their leaders from influencing foreign leaders with monetary gains or gifts, which is essentially a prohibition against bribes. The second part of the act requires these companies to maintain accurate records of all financial transactions and make these records available for review by one of two federal governmental offices: the United States Securities and Exchange Commission or the Department of Justice. Either of these organizations has the power to enforce the law by imposing hefty fines on the company and filing criminal charges against company leaders.

However, some businesses find loopholes to get around these laws. For example, compensation referred to as "greased payments" is exempt from FCPA. These payments are supposed to be given to government officials for the purpose of expediting the performance of legal duties. The payments are supposed to be an incentive to work quickly, but within the law. The lines between lawful and unlawful can quickly become blurred when any financial incentive is given to a foreign government, especially notoriously corrupt nations where bribes are a prerequisite to conducting business.

FCPA does not necessarily deal with the cause of the problem of corruption. As we have discussed in this book, corruption is rampant in the majority of the world, where it is part of everyday life. Instead of the United States creating laws that limit U.S. corporations from conducting business in a manner that is considered routine practice in these countries, the U.S. needs to focus on getting rid of the corrupt systems before allowing U.S. corporations to compete in these countries. Bribes are a standard mode of operation in these nations. If U.S. businesses are told to use U.S.-based laws to operate in foreign countries, they do not succeed. Penalizing bribes and other funding of foreign corporate leaders is inadequate. The U.S. can solve the core issue by removing the corruption involving the concentration of power that permeates third-world countries.

Since U.S. businesses are unable to legally bribe foreign leaders, large companies win contracts by using the power of the U.S. military to influence them. This leads to additional justification of military spending. For example, a $350 billion arms deal with Saudi Arabia during President Trump's visit was not based on open competition.[247] This use of military power unfairly limits smaller U.S. companies from winning international business contracts. A law that is impractical and unsustainable creates poor outcomes, both unintended and undesired.

Racism and Police Misconduct

A longstanding embedded flaw in U.S. society is systemic racism directed toward people of color, especially African Americans. With roots stretching back four centuries to the country's colonial era, the legacy of slavery continues to be painful and promote injustice. Other significant examples include the forced displacement of Native Americans, the Chinese Exclusion Act, the internment of Japanese Americans, and the U.S. prison system have contributed to the discrimination that minorities continue to experience. For centuries, white Americans have been afforded legal and social privileges, while African Americans and other minorities were denied the same rights. The landmark Civil Rights Act of 1964 prohibited discrimination in public places, the segregation of schools, and employment discrimination. Though it was intended to protect the civil rights of all Americans, the cultural and societal discrimination it was meant to discourage persists in more subtle forms. Even with legal protections in place, deeply ingrained attitudes and fear of "the other," combined with loopholes, bad policies, and uneven enforcement allow discrimination to propagate.

Institutional racism manifests in a variety of ways. While blatant aggression and hate crimes are the easiest to identify, microaggressions, and systematic disparities related to employment, housing, education, healthcare, law enforcement, and criminal justice are widespread in America. These disparities and injustices work together, creating a cycle of poverty that is evident in African Americans' continued economic struggles. High levels of poverty, disenfranchisement, and hopelessness can lead to the types of activities and behaviors that result in elevated incarceration rates. A 2015 report published by the Prison Policy Initiative examined the incomes of incarcerated individuals before imprisonment.[248] Researchers determined that incarcerated people ages 27–42 had a median annual income of $19,185 before being incarcerated, which is 41% less than similarly aged non-incarcerated people. Conversely, incarceration contributes to poverty by creating barriers to employment, causing debt through court fines and fees, impeding educational opportunities, and disrupting communities. In the U.S., a felony conviction can bar an individual from employment and housing opportunities. Even a minor felony, like a teenager stealing a bicycle, can have lifelong economic consequences. This is a policy issue. Legal requirements should be imposed on employers and landlords, similar to the ban on discrimination based on race, religion, ethnicity, gender, and sexual orientation, that prohibit discrimination based on minor felony records.

Two additional policy areas illuminate the connection between racism, injustices, and the criminal justice system in America: the management of police officers and the prison system. As the police force is the first line of justice, flaws in the training, management, and conduct of these law enforcement agencies gravely impacts the entire judicial process and society as a whole. While victims of police misconduct experience the physical ramifications, these actions take a mental and emotional toll on the community as a whole, permanently straining the relationship between law enforcement and citizens. Studies consistently show that minority communities are particularly distrustful of the police, viewing them with suspicion at a much higher rate than white communities. People of color often experience being disproportionally targeted by law enforcement because of their race or ethnicity even for very minor offences like jaywalking that have escalated into violence. When people distrust the police and perceive them as discriminatory and illegitimate, it leads to an unstable relationship between police officers and the people they serve. If citizens do not see law enforcement as legitimate, they are less willing to abide by their authority.

Protests about police brutality against minorities has become more common, especially as citizens have been able to provide video proof of abuses and misconduct. Many have pointed to inadequate police training as one cause of these societal problems. Seth Stoughton is a former law enforcement officer and an associate professor at the University of Southern California School of Law. He explained that, while American law enforcement officers are one of the best trained in the world, their training is based more on fear and violence rather than protecting and serving. He said that officers are trained to act instantly, even before an actual threat emerges.[249] An August 2015 study by the Police Executive Research Forum found that American officers generally receive only eight hours of conflict de-escalation training compared to 129 hours of weapons and fighting training. This type of fear-based training makes violence a standard policing tool for preventing a possible threat that may not have ever materialized instead of a device that is only used in response to an imminent danger of harm or death.

Since many law enforcement officers typically exhibit these higher levels of aggression toward minorities, African Americans are disproportionately represented among the U.S. prison populations. Based on 2010 U.S. Census results, Prison Policy Initiative found that 2,306 of every 100,000 African Americans were incarcerated compared to 1,291 of Native Americans, 831 of Latino, and 450 of white Americans.[250] Ac-

cording to the National Association for Advancement of Color People
(NAACP), African Americans are incarcerated at more than five times
the rate of whites. Additionally, the imprisonment rate for African American women is twice that of white women. African American children
represent 42% of children who are detained, and 52% of children whose
cases are judicially transferred to criminal court.[251]

With such high incarceration rates, it is essential to consider how
the prison system affects the prisoner as well as society as a whole. What
is the purpose of the prison system? Historically, prisons were created
for housing inmates and deterring people from committing crimes. Cer-
tainly when someone does a criminal act, they should be held accountable. However, that accountability should not be at a level that ruins
their life and impedes them from ever becoming a productive contributor to society, unable to vote, get a job, or buy a home. Rehabilitation
should play a significant role in the prison system. But the U.S. prison
system has become a profitable enterprise for private corporations who
are not incented to put people back into society. Prison privatization
occurs when the functions of running a prison are transferred from the
government sector to the private sector. In some cases, operations of
the entire jail are taken over by a private corporation. U.S. Corrections
Corporation is a private company headquartered in Kentucky. Established in 1986, it was the first private company to own and operate an
adult state prison.[252] As of May 2020, the company is worth more than
$1.4 billion.

The U.S. has the highest rate of incarceration in the world, with over
2.2 million prisoners. This number represents an incredible loss of resources that these human beings could be contributing instead of bur-
dening taxpayers with their upkeep as inmates. To house these millions
of prisoners, the U.S. spends over $43 billion annually for security, ad-
ministrative staff costs, food, infrastructure costs, and healthcare. The
total cost per inmate averaged $33,274. Even with this much spending,
America is widely viewed as having one of the most ineffective and unsuccessful prison systems in the world.

Recidivism is the return of previously imprisoned individuals to
jail after release. The recidivism rate in Sweden after three years is 29%
compared to 68% in the United States. When the higher recidivism rate

of the U.S. prisons is analyzed, the differences in treatment of prisoners easily explains why the two countries experience such different outcomes.[253] In Swedish jails, prisoners are housed in dormitories, where
they are allowed certain freedoms. For example, inmates wearing an
ankle bracelet location monitor are permitted to leave the facility for
employment and educational opportunities. In the U.S., inmates are
stuffed into overcrowded jails, often with nothing more than the bare
necessities and little outside contact. These poor conditions lead to
poor health, more significant mental health challenges, and increased
levels of inmate-on-inmate violence. Correctional officers act as advocates and progress counselors in Sweden. In the U.S., prison guards are
solely there to enforce rules and punish undesirable conduct. Swedish
guards guide the prisoners in their rehabilitation and even eat with them
in a communal setting. As a result, the instances of violence against correctional officers are extremely low. Solitary confinement is viewed as
an absolute last resort in Swedish prisons, while it is routinely used as a
method of punishment in America. The Swedish prison system is seen
as a vehicle for reform and rehabilitation, and less of a vehicle for punishment. Conversely, the American prison system leaves first-time offenders to sit in jail for years without improvement, teaching them to
become hardened criminals.

As discussed throughout earlier chapters, we behave in response
to our environment. Even if someone breaks the law and commits a
crime, they likely experienced some dire circumstances to stoop to that
behavior. When we understand that, we recognize the importance of
showing empathy toward our fellow man. This important topic warrants
another book; however, I will suggest briefly here that instead of only
punishing a wrongdoer, experts must do some analysis on what it will
take for the person to become a productive member of society. Then
the systems in place should encourage the person to achieve those goals
and hold them accountable until they are met. How can this be done?
First, offenders should be given specific educational tests and the opportunity to learn online or participate in classes held inside the prison
or at colleges. Education will make the person more employable and
productive after leaving the prison system. For those who are released,
a tracking device on their person for a defined period can assist in sup-

porting their rehabilitation and/or identifying a potential trend toward re reoffending. Artificial intelligence could be employed for a period to track their movements and life activities, and monitor their bank accounts, employment records, paychecks, etc. The technology must be designed without embedding discrimination practices that would result in uneven treatment of former prisoners.

The need for police reform, particularly in relation to racial discrimination, has become a widely discussed issue within American society and around the globe, as people examine the vast differences between the purported role of the police force and the systematic deficiencies that have undermined the credibility and effectiveness of police departments. The calls for change require initiatives that will refocus police actions onto their intended purpose of protecting and serving.

The most effective police departments have the support of the communities they serve. When citizens trust their law enforcement officials, they are more likely to cooperate and work collectively to promote their neighborhoods' safety. Community policing is about building relationships between law enforcement and community members so that each side at least tries to understand the perspective of the other, earning respect and listening to one another. Community policing also involves peaceful conflict resolution and breaking down the biases that police officers and community members hold about one another. While the value of community policing is well researched and documented, some local and state governments still fail to recognize the need for these programs. Many states and localities have drastically cut funding for community policing over the last twenty years. This translates to fewer officers within neighborhoods, getting to know the residents, and building mutually respectful relationships.

One way to foster these valuable relationships is to mandate that police officers reside within the neighborhoods where they serve. Many localities do not even require officers to live within the cities where they work. In about two-thirds of U.S. cities with the largest police forces, the majority of police officers live in neighboring towns and commute to work. On average, among the 75 largest law enforcement agencies, 60% of the officers lived outside the city limits.[254] This disconnect often results in a police force that does not represent the racial makeup of the community it serves. A U.S. Bureau of Justice Statistics survey of 100 police departments nationwide found that the percentage of white officers in these departments was more than 30% higher than white citizens within communities they served, i.e., in a city where white residents make up 10% of the population, the racial makeup of the police department is 40% white. While minority officers make up less than 25% of police departments, the national minority population is nearly 40% and rapidly growing.[255] The police force should represent the makeup of their district. For example, if a police district has 20% African Americans, it should also have 20% African American police officers. Diversity contributes to increased awareness about the culture of a neighborhood and its residents, which can sometimes be the difference between a minor police interaction and a life-ending tragedy. Studies show that minorities tend to have a less favorable opinions of police departments when they do not represent the community's diversity. This distrust and animosity create tension between police officers and the people they are supposed to serve, ultimately making the department less effective. Residency requirements give police officers a stake in the cities they serve and a vested interest in the area and are less likely to see it as nothing more than a job.

Bringing officers and citizens together can also be accomplished with the implementation of smaller police districts. These districts can be narrowly defined to ensure an adequate number of officers in proportion to the community's population. Smaller districts would improve response times for emergency calls, while also fostering an environment where officers and the citizens they serve can form relationships with one another. Each police district can be overseen by an elected citizen council representing the residents of the police district. These local residents can oversee the policing of their respective districts, providing insights and guidance about their actions and contributions to the community. Similar to political wards where a city is divided into separate districts, each police district would have a separate advisory council. These smaller districts promote greater interaction with community members in non-enforcement situations. Police agencies should welcome citizens to participate in regular town hall meetings to ensure that they are effectively serving their communities.

Community trust is earned when citizens stop viewing law enforcement as solely punitive and start seeing it as rehabilitative. When citizens only think of the repressive nature of policing, they begin to fear the police instead of trusting them to help and protect them. We end up with entire communities where people do not call the police, even when they are in danger or have information about a crime. Each interaction with a police officer becomes a heightened chance that they will end up arrested and incarcerated, so they would rather not have any interaction at all. A way to address this relationship problem is by employing social workers and mental health professionals to assess situations and mitigate problems when the police are called.

When the City of San Francisco, California, announced plans to reform its police force, part of the plan ended police responses to emergency calls for noncriminal activity. That means that instead of a police officer responding to a domestic disturbance or mental health crisis, a trained therapist would respond. A small group of localities across the nation have been utilizing similar strategies for years. In Eugene, Oregon, psychologists respond to mental health calls instead of police officers. These reforms are useful at preventing nonviolent situations from escalating, which can happen when distressed people come in contact with police officers who have more training in weaponry than conflict resolution. These measures also help change the systems that currently convert first-time offenders into hard-core criminals. Many first-time offenders, especially those in violation of drug laws, are better served with counseling and rehabilitation instead of incarceration. By identifying and addressing problems early with appropriate services, instead of throwing people in jail for minor infractions, we can start to break the chain of first-time offenders becoming reoffenders.

Even with the most effective systems in place, police misconduct will still occur. When this happens, we need policies in place to address the problems openly and honestly. Body-cameras offer a solution to documenting the incidents. These cameras should be worn by every police officer in the country to ensure accountability. Though many law enforcement agencies resist the use of body cameras, they actually protect both the community and the officers. The citizens receive protection from unjustified use of force, and officers receive protection against unwarranted complaints. According to a California study, the use of body cameras led to a 60% reduction in the use of force, and an 88% reduction in the number of citizen complaints against officers.

Law enforcement agencies should make these recordings available to the public promptly when incidents occur. It is common that the footage from the body-cameras is kept from public viewing for weeks or even months. Judges may block the footage because of its possible effect on future trials of involved officers or prosecutors that may prevent the release of footage because it could taint a potential jury. There could also be privacy issues involving bystanders included in the footage. When body camera tapes are kept private, it gives the impression that the agency is trying to protect corrupt officers. Transparency by making recordings available to the public via the internet increases the trust in the police.

Policies and organizational structure should be in place to ensure unbiased investigation and prosecution of police misconduct. Many localities and states rely on local prosecutors to investigate, charge, and prosecute law enforcement officials. However, the prior relationship between prosecutors and police officers compromises this duty. Prosecutors depend on their local police to help them when prosecuting a case.[256] These same police officers rely on prosecutors to assist them with their investigations to convict the criminals. In cases involving police misconduct, these relationships can keep the prosecutor from indicting the coworker police officer without prejudice. As some states have looked to address these concerns, they have come up with various reforms. Some jurisdictions maintain a permanent special prosecutor's office that solely investigates allegations of police misconduct. Other states mandate independent investigations of police-involved shootings, while others automatically refer these cases to outside jurisdictions.

Half of U.S. states operate under a system that keeps incidents of police misconduct confidential and out of public view. Without a national database of unlawful acts, the history of a police officer's misconduct is not scrutinized. Many studies have identified problems in the collection of data on killings by police officers. The primary source for data about homicides in the U.S. is the FBI's Uniform Crime Reporting (UCR) program. Under this system, federal, state, and local law enforcement agencies only voluntarily report crimes, including homicides. Unfortunately, participation in the program is voluntary, and many police departments choose not to participate, or pick and choose which crimes to report. The federal government should mandate that local law enforcement agencies report to the UCR.

Many citizens feel that the police get to operate under a different set of rules, shielded from accountability for their harmful actions. For example, an American legal concept called "qualified immunity" makes it virtually impossible to sue police officers for the harms they cause while on duty. Police unions also work hard to shield their members from the consequences of their actions. Many include provisions in their agreements with the governments to constraint investigations on police officers, delay investigations, reduce disciplinary actions, and clear officer records of bad behavior. Many have persuaded state governments to turn these police protections into law by implementing Officer Bill of Rights statutes. These police unions stand and protect corrupt officers even if it means obstructing justice.

Summary

The United States governmental structure is the most successful worldwide, but there are still many opportunities for improvement. Campaign contributions by corporations, along with excessive military spending, support and expand corruption instead of preventing it. Moreover, the injustices caused by racism-driven law enforcement behavior continue to propagate poverty for minorities and affect the overall economy and quality of life.

ACT NOW: JOIN THE MOVEMENT

10

"I have the audacity to believe that people everywhere can have three meals a day for their bodies, education and culture for their minds, and dignity, equality, and freedom for their spirits. I still believe that one day mankind will bow before the altars of God and be crowned triumphant over war and bloodshed, and nonviolent redemptive goodwill will proclaim the rule of the land."

—Dr. Martin Luther King Jr.

The time has come to reawaken the message of Martin Luther King Jr.—to make a world where all people triumph over war and bloodshed, and nonviolent goodwill rules.

Every person must come to know and fully believe that we are all created equal, and together we can benefit from the existence and capabilities of other human beings. Unfortunately, we are living in a world where 75% of the population must fight to survive the challenges of living in societies where their lives are compromised and treated as insignificant. These tragedies are allowed to continue because the other 25% of the world is unaware of the gravity of the problem. There is nothing

225

inherently wrong with any of us. The root cause is injustice, which manifests as corruption. Injustice also kills the innate desire of a human soul to excel.

When we look closely at Maslow's hierarchy of needs and how individuals in kleptocracies are prevented from reaching self-actualization—the highest level in the hierarchy of human need. The basic tenet of this theory is that when individuals live in societies where daily life is consumed with meeting basic needs for themselves and their families, they are unable to strengthen their self-esteem or reach self-actualization.

The average person living in a prosperous and just country has reasonable access to daily necessities such as food and housing, and their safety and security are not in constant jeopardy. Therefore, achieving the basic needs of Maslow's hierarchy does not require a significant percentage of their time and effort. However, the average individual living within a kleptocracy continually struggles to meet their physiological and safety needs. In fact, they spend so much time fulfilling these fundamental needs that there is no opportunity to even think about the higher levels of human desires described in Maslow's hierarchy.

We can no longer allow ourselves to ignore the fact that this is the reality for the majority of people on Earth. Globalization has connected people in a way that we have never experienced before, with the Internet providing the ability to see firsthand the living conditions of people around the world. People living in more advanced countries have come face-to-face with the challenges of people living in underdeveloped nations. We are witnessing the physiological deficiencies of children and families living without adequate shelter, food, and water. Our news outlets continuously show us the tragedies of war-torn nations and innocent people caught in the deadly consequences of their corrupt government's actions and policies.

The Internet has changed the world by providing people living in these oppressed societies a different perspective on their circumstances. They can now see that people in developed countries are living a much better life. The mental impact of their daily challenges is further amplified when they learn that hunger and poverty are not the typical way of living in advanced countries around the world. They see the opportunities that they must do without and it heightens the pain of their adversity. Globalization proves the theory that when any nation fails, it impacts other countries. People's frustrations fuel extremist groups, which resort to violence to revolt against injustice and corruption.

Just and moral governing structures are the only way to counter injustice and corruption. Merely implementing democratic structure is insufficient. We must also ensure that we have checks and balances in place to promote true equality and opportunity for all people. The world is missing out on the untapped contributions of most of its population. If we implement policies and laws that release these individuals from the corruption and oppression that binds them, they will be free to pursue and reach their full potential.

Numerous myths surround the causes and remedies of corrupt governments. It is often argued that democracy is the answer to corruption, but corruption occurs under all political systems. While the principles of democracy promote increased equality, they alone are not sufficient without additional structures in place to regulate the actions of citizens. Throughout history, numerous oppressive governments came to power under democratic elections. Adolph Hitler was technically elected to his position, and he went on to commit some of the worst atrocities in history.

Transition to democracy without a distributed government structure of checks and balances leads countries to chaos and anarchy. As a reaction to chaos, countries revert to autocratic rule. For example, the Arab Spring movement for democratic rule failed in Egypt. It is now back to the authoritarian security state that existed under President Hosni Mubarak. Unchecked power under any system causes tyranny.

Literacy rates and educational deficiencies are also used to explain the problems of these nations. Though low literacy rates negatively impact a country's success, if a country is prosperous, it will have resources to enable its population to become educated and increase the literacy rate. Having a high literacy rate by itself does not lead to economic prosperity. For example, Sri Lanka has the extremely high literacy rate of 91.2%, yet its economy continuously struggles with ongoing reliance on assistance from the International Monetary Fund.[257] Numerous nations with high literacy rates are poor, including Lebanon and Cuba.

Africa is full of countries with a wealth of natural resources due to their geography. However, rich and powerful nations have extracted the resources of Africa for hundreds of years, using them for their own benefit.

Several factors contribute to the current situation in the world. Up until recent history, almost all world leaders were monarchs and other types of dictators. They used their power for personal gain. Leaders in France, Spain, and the British Empire exerted these corrupt behaviors through history as they occupied land and extracted resources from less powerful nations for personal gain. Spanish invasions of the Aztecs of Mexico and Incas of Peru resulted in the virtual extinction of entire populations, while gold and silver were forcibly extracted from these rich lands and sent back to appease the Spanish throne. In its quest for riches and control, the British Empire colonized more than 20 nations, including India, Egypt, Sudan, and Nigeria.

Even when the countries were decolonized, the new leaders continued the inherited governance of command and control, taking command of the people for the purpose of controlling the country's resources. When citizens become tired of the low quality of life beneath oppression and injustice, they revolt. Recent attempts at revolution demonstrate the widespread dissatisfaction that exists around the world today, but these efforts have failed to effect lasting change because people do not truly understand what is necessary to bring about long-lasting prosperity within their countries.

Corruption stems from the lack of checks on wrongdoing. A corrupt nation operates through internal systems of fraudulent activities. Within a kleptocracy, the goal of the leaders is not to serve the needs of the people. Their goal is to increase their wealth as a vertically integrated enterprise, i.e., everyone in the chain of command feeds a share of their bribes to the next higher-ranking person. Even if a few uncorrupted leaders are elected to office, fraud is so embedded in the bureaucratic system that their efforts to correct the problem are ineffective. This translates into overwhelming problems for the citizens of these countries. Every day presents insurmountable challenges, including the difficult choice of standing their moral ground or participating in the system of corruption. They are forced to pay bribes for such basic needs as education, utilities, public services, and healthcare. These corrupt practices also complicate foreign investment opportunities by either discouraging potential investors or attracting even more corruption. Entrepreneurs and businesses are also stifled by corruption, constantly faced with the requirement to pay bribes to do business. National resources are extracted, and sometimes sold in the name of privatization to the highest briber, instead of being used to benefit the citizens. Together, all of these systems work to ensure that only a few retain the wealth of a nation. As the nation's resources are extracted, money is stashed in international safe locations as foreign investments, including Swiss bank accounts. The actions of these leaders ensure that the nation and its citizens do not benefit from the country's resources.

To sustain this system of corruption within the kleptocratic structure, law enforcement must be subservient to corrupt leaders by insulating them from legal ramifications. Law enforcement members are given no choice but to follow the directives of their superiors, even when they don't follow the law. If law-enforcement personnel refuse to meet the demands of their superiors and powerful interests, they are punished with transfers to remote areas or loss of their jobs. Their rights are not protected, so they are made to become part of the corruption that drives the government. Law enforcement is routinely prevented from investigating crimes or forced to arrest innocent people.

The judiciary is also part of this systematic corruption, with judges purposely delaying cases or handing down decisions as instructed by government officials.

Citizens of corrupt countries live under a set of unwritten rules that drives their behavior. These people experience oppression at the macro and micro levels of their lives, which affects the decisions they make each day. All of us are driven by our environments and individual experiences. We make decisions based on our fundamental needs, shaped and constrained by the acceptable practices of our environment. Remember the water example we discussed in Chapter 6? Individuals routinely break the law to access water, a necessity that people in developed nations take for granted. This is a perfect example of the hierarchy of needs. These individuals must spend an incredible amount of time on level one, trying to meet their physiological needs, so they do not have the time or drive to focus on self-actualization.

Life in unjust countries drastically differs from life in a just society, where people have the opportunity to flourish and spend their energy on their self-esteem and growth. Equality makes people feel that they are valued as human beings. It creates hope, reducing the feelings of helplessness that limit drive for human achievement. A just society promotes individual contributions via meritocracy, encouraging people to work hard and thrive. In a society that promotes just actions and adequately punishes corrupt actions, people act positively. In a just society, individuals thrive, along with the economy. Foreign investments flow into the country, and resources are used to benefit the citizens of the nation. The rule of law is also in place, applying justice for all people, regardless of their status. In addition, checks and balances ensure that all levels and branches of the government serve the citizens according to the law and the constitution. Tax collection is handled justly, with all people contributing to the national economy proportionately. Finally, revenue collected through taxation is for the benefit of all citizens.

Creating a just environment for all citizens requires a system of checks and balances, where no one is above the law. I believe the best structure and system of government can be found in the United States Constitution. The system of checks and balances implemented at the federal level is replicated in state and local governments. Individuals in leadership positions, from the president and members of Congress to mayors, county commissioners, and local judges, are held accountable for their actions and decisions.

The United States, though not perfect, provides the best example of a system that protects the environment of every person by utilizing a government structure designed for equality through systems of checks and balances. Since the system does not support corrupt behavior, leaders who serve out of a commitment to public service can become politically prominent. The checks and balances prevent leaders from increasing their wealth by corruption. Political candidates are elected through a fair election process, where citizens participate even at the party level and have their voices heard. Leaders do not buy their offices or use intimidation to force themselves into their positions. A system of checks and balances keeps the executive, legislative, and judicial branches from usurping powers and acting unjustly. These same systems exist at the state and local levels, which are closer to the people and the feelings they have about their everyday lives. The U.S. structure creates an environment that encourages people to *achieve good*.

The basic premise of democracy is that citizens elect their leaders. However, the act of electing leaders does not in itself protect individuals' rights. Throughout this book, I emphasize the need to protect every individual and give each an environment that provides each person with the most opportunities. Accomplishing a just environment requires a specific structure designed for the protection of individual rights that guarantees equality to all. The U.S. governmental structure is designed to protect individual rights.

Again, no system guarantees success for every individual, but an environment can guarantee opportunities for success and protect those opportunities from the unjust actions of others. An opportunity to succeed triggers the human imagination to strive for more and to achieve self-actualization.

While the U.S. government gives us a good example of an ideal government structure, it does have its weaknesses and areas for improvement. As in all parts of the world, in the United States, money influences who has power. Creating a more effective democracy requires reducing the influence of money on government and maintaining an environment that invites participation from all citizens. Individuals should be limited in the amount of money they can donate to a political candidate, and corporations should not be allowed to contribute at all. These changes are proposed by many political pundits to reduce the influence of money in the political system. All contributions should be made public. Interest groups and lobbyists must also be kept under stringent regulation.

Kleptocracies do not utilize systems of public funding for political elections, which creates an environment where only the wealthiest individuals can secure public office. While running for American elections does require money, even poor individuals can dream of becoming leaders and raise the money for their political success. Even though a limited number of people participate in the U.S. democratic process, knowing that all citizens have equal opportunity to participate cultivates a feeling of equality and well-being.

My dream is to live in a world where everyone lives in an environment that allows them to prosper. We need to look beyond our borders and understand that the world is interconnected; any wrong in the world will resonate and impact the rest of the world. Anything wrong in the world makes us all feel bad. Similarly, by not leveraging the potential of other human beings in a positive fashion, we are missing out on growth opportunities for us all.

In his book *Thank You for Being Late*, Tom Friedman warns that, if we don't take action, our world will run into potential disaster, with the population forecasted to reach nine billion in the next 30 years. Population growth and global warming will leave more people without adequate food sources. According to a report by the Food and Agriculture Organization of the United Nations, global warming will significantly decrease the availability of food in the world's poorest nations.[258] Additionally, automation and technology will have a negative impact on jobs, furthering the need for immediate action. We must address the needs of people and the root causes of desperate acts. We also must understand that all humans behave similarly under the same circumstances, and desperation is not driven by a person's religion, race, country, or culture. Like an interconnected system, if a single piece is held down, the rest of the system also gets held down.

With the help of every person I can reach, I want to rekindle King's dream of creating centers of enlightenment across the globe instead of wasting $1.7 trillion annually on the world's militaries.

We need to recognize that our actions reflect what is in our heads. Our thoughts are determined by what is around us because survival skills drive us. We are always watching the world around us and autonomously adjusting and responding to our environment. To liberate all human beings for success, we need to protect the environment of each human being. Each person must feel equal in and empowered by their environment. For human beings to be happy in their environment, they need justice, equality, and equal access to opportunities. If people are unhappy and have negative feelings, they are not going to contribute positively to their lives or to the lives of others.

Again, the dream is living in an environment that allows us the liberty to do good but only to do good. Based on this dream, my goal is to create an Internet-based organization that connects people across the

globe, bringing together those suffering due to injustice and those enjoying the fruits of justice.

Know Who You Are

Moving toward action first requires that you recognize the circumstances under which you live. You need to understand what side of the fence
you stand on, whether or not you are living in a just society. If you are
unclear, the following list will help you evaluate whether or not your
rights are being protected under your current government system.

▶ You do not trust the police or law enforcement that are
   supposed to be serving you.

▶ You do not trust the legal system and would not pursue
   legal action, even if your rights are violated, because you
   know justice would not be served.

▶ The leaders of your nation are extremely rich compared to
   average citizens. The leaders live lavish lifestyles without
   any checks and balances on their ability to steal the nation's
   resources.

▶ Corruption is widespread, and you have experienced it firsthand when dealing with government officials or the police.

▶ Your country is struggling financially compared to the rest
   of the world, especially more highly developed nations.

▶ Your country maintains high levels of unemployment, and
   many people look for opportunities in other countries due
   to the lack of local jobs.

▶ Your day-to-day activities are focused on survival, such as
   the ability to get essential services like electricity, water,
   natural gas, and gasoline.

▶ Job opportunities are offered to people who know someone
   in power instead of people with the most knowledge and
   experience.

▶ In general, you are frustrated about your well-being and
   future opportunities for your children.

If these circumstances do not apply to your personal life, you likely
reside in a just and prosperous nation. However, this does not lessen
your responsibility to those living in these miserable conditions. Your
role in this effort requires that you acknowledge the following:

1. Realize that most countries are operating as kleptocracies
   due to a lack of structural checks and balances.

2. The world is much more connected today than in the past,
   creating a situation where issues in one part of the world
   can and do ripple throughout the rest of the world.

3. Instead of relying on the government, we as individuals
   need to take this movement into our own hands and leverage the Internet to collaborate with one another and create
   justice across the globe.

4. The world is spending $1.7 trillion annually on military, and
   we need to turn this waste into an investment in a just and
   productive world.

5. Due to advances in technology, each human being has become extremely powerful. For example, using the Internet,
   one person can change the world for the better or impact
   the world for the worse. In 2015, the British insurance company Lloyd's estimated that cyberattacks cost businesses
   and the economy more than $400 billion a year, while many
   estimates suggest that this number is actually much higher.

6. Climate change will continue to have a real impact on the
   migration of large populations due to droughts and de-
   pleting food sources. This growing climate disaster needs
   attention and should be addressed immediately.

7. If we can free billions of people in this world to meet their
   full potential, the nations that can provide more will reap
   greater benefit. We need to look at all people as human

resources. Each one of us can bring our strength to the global table. Conversely, if not empowered, each of us can weaken our world.

The primary purpose of this book is to help others understand that the majority of this world is suffering from corruption due to structural weaknesses. Unless it is recognized as the fundamental problem driving human suffering, it will not be solved. The solution requires the creation of just environments with a structure of checks and balances that would not allow anyone to do wrong. I hope and expect that the information provided in this book will compel you to take action, not only on behalf of these suffering individuals, but also on behalf of the entire world. Once people understand these issues, we can collaborate via the Internet and work together to create a mass awareness movement across the globe.

Taking action is no small feat. I need your help and support. I believe that people are desperate for a solution. When they understand the right direction, they will move toward it.

Goal

We need the involvement of every person who reads this book. Access www.prosperityweb.org and become a member.

The purpose of ProsperityWeb is to create an online movement of awareness. Through crowdsourcing and crowdfunding, we will take this recipe for creating a just environment to every individual in the world. It will be a nonprofit organization that will be above greed, similar to National Public Radio in the United States, a nonprofit membership organization designed to provide unbiased news to over one thousand local public radio stations.

We are at a tipping point. The Internet has enabled people across the globe to connect independent of their governments and to create a movement to enforce the will of the people. Our innate desire is to do good. We all need to connect on a human level so we are acting above the corruption of any government. The Internet, with more than three billion users and growing rapidly, creates the largest body of connected people, bigger than any one country in the world. Please stop letting the government dictate your life. Take action.

With your support, ProsperityWeb will be a multilingual social media platform dedicated to global prosperity. When we list our information on LinkedIn, for example, we list our professional accomplishments and organizations. On ProsperityWeb, people share thoughts about how to help other people suffering in the world. It is all about creating, not a professional accomplishment directory, but a common place to discuss ideas about how to make this world a better place. Think of it as a site that facilitates a meeting of the minds to do good, where we brainstorm how to fund projects to restructure governments. ProsperityWeb is the place where you describe your dreams about and your accomplishments toward improving human lives, and get support from others on how we can work together to meet our common goals of world peace and prosperity.

Facebook can garner two billion users for social interaction. I need your help to connect significant numbers of people to exchange ideas on how to accomplish global prosperity. This global online network will work to achieve world peace and prosperity for all, connecting people across borders. The purpose of ProsperityWeb is to overcome the challenge created by those benefiting from kleptocratic governments. Unfortunately, unjust governments will not support this effort because the people who lead them are not interested in changes that would benefit their people. However, we will use the Internet to empower the people to realize that they are in control of their lives and there is no force that can resist the organized will of the people.

Public Awareness Projects

The goal of ProsperityWeb is to create awareness that structural checks and balances are necessary in order to ensure that people in positions of authority are working for the benefit of all people, not just a select few. We all benefit if the structure keeps everyone in check.

We want to spread the belief that all people are equal and we are all better off helping each other. Humans are our greatest resource; we all gain if we leverage all human resources to their fullest. Just imagine if the oppressed 75% of the world were able to move from the desperation of survival to self-actualization and the ability to become consumers of everything that is currently available only to people in prosperous countries.

Think about the possibility of living in a peaceful world where we can all feel safe traveling globally and doing business in any part of the world. Let's work together to convert the $1.7 trillion annual military spending toward dealing with the root cause of war: the injustice that leads to poverty, which results in desperate revolts, terrorist and criminal activities, and the displacement of large numbers of refugees.

Instead of listening to doomsday scenarios, we can choose to organize ourselves for a prosperous future. Ultimate prosperity will be achieved when there is no hunger or war, when we have compassion for every human being, when we can enjoy visiting any part of the world, and when we are making use of the contributions of all human beings. The world would become a big party to which everyone is invited. Let's call it the World United.

ProsperityWeb in Action

- ▶ **Crowdsourcing**—Engage people across the world via the Internet to support this cause by becoming ambassadors of the message. Anyone in any country can propose an awareness project to the members of ProsperityWeb, and members would help create this awareness. For example, a person in Uganda could propose the distribution of either this book or a summary of it translated into their local language. The rest of the people in the network would help carry out this task by providing the human resources, funding, and any other help needed to complete the project.

- ▶ **Crowdfunding**—People who believe that the root cause of most human suffering is injustice will be asked to fund ProsperityWeb, both in general and for specific awareness projects. We will count on the people in the first world who are blessed with resources to help financially. Most of these people are living in successful democracies and will understand that structural checks and balances are crucial in any form of government in order to have the justice that will ultimately lead to world peace.

▶ **Activist Groups**—Facilitate the creation of local groups across the globe to create a unified voice for justice and prosperity for all. The purpose of these groups will be to provide awareness of the principles of checks and balances required for justice. This will be a better venue for the poor people who are suffering and presently can only vent to and hear solutions from religious scholars who are not educated in government structures. Currently, many blame Western nations for maintaining the kleptocratic governments that inflict injustice and poverty upon them. My belief is that if these religious scholars understand the need for the structural changes described in this book, they will support them and become the voices for this change to create a world of justice.

Summary

By working together, we can make the world more prosperous for everyone. By joining ProspertyWeb, we can help billions of humans have more fulfilling lives. Let's commit to feel better ourselves as well by helping the 75% of those suffering in the world to be able to rise to their full potential.

"We all do better when we all do better."
—Paul Wellstone

Please join
www.prosperityweb.org

ENDNOTES

1   Khoun Theara, "Cambodia Ranked Most Corrupt Country in the Region," *VOA Cambodia*, 2013, http://www.voacambodia.com/content/cambodia-ranked-most-corrupt-country-in-the-region/1802720.html (accessed May 28, 2019).

2   "How Corrupt Is Your Country?" *2013 Corruption Perceptions Index—Results*, Transparency International, http://www.transparency.org/cpi2013/results (accessed May 28, 2019).

3   "Poverty Facts and Stats," *Global Issues: Poverty Stats and Facts*, http://www.globalissues.org/article/26/poverty-facts-and-stats#src1 (accessed May 28, 2019).

4   "UN Sustainable Development Goals," https://www.un.org/sustainabledevelopment/poverty/ (accessed May 31, 2018).

5   "Poverty Facts and Stats," WHO World Water Day Report, http://www.globalissues.org/article/26/poverty-facts-and-stats#src1 (accessed May 28, 2019).

6   Global Terrorism Index 2014, Institute for Economics & Peace, November 16, 2014, http://economicsandpeace.org/wp-content/uploads/2015/06/Global-Terrorism-Index-Report-2014.pdf (accessed August 21, 2019).

7   "Total Killed in Terrorist & Rebel Incidents by Country in 2014," www.Intelcenter.com (accessed May 28, 2019).

8   "Total Killed in Terrorist & Rebel Incidents by Country in 2014," www.Intelcenter.com (accessed May 28, 2019).

9   Amir Wasim, "Terrorism Dogs Pakistan in '06: Over 900 Killed in 657 Attacks," *Dawn*, January 7, 2007, https://www.dawn.com/news/226760/terrorism-dogs-pakistan-in (accessed August 21, 2019).

10 Peace Institute for Peace Studies (PIPS) 2007 Annual Report. See https://www.pakpips.com/pips-annual-report.

11 "Over 12,800 Militants Caught in 2009," *Dawn*, January 11, 2010, https://www.dawn.com/news/857972/over-12-800-militants-caught-in-2009 (accessed August 21, 2010).

12 Jane Onyanga-Omara, "Nearly 50 Killed within 24 Hours in Multiple Nigerian Terror Attacks," *USA Today*, 2015, https://www.usatoday.com/story/news/world/2015/11/18/nigeria-former-official-arrest/75978406/ (accessed May 28, 2019).

13 "Death Tolls," I Am Syria, www.iamsyria.org/death-tolls.html (accessed May 28, 2019).

14 Amir Wasim, "Terrorism dogs Pakistan in '06: Over 900 killed in 657 attacks," *Dawn*, January 7, 2007, https://www.dawn.com/news/226760/terrorism-dogs-pakistan-in (accessed August 21, 2019).

15 Peace Institute for Peace Studies (PIPS) 2001 Annual Report. See https://www.pakpips.com/pips-annual-report.

16   "Over 12,800 militants caught in 2009," *Dawn*, January 11, 2010, https://www.dawn.com/news/857972/over-12-800-militants-caught-in-2009 (accessed August 21, 2010).

17   Universal Declaration of Human Rights, United Nations, http://www.un.org/en/universal-declaration-human-rights/ (accessed May 28, 2019).

18   International Religious Freedom Report for 2016, U.S. Department of State, https://www.state.gov/international-religious-freedom-report-for-2016/ (accessed June 1, 2019).

19   K. Alan Kronstadt, "India: Religious Freedom Issues," Congressional Research Service, August 30, 2018, https://fas.org/sgp/crs/row/R45303.pdf (accessed July 21, 2019).

20   "Sudan," *Human Rights Watch*, www.hrw.org/africa/sudan (accessed May 28, 2019).

21   Ewelina Ochab, "Situation of Girls and Women in Pakistan," *Forbes*, March 6, 2017, www.forbes.com/sites/ewelinaochab/2017/03/06/situation-of-girls-and-women-in-pakistan/#23e4c306128a (accessed May 28, 2019).

22   "War's Overlooked Victims," *The Economist*, January 15, 2011, www.economist.com/node/17900482 (accessed May 28, 2019).

23   Frank G. Njenga et al., "War and Mental Disorders in Africa," *World Psychiatry*, February 2006, www.ncbi.nlm.nih.gov/pmc/articles/PMC1472262/ (accessed May 28, 2019).

24   See https://www.ncbi.nlm.nih.gov/pmc/articles/PMC1472262/.

25   Jake Silverstein, "The Displaced: Introduction," *The New York Times*, November 7, 2015, www.nytimes.com/2015/11/08/magazine/the-displaced-introduction.html?_r=0 (accessed May 28, 2019).

26   Rachel Hanna, "Fighting Corruption in India," *Harvard Political Review*, May 15, 2013, harvardpolitics.com/world/fighting-corruption-in-india/ (accessed May 28, 2019).

27   Jason Burke, "Corruption in India: 'All Your Life You Pay for Things That Should be Free,'" *The Guardian*, August 19, 2011, www.theguardian.com/world/2011/aug/19/corruption-india-anna-hazare (accessed May 28, 2019).

28   Josh Cohen, "Corruption in Ukraine is So Bad, a Nigerian Prince Would Be Embarrassed," *Reuters*, December 30, 2015, blogs.reuters.com/great-debate/2015/12/30/corruption-in-ukraine-is-so-bad-a-nigerian-prince-would-be-embarrassed-2/ (accessed May 28, 2019).

29   Paul Waldie, "Globe in Kiev: In Ukraine, corruption Is a Fact of Daily Life," *The Globe and Mail*, March 25, 2017, http://www.theglobeandmail.com/news/world/globe-in-kiev-in-ukraine-corruption-is-a-fact-of-daily-life/article17076395/ (accessed May 28, 2019).

30   Alan Tovey, "$1,570,000,000,000: How Much the World Spent on Arms This Year," *The Telegraph*, 2016, http://www.telegraph.co.uk/business/2016/12/12/1570000000000-much-world-spent-arms-year/ (accessed May 30, 2019).

31   John F. Kennedy *Address to the United Nations General Assembly* delivered 25 September 1961 https://americanrhetoric.com/speeches/jfkunitednations.htm (accessed Dec 28, 2019)

32   S. Mintz and S. McNeil, "The Great Depression in Global Perspective," *Digital History*, 2016, http://www.digitalhistory.uh.edu//disp_textbook.cfm?smtID=2&psid=3433 (accessed May 30, 2019).

33   "Global Impact 1929–1939," Historic Events for Students: The Great Depression, http://www.encyclopedia.com/article-1G2-3424800042/global-impact-1929-1939.html (accessed May 30, 2019).

34   S. Mintz and S. McNeil, "The Great Depression in Global Perspective," *Digital History*, 2016, http://www.digitalhistory.uh.edu//disp_textbook.cfm?smtID=2&psid=3433 (accessed May 30, 2019).

35   "The Taliban in Afghanistan," Council on Foreign Relations, http://www.cfr.org/afghanistan/taliban-afghanistan/p10551 (accessed May 31, 2019).

36   Tara John, "ISIS: Timeline of the Rise of the Islamic State," *Time*, http://time.com/4030714/isis-timeline-islamic-state/ (accessed May 31, 2019).

37   "Timeline: Rise and Spread of the Islamic State," Wilson Center, 2016, https://www.wilson
      center.org/article/timeline-rise-and-spread-the-islamic-state (accessed May 31, 2019).

38   Ken Sofer Addison and Jennifer Sofer Addison, "The Unaddressed Threat of Female Suicide
      Bombers," Center for American Progress, 2012, https://www.americanprogress.org/issues/
      security/news/2012/01/05/10992/the-unaddressed-threat-of-female-suicide-bombers/ (ac-
      cessed May 31, 2019).

39   "National Liberation Front of Tripura (NLFT)," National Liberation Front of Tripura
      (NLFT) | Terrorist Groups | TRAC, http://www.trackingterrorism.org/group/national-liber
      ation-front-tripura-nlft (accessed May 30, 2019).

40   "Who are Nigeria's Boko Haram Islamist groups?" *BBC News*, 2016, http://www.bbc.com/
      news/world-africa-13809501 (accessed May 30, 2019).

41   Freedom Onuoha, "Why Do Youth Join Boko Haram?" United States Institute of Peace Spe-
      cial Report, 2014, http://www.usip.org/sites/default/files/SR348-Why_do_Youth_Join_Boko_
      Haram.pdf (accessed May 30, 2019).

42   Martin Luther King Jr., "Address at the Freedom Rally at Cobo Hall," https://kinginstitute.
      stanford.edu/king-papers/documents/address-freedom-rally-cobo-hall (accessed September
      1, 2019).

43   Leonard J. Hoenig, MD, "The Branding of African American Slaves," ResearchGate, Febru-
      ary 2012. https://www.researchgate.net/publication/221848902_The_Branding_of_African_
      American_Slaves (accessed July 21, 2019).

44   Maria Popova, "Compassion and the Real Meaning of the Golden Rule," Brain Pickings, 2016,
      https://www.brainpickings.org/2015/01/08/karen-armstrong-compassion/ (accessed May 31,
      2019).

45   Gregg Zoroya, "How the IED Changed the U.S. Military," *USA Today*, https://www.usatoday.
      com/story/news/nation/2013/12/18/ied-10-years-blast-wounds-amputations/3803017/ (ac-
      cessed May 31, 2019).

46   Katie Fullerton, "Birth Rates Decrease as People Rise Out of Poverty," The Borgen Project,
      2017, https://borgenproject.org/birth-rates-decrease-as-people-rise-out-of-poverty/ (accessed
      May 31, 2019).

47   "How Will a Population Boom Change Africa?" *BBC News*, 2015, http://www.bbc.com/news/
      world-africa-34188248 (accessed May 31, 2019).

48   "Africa's Population Growth Could Undermine Sustainability Goals," *YaleGlobal Online*, 2016,
      http://yaleglobal.yale.edu/content/africas-population-growth-could-undermine-sustainabili-
      ty-goals (accessed May 31, 2019).

49   "Five Years after a Revolution, Egypt Is Far from 'Restoring Democracy,'" *The Washington Post*,
      January 25, 2016, www.washingtonpost.com/opinions/5-years-after-a-revolution-egypts-re
      gime-is-far-from-restoring-democracy/2016/01/25/cb18a75e-c389-11e5-a4aa-f25866ba0dc6_
      story.html?utm_term=.cac92a39ffbd (accessed June 5, 2019).

50   "5.3 Lakh Families in the Country Are Homeless: Maken," *The Indian Express*, March 7,
      2013, archive.indianexpress.com/news/5.3-lakh-families-in-the-country-are-homeless-mak-
      en/1084676/ (accessed June 5, 2019).

51   John Elliott, "Democracy Has Become a Fig leaf to Cover India's Failures," *The Times of India*,
      March 30, 2014, timesofindia.indiatimes.com/home/sunday-times/all-that-matters/Democra
      cy-has-become-a-fig-leaf-to-cover-Indias-failures/articleshow/32938440.cms (accessed June
      5, 2019).

52   Salman Masood, "More Bodies Pulled from Hotel Rubble in Pakistan," *The New York Times*,
      September 21, 2008, www.nytimes.com/2008/09/22/world/asia/22marriott.html (accessed
      June 5, 2019).

53   Moeed Yusuf, "The Future of Democracy in Pakistan and Afghanistan," *YouTube*, September 23, 2014, https://www.youtube.com/watch?v=gPFo-hU6NWU#action=share (accessed June 5, 2019).

54   UNESCO Institute for Statistics, 2015. "Literacy Statistics Metadata Information Table."

55   "Level of 'Shadow Economy' in Ukraine down to 34% of GDP in 2016—Economy Ministry," Interfax-Ukraine, March 7, 2017, http://en.interfax.com.ua/news/economic/433408.html (accessed June 5, 2019).

56   Philippa Stewart, "Ukraine's 'Shadow Economy' Is One of the Largest in the World and It's Still Growing," *Business Insider*, December 23, 2015, http://www.businessinsider.com/ukraines-shadow-economy-is-one-of-the-largest-in-the-world-and-its-still-growing-2015-12?pundits_only=0&get_all_comments=1&no_reply_filter=1 (accessed June 5, 2017).

57   C.W., "Why is Ukraine's Economy in Such a Mess?" *The Economist,* March 5, 2014, https://www.economist.com/blogs/freeexchange/2014/03/ukraine-and-russia (accessed June 5, 2019).

58   Maxim Tucker, "Ukraine's Fallen Leader Viktor Yanukovych 'Paid Bribes of $2 Billion'—or $1.4 Million for Every Day He Was President," *The Telegraph*, May 31, 2016, http://www.telegraph.co.uk/news/2016/05/31/ukraines-fallen-leader-viktor-yanukovych-paid-bribes-of-2-billio/ (accessed June 5, 2019).

59   Zimbabwe GDP per Capita, Trading Economics, https://tradingeconomics.com/zimbabwe/gdp-per-capita (accessed June 5, 2019.

60   "Doctors Killed in Pakistan: 2001–2017," Institute for Conflict Management, www.satp.org/satporgtp/countries/pakistan/database/Doctors_killed_Pakistan.htm (accessed June 5, 2019).

61   Central Intelligence Agency, "Contact CIA," The World Factbook, https://www.cia.gov/library/publications/resources/the-world-factbook/geos/print_ja.html (accessed June 27, 2019).

62   Chelsea Evans, "Poverty in Afghanistan: 5 Facts You Might Not Know," The Borgen Project, February 16, 2015, https://borgenproject.org/poverty-afghanistan-5-facts-might-know/ (accessed June 5, 2019).

63   "World's Top 10 Proven Oil Reserves," Arabian Industry, https://www.arabianindustry.com/oil-gas/united-arab-emirates/photos/2014/may/4/gallery-worlds-top-10-proven-oil-reserves-4685148/ (accessed June 5, 2019).

64   "A Concentrated Mining Sector," Mining for Zambia, https://miningforzambia.com/a-concentrated-mining-sector/ (accessed June 5, 2019).

65   Siji Jabbar, "How the Swiss Get Rich at Zambia's Expense," This Is Africa, December 11, 2012, https://thisisafrica.me/how-the-swiss-get-rich-at-zambias-expense/ (accessed June 5, 2019).

66   "Zimbabwe's River System Heavily Polluted," *The Standard,* April 7, 2013, https://www.thestandard.co.zw/2013/04/07/zimbabwes-river-system-heavily-polluted/ (accessed June 5, 2019).

67   Samuel Cartwright, "Diseases and Peculiarities of the Negro Race" (1851), *Africans in America*, PBS, www.pbs.org/wgbh/aia/part4/4h3106t.html (accessed June 5, 2019).

68   Prableen Bajpai, "North Korean vs. South Korean Economies: What's the Difference?" *Investopedia*, April 14, 2019, http://www.investopedia.com/articles/forex/040515/north-korean-vs-south-korean-economies.asp (accessed June 5, 2019).

69   Daron Acemoglu and James A. Robinson, *Why Nations Fail: The Origins of Power, Prosperity, and Poverty* (New York: Crown Books, 2012).

70   The Three Estates Information Sheet, *UCL Culture*, https://www.ucl.ac.uk/culture/sites/culture/files/three-estates-student-sheets.pdf (accessed June 7, 2019).

71   Kallie Szczepanski, "Nutmeg: The Unsavory History of a Tasty Spice," *ThoughtCo.*, August 26, 2018, https://www.thoughtco.com/nutmeg-the-unsavory-history-195274 (accessed June 7, 2019).

72 Central America: Economics, Global Perspectives: A Remote Sensing and World Issues Site, 1999–2002, http://www.cotf.edu/earthinfo/camerica/caeco.html (accessed June 7, 2019).

73 Lateef Mungin, "Amnesty: Egypt far from Justice over Unrest That Killed More Than 800," *CNN*, May 19, 2011, http://www.cnn.com/2011/WORLD/africa/05/19/egypt.revolution.report/ (accessed June 7, 2019).

74 Japan Overview, National Center on Education and the Economy, http://www.ncee.org/programs-affiliates/center-on-international-education-benchmarking/top-performing-countries/japan-overview/ (accessed June 7, 2019).

75 See https://www.forbes.com/powerful-brands/list/

76 Alissa J. Rubin, "Karzai Vows Corruption Fight, But Avoids Details," *The New York Times*, November 3, 2003, http://www.nytimes.com/2009/11/04/world/asia/04afghan.html?_r=0 (accessed June 10,2019).

77 Jacques Morisset and Victoria Cunningham, "Why Isn't Anyone Paying Taxes in Low-Income Countries?" Brookings, April 30, 2015, https://www.brookings.edu/blog/future-development/2015/04/30/why-isnt-anyone-paying-taxes-in-low-income-countries/ (accessed June 10, 2019).

78 "Tax Them and They Will Grow," *The Economist*, July 11, 2015, http://www.economist.com/news/finance-and-economics/21657433-poor-countries-need-get-better-raising-tax-and-multi national-firms-need (accessed June 10, 2019).

79 Andrew Grice, "Criminals and Corrupt Politicians Steal $1trl a Year from the World's Poorest Countries," *The Independent*, September 3, 2014, http://www.independent.co.uk/news/world/politics/criminals-and-corrupt-politicians-steal-1trn-a-year-from-the-worlds-poorest-countries-9707104.html (accessed June 10, 2019).

80 Dia Rekhi, "Everything You Want to Know about P-Notes," *ET Markets*, July 29, 2016, http://economictimes.indiatimes.com/markets/stocks/policy/everything-you-want-to-know-about-p-notes/articleshow/53442336.cms (accessed June 10, 2019).

81 "Dr. Subramanian Swamy Explains How Participatory Notes are Destroying Indian Share Market," *YouTube*, March 29, 2012, https://www.youtube.com/watch?v=cYDREaLOqyM (accessed June 10, 2019).

82 Palak Shah, "P-Note Unwinding to Weight on Equity Market," *BusinessLine*, July 9, 2017, http://www.thehindubusinessline.com/economy/pnote-unwinding-to-weigh-on-equity-mar ket/article9756513.ece (accessed June 10, 2019).

83 Julia Kagan, "Hawala," Investopedia, May 7, 2019, http://www.investopedia.com/terms/h/ha wala.asp (accessed June 10, 2019).

84 "Money Laundering," Financial Action Task Force, http://www.fatf-gafi.org/faq/moneylaun dering/ (accessed June 10, 2019).

85 "Russia's Former Largest Foreign Investor Putin is Worth 200 Billion," *Business Insider*, https://www.businessinsider.com/russias-former-largest-foreign-investor-putin-is-worth-200-billion-2015-2

86 "8 of the Richest Dictators in History," *Investopedia*, https://www.investopedia.com/financial-edge/0912/8-of-the-richest-dictators-in-history.aspx

87 "Asif Ali Zardari Net Worth," The Richest, https://www.therichest.com/celebnetworth/polit ician/president/asif-ali-zardari-net-worth/

88 "8 of the Richest Dictators in History, *Investopedia*, https://www.investopedia.com/financial-edge/0912/8-of-the-richest-dictators-in-history.aspx

89 "Nawaz Sharif Net Worth," *NetWorthBox*, https://networthbox.com/nawaz-sharif-politician-net-worth/

90 "10 Richest People in Pakistan," *Historypak*, https://historypak.com/10-richest-people-paki stan/

91 Conor Gaffey, "How the Panama Papers Brought down Pakistan's Prime Minister Nawaz Sharif," *Newsweek*, July 28, 2017, http://www.newsweek.com/panama-papers-pakistan-prime -minister-nawaz-sharif-643230 (accessed June 10, 2019).

92 "CIA Bribes Karzai: Millions in 'Ghost Money' Paid to Afghanistan President's Office, New York Times Reports," *The Huffington Post*, April 29, 2013, https://www.huffingtonpost. com/2013/04/29/cia-bribes-karzai-millions-ghost-money-paid-afghanistan-president-new-york-times_n_3176956.html (accessed June 10, 2019).

93 Carol Kearney, "Hamid Karzai Highest-Paid Politician in the World," *MediaMass*, June 10, 2019, https://en.mediamass.net/people/hamid-karzai/highest-paid.html (accessed June 10, 2019).

94 John F. Burns, "House of Graft: Tracing the Bhutto Millions," *The New York Times*, January 9, 1998, http://www.nytimes.com/1998/01/09/world/house-graft-tracing-bhutto-millions-special-report-bhutto-clan-leaves-trail.html (accessed June 10, 2019).

95 Global Corruption Report 2004: Political Corruption, Transparency International, March 25, 2004, https://www.transparency.org/whatwedo/publication/global_corruption_report_2004_political_corruption (accessed August 21, 2019).

96 Majlinda Aliu, "How Wealthy are Kosovo Politicians Really?" *Balkan Insight*, June 7, 2011, http://www.balkaninsight.com/en/article/how-wealthy-are-kosovo-politicians-really (accessed June 10, 2019).

97 "Detention on Remand against German Citizen," European Union External Action, November 15, 2012, http://www.eulex-kosovo.eu/en/pressreleases/0371.php (accessed June 10, 2019).

98 "EU Prosecutors Indict Kosovo Ex-minister for Corruption," *EU Business*, http://www.eubusiness.com/news-eu/kosovo-politics.ksn (accessed June 10, 2019).

99 David Barboza, "Billions in Hidden Riches for Family of Chinese Leader," *The New York Times*, October 25, 2012, https://www.nytimes.com/2012/10/26/business/global/family-of-wen-jia-bao-holds-a-hidden-fortune-in-china.html (accessed June 10, 2019).

100 Nash Jenkins, "The U.S. Is Point-Blank Accusing Vladimir Putin of Corruption," *Time*, January 26, 2016, http://time.com/4193567/us-vladimir-putin-corrupt-corruption/ (accessed June 10, 2019).

101 "New Wealth Rubs Shoulders with Old Poverty in Morocco," *The New Arab*, August 17, 2015, https://www.alaraby.co.uk/english/politics/2015/8/17/new-wealth-rubs-shoulders-with-old-poverty-in-morocco (accessed June 10, 2019).

102 Leyal Khalife, "Collective Wealth of 3 Moroccan Billionaires Equals that of the Poorest 375,000," *StepFeed*, January 24, 2018, https://stepfeed.com/collective-wealth-of-3-moroccan-billionaires-equals-that-of-poorest-375-000-5140 (accessed June 10, 2019).

103 Tecee Boley, "Liberia: Very Rich, or Very Poor," *New Narratives*, June 14, 2011, http://www.newnarratives.org/stories/tecee-boley/liberia-very-rich-or-very-poor/ (accessed June 10, 2019).

104 Yomi Kazeem, "George Weah is Trying to Kick-Start a Pay-Cut Revolution for Liberia's Highly Paid Political Class," *Quartz Africa*, February 1, 2018, https://qz.com/africa/1195630/liberias-president-george-weah-has-taken-a-pay-cut/ (accessed June 10, 2019).

105 "Poverty in Guatemala," *Avivara*, http://www.avivara.org/aboutguatemala/povertyinguatemala.html (accessed June 10, 2019).

106 "Guatemalan Capital's Wealthy Offered Haven in Gated City," *The Guardian,* January 9, 2013, https://www.theguardian.com/world/2013/jan/09/guatemalan-capital-wealthy-haven-city (accessed June 10, 2019).

107 Sarah Chayes, *Thieves of State: Why Corruption Threatens Global Security* (New York: Norton, 2016).

108 "World Health Day: Challenging Healthcare Corruption around the World," *Transparency International*, April 7, 2014, http://www.transparency.org/news/feature/world_health_day_challenging_healthcare_corruption_around_the_world (accessed June 10, 2019).

109 "Emergency Help," *Transparency International*, http://www.transparency.org/news/story/emergency_help (accessed June 10, 2019).

110 "People and Corruption: Asia Pacific Global Corruption Barometer," *Transparency International*, March 7, 2017, https://www.transparency.org/whatwedo/publication/people_and_corruption_asia_pacific_global_corruption_barometer (accessed June 10, 2019).

111 "Education: Problem/Solution," *Transparency International*, https://www.transparency.org/topic/detail/education/ (accessed June 10, 2019).

112 Mary Penn, "Food Corruption in India," *The Borgen Project*, September 4, 2013, http://borgenproject.org/food-corruption-india/ (accessed June 10, 2019).

113 Yanzhong Huang, "China's Corrupt Food Chain," *The New York Times*, August 17, 2012, http://www.nytimes.com/2012/08/18/opinion/chinas-corrupt-food-chain.html?_r=0 (accessed June 10, 2019).

114 "How Fish Stored in Pakistan?" *Dunya News*, March 3, 2016, http://video.dunyanews.tv/index.php/en/mustwatch/42255/How-Fish-stored-in-Pakistan#.WSC4YGjyu70 (accessed June 10, 2019).

115 S. Akhtar, "Food Safety Challenges—A Pakistan's Perspective," *PubMed*, 2015, https://www.ncbi.nlm.nih.gov/pubmed/24915401 (accessed June 10, 2019).

116 Kenya Corruption Report, *GAN Business Anti-Corruption Portal*, June 2017, http://www.business-anti-corruption.com/country-profiles/kenya (accessed June 10, 2019).

117 Foreign Corrupt Practices Act, U.S. Department of Justice, February 3, 2017, https://www.justice.gov/criminal-fraud/foreign-corrupt-practices-act (accessed June 10, 2019).

118 Beata S. Javorcik and Shang-Jin Wei, "Corruption and Cross-Border Investment in Emerging Markets: Firm-Level Evidence," https://www.cass.city.ac.uk/__data/assets/pdf_file/0011/76970/Corruption-2008-06-19.pdf (accessed August 21, 2019).

119 Global Corruption Report 2004: Political Corruption, *Transparency International*, March 25, 2004, https://www.transparency.org/whatwedo/publication/global_corruption_report_2004_political_corruption (accessed August 21, 2019).

120 "Police, Then Judiciary Most Corrupt Public Institutions in South Asia, Reveals TI Survey," *Transparency International*, December 16, 2002, https://www.transparency.org/news/press-release/police_then_judiciary_most_corrupt_public_institutions_in_south_asia_reveal (accessed August 21, 2019).

121 Parker Asmann, "Mexico Police Collude with Criminal to Kidnap, Extort Migrant," *InSight Crime*, June 20, 2019, https://www.insightcrime.org/news/brief/mexico-police-collude-criminals-kidnap-migrant/ (accessed August 21, 2019).

122 Claire O'Neill McCleskey, "92% of Crimes in Mexico Go Unreported: Survey," *InSight Crime*, September 28, 2012, https://www.insightcrime.org/news/brief/crimes-mexico-unreported-in-egi/ (accessed August 21, 2019).

123 Robert Wanjala, "Tackling Police Corruption in Kenya," *Institute for War & Peace Reporting*, https://iwpr.net/global-voices/tackling-police-corruption-kenya (accessed August 21, 2019).

124 "Citizens Speak Out about Corruption in Africa," *Transparency International*, July 11, 2019, https://www.transparency.org/news/feature/citizens_speak_out_about_corruption_in_africa (accessed August 21, 2019).

125 "Six Questions on the Cost of Corruption with World Bank Institute Global Governance Director Daniel Kaufmann," *News & Broadcast*, http://web.worldbank.org/WBSITE/EXTERNAL/NEWS/0,,contentMDK:20190295~menuPK:34457~pagePK:34370~piPK:34424~theSitePK:4607,00.html (accessed June 10, 2019).

126 Elisabeth Rosenthal and Andrew Martin, "UN Says Solving Food Crisis Could Cost $30 Billion," *The New York Times,* June 4, 2008, http://www.nytimes.com/2008/06/04/news/04i-ht-04food.13446176.html (accessed June 10, 2019).

127 "What's the Cost? A Holistic Approach," *Water Wells for Africa,* http://waterwellsforafrica.org/whats-the-cost/ (accessed June 10, 2019).

128 "Vaccines: The Price of Protecting a Child from Killer Diseases," *Doctors Without Borders,* December 3, 2012, https://www.doctorswithoutborders.org/what-we-do/news-stories/research/vaccines-price-protecting-child-killer-diseases (accessed July 7, 2019).

129 Christina Majaski, "Invisible Hand Definition," *Investopedia,* May 5, 2019, https://www.investopedia.com/terms/i/invisiblehand.asp (accessed June 24, 2019).

130 Chris Gowans, "Moral Relativism," *Stanford Encyclopedia of Philosophy,* April 20, 2015, http://plato.stanford.edu/entries/moral-relativism/ (accessed June 24, 2019).

131 American Anthropological Association, "Statement on Human Rights," *American Anthropologist* 49, no. 4:1 (October–December 1947): 539–543, https://lucian.uchicago.edu/blogs/around1948/files/2012/09/1947-Statement-on-Human-Rights-American-Anthropological-Association.pdf (accessed August 21, 2019).

132 Dario Berrebi, "Corruption in India: A Cause of Instability & Inequalities," *Poverties,* February 20, 2013, http://www.poverties.org/blog/corruption-in-india (accessed June 24, 2019).

133 Celeste Friend, "Social Contract Theory," *Internet Encyclopedia of Philosophy,* http://www.iep.utm.edu/soc-cont/ (accessed June 24, 2019).

134 Mark Bond, "Criminology: Broken Window Theory Explained," *E-Roll Call Magazine,* January 23, 2017, https://andragogytheory.com/2017/01/23/criminology-broken-window-theory-explain/ (accessed June 24, 2019).

135 Philip G. Zimbardo, "Setting Up," Stanford Prison Experiment, http://www.prisonexp.org/setting-up (accessed June 24, 2019).

136 Zimbardo, "Arrival," Stanford Prison Experiment, http://www.prisonexp.org/arrival (accessed June 24, 2019).

137 9 Zimbardo, "Guards," Stanford Prison Experiment, http://www.prisonexp.org/guards (accessed June 24, 2019).

138 Zimbardo, "Conclusion," Stanford Prison Experiment, http://www.prisonexp.org/conclusion (accessed June 24, 2019).

139 Jennifer Latson, "Why the 1977 Blackout Was One of New York's Darkest Hours," *Time,* July 13, 2015, http://time.com/3949986/1977-blackout-new-york-history/ (accessed June 24, 2019).

140 Carl Wilms, "Oppression," *Liberatory Science Education,* 2006–2007, http://www.users.miamioh.edu/wilmsce/oppression.html (accessed June 24, 2019).

141 "Profiles: Uganda," *Anti-Corruption Authorities,* December 2014, https://www.acauthorities.org/country/ug (accessed June 24, 2019).

142 "'Letting the Big Fish Swim': Failures to Prosecute High-Level Corruption in Uganda," *Human Rights Watch,* October 21, 2013, https://www.hrw.org/report/2013/10/21/letting-big-fish-swim/failures-prosecute-high-level-corruption-uganda (accessed June 24, 2019).

143 Mubasher Bukhari, "Pakistan Gets First Women-Only Auto-Rickshaw to Beat Male Pests," *Reuters,* April 9, 2015, https://in.reuters.com/article/pakistan-rickshaws/pakistan-gets-first-women-only-auto-rickshaw-to-beat-male-pests-idINKBN0N103L20150410 (accessed June 24, 2019).

144 Zar Aslam, "The Pink Rickshaw; Putting Women in the Driving Seat," GoGetFunding, https://gogetfunding.com/the-pink-rickshaw-putting-women-in-the-driving-seat/ (accessed August 21, 2019).

145 Ashraf Javed, "Pink Rickshaw Recipients Robbed," *The Nation,* March 5, 2016, http://nation.com.pk/05-Mar-2016/pink-rickshaw-recipients-robbed (accessed June 24, 2019).

146 "10 Most Corrupt Police Forces in the World," *Criminal Justice Degrees Guide*, 2019, http://www.criminaljusticedegreesguide.com/features/10-most-corrupt-police-forces-in-the-world.html (accessed June 24, 2019).

147 Jonathan Strong, "Haitian Corruption and Graft Delay Earthquake Relief Efforts, Punishes Destitute Refugees," *Daily Caller*, April 21, 2010, http://dailycaller.com/2010/04/21/haitian-corruption-and-graft-delay-earthquake-relief-efforts-punishes-destitute-refugees/ (accessed June 24, 2019).

148 Transparency International, Global Corruption Report 2007: Corruption in Judicial Systems, *ISSUU*, https://issuu.com/transparencyinternational/docs/global_corruption_report_2007_english?backgroundColor= (accessed June 24, 2019).

149 Ethan S. Burger, "Corruption in the Arbitrazh Courts: Will There Be Significant Progress in the Near Term?" *The International Lawyer* 38, no. 1 (Spring 2004): 15–34, https://scholar.smu.edu/cgi/viewcontent.cgi?article=2260&context=til (accessed August 21, 2019).

150 Gary Haugen, "The Hidden Reason for Poverty the World Needs to Address Now," *TED Talk*, 2015, https://www.ted.com/talks/gary_haugen_the_hidden_reason_for_poverty_the_world_needs_to_address_now (accessed June 24, 2019).

151 Sabrina Toppa, "Dry Dams, Leaky Pipes, and Tanker Mafias—Karachi's Water Crisis," *The Guardian*, June 28, 2016, https://www.theguardian.com/global-development-professionals-network/2016/jun/28/karachi-pakistan-water-crisis (accessed August 21, 2019).

152 Lord Acton, Acton Institute, https://acton.org/research/lord-acton-quote-archive (accessed June 24, 2019).

153 Tim Jackins, "The Effects of Oppressive Societies," *Liberation Theory*, May 2, 2019, https://www.rc.org/page/liberationtheory/pt131_023_tj (accessed June 26, 2019).

154 Gleb Tsipursky, "Autopilot vs. Intentional System: The Rider and the Elephant," *Intentional Insights*, November 14, 2014, https://intentionalinsights.org/autopilot-vs-intentional-system-the-rider-and-the-elephant/ (accessed June 26, 2019).

155 Eric R. Pianka, "Adaptation," *Biology Encyclopedia*, 2019, http://www.biologyreference.com/A-Ar/Adaptation.html (accessed June 26, 2019).

156 Ernie Capobianco, "Rewards and Recognition: Two Highly Effective Ways to Motivate Your Employees," *Entrepreneur*, October 9, 2014, http://thenextweb.com/entrepreneur/2014/10/09/recognizing-your-employees/ (accessed June 26, 2019).

157 Bryan Stevenson, "We Need to Talk about an Injustice," *TED Talks*, March 2012, https://www.ted.com/talks/bryan_stevenson_we_need_to_talk_about_an_injustice (accessed June 26, 2019).

158 Melinda Wenner, "Study: Doing Good Makes You Feel Good," *Live Science*, May 4, 2007, https://www.livescience.com/4443-study-good-feel-good.html (accessed June 26, 2019).

159 "Pakistan Army Rescues Chief Justice's Son, Kidnapped in June," *CBS News*, July 19, 2016, http://www.cbsnews.com/news/pakistan-army-rescues-chief-justices-son-kidnapped-in-june/ (accessed June 26, 2019).

160 Pramit Bhattacharya and Tadit Kundu, "99% Cases of Sexual Assaults Go Unreported, Govt Data Shows," liveMint, April 24, 2018, https://www.livemint.com/Politics/AV3sIKoEBAG-ZozALMX8THK/99-cases-of-sexual-assaults-go-unreported-govt-data-shows.html (accessed August 21, 2019).

161 "SOI Tax Stats—IRS Data Book," The Internal Revenue Service (IRS), (accessed December 28, 2019).

162 "Taxing Wages 2019," OECD, Centre for Tax Policy and Administration, https://www.oecd.org/unitedstates/taxing-wages-united-states.pdf (accessed Dec 28, 2019).

163 Julie McCarthy, "Why So Few Indians Pay Taxes," *NPR*, March 22, 2017, https://www.npr.org/2017/03/22/521056987/why-so-few-indians-pay-taxes (accessed August 21, 2019).

164 Mubarak Zeb Khan, "Income Tax Paid by Legislators Revealed," *Dawn*, February 16, 2014, https://www.dawn.com/news/1087338 (accessed June 26, 2019).

165 Stuart Yikona, "How Corruption and Tax Evasion Distort Development," *World Bank Blogs*, December 6, 2011, http://blogs.worldbank.org/governance/how-corruption-and-tax-evasion-distort-development (accessed June 26, 2019).

166 "What Are the Panama Papers?" *The New York Times*, April 4, 2016, http://www.nytimes.com/2016/04/05/world/panama-papers-explainer.html?_r=0 (accessed June 26, 2019).

167 "Half of Pakistani Lawmakers Don't Pay Taxes," *Newsweek*, December 23, 2013, https://www.newsweek.com/half-pakistani-lawmakers-dont-pay-taxes-report-224968 (accessed August 21, 2019).

168 "Greece: The Cost of a Bribe," *Transparency International*, April 3, 2012, http://www.transparency.org/news/feature/greece_the_cost_of_a_bribe (accessed June 26, 2019).

169 Vito Tanzi and Hamid Davoodi, "Roads to Nowhere: How Corruption in Public Investment Hurts Growth," International Monetary Fund, March 1998, http://www.imf.org/external/pubs/ft/issues12/ (accessed June 26, 2019).

170 Sudan Public Expenditure Review, Poverty Reduction and Economic Management Unit, World Banks, December 2007, https://siteresources.worldbank.org/INTSUDAN/Resources/SD_PER_synthesis_report.pdf (accessed August 21, 2019).

171 Utz Pape, Julius Gunnemann, Luca Parisotto, and Mario Di Fillipo, South Sudan Poverty Profile 2015 (Washington: The World Bank, 2016).

172 "Africa Rising? Inequalities and the Essential Role of Fair Taxation," *Christian Aid*, February 1, 2014, https://www.christianaid.org.uk/resources/about-us/africa-rising-inequalities-and-essential-role-fair-taxation (accessed June 26, 2019).

173 Lesley Stahl, "Arafat's Billions: One Man's Quest to Track Down Unaccounted For Funds," *60 Minutes*, 2003, https://www.cbsnews.com/news/arafats-billions/ (accessed June 26, 2019).

174 John F. Burns, "House of Graft: Tracing the Bhutto Millions," *The New York Times*, January 9, 1998, http://www.nytimes.com/1998/01/09/world/house-graft-tracing-bhutto-millions-special-report-bhutto-clan-leaves-trail.html (accessed June 26, 2019).

175 David Barboza, "Billions in Hidden Riches for Family of Chinese Leader," *The New York Times*, October 25, 2012, http://www.nytimes.com/2012/10/26/business/global/family-of-wen-jia-bao-holds-a-hidden-fortune-in-china.html (accessed June 26, 2019).

176 Majlinda Aliu, "How Wealthy Are Kosovo Politicians Really?" *Balkan Insight*, June 7, 2011, http://www.balkaninsight.com/en/article/how-wealthy-are-kosovo-politicians-really (accessed June 26, 2019).

177 "Detention on Remand against German Citizen," *European Union External Action*, November 15, 2012, http://www.eulex-kosovo.eu/en/pressreleases/0371.php (accessed June 26, 2019).

178 Vladimir Putin Biography, Biography.com, April 2, 2014, https://www.biography.com/people/vladimir-putin-9448807 (accessed June 26, 2019).

179 Selma Kurtishi-Kastrati, "The Effects of Foreign Direct Investments for Host Country's Economy," *European Journal of Interdisciplinary Studies* 5, no. 1 (2013), http://www.ejist.ro/files/pdf/369.pdf (accessed June 26, 2019).

180 John Menadue, "Four Waves of Australia's Relationships: UK, US, Japan, and China," Australian Institute of International Affairs, June 6, 2018, https://www.internationalaffairs.org.au/australianoutlook/australianoutlook-four-waves-australia-relationships-uk-us-japan-china/ (accessed August 21, 2019).

181 Joseph E. Stiglitz, "Resource Rich, Cash Poor: Why New Discoveries of Natural Resources Probably Won't Help Ghana, Uganda, Tanzania, or Mozambique," *Slate*, August 12, 2012,

http://www.slate.com/articles/business/project_syndicate/2012/08/why_resource_rich_countries_usually_end_up_poor_.html (accessed June 26, 2019).

182 Mark Curtis, "Extracting Minerals, Extracting Wealth: How Zambia is Losing $3 Billion a Year from Corporate Tax Dodging," WarOnWant.org, October 2015, http://www.waronwant.org/sites/default/files/WarOnWant_ZambiaTaxReport_web.pdf (accessed June 26, 2019).

183 Kevin Baxter and Summer Said, "Could Saudi Aramco Be Worth 20 Times Exxon?" *The Wall Street Journal*, January 8, 2016, https://www.wsj.com/articles/saudi-aramco-confirms-ipo-study-1452254819 (accessed June 26, 2019).

184 Michael Kugelman, "Pakistan's fixation with feudalism," *Dawn*, January 3, 2013, https://www.dawn.com/news/775988/pakistans-fixation-with-feudalism (accessed June 26, 2019).

185 Nicholas Kristof, "Feudalism in Pakistan," *The New York Times*, August 1, 2009, http://kristof.blogs.nytimes.com/2009/08/01/feudalism-in-pakistan/?_r=0 (accessed June 26, 2019).

186 David Wilson, "Land Reform—Success and Failure," *New Internationalist*, November 2, 1979, https://newint.org/features/1979/11/01/land-reform/ (accessed June 26, 2019).

187 Dexter Roberts, "China and Schumpeter's 'Creative Destruction,'" *Bloomberg*, February 18, 2014, https://www.bloomberg.com/news/articles/2014-02-18/china-and-schumpeters-creative-destruction (accessed June 26, 2019).

188 Sunita Dodani and Ronald E. LaPorte, "BrainDrain from Developing Countries: How Can Brain Drain Be Converted into Wisdom Gain?" *Journal of the Royal Society of Medicine* 98, no. 11 (November 2005): 487–491, https://www.ncbi.nlm.nih.gov/pmc/articles/PMC1275994/ (accessed June 26, 2019).

189 Michael Grothaus, "Some of the U.S.'s Biggest Companies are Founded by Immigrants," *Fast Company*, July 26, 2018, https://www.fastcompany.com/90202816/some-of-the-u-s-s-biggest-companies-are-founded-by-immigrants (accessed August 21, 2019).

190 Johana Bhuiyan, "Half of the Most Highly Valued Tech Companies in the U.S. Were Founded by Immigrants," *Vox*, May 31, 2017, https://www.recode.net/2017/5/31/15720198/immigrants-tech-innovation-good-for-america (accessed June 26, 2019).

191 Monica Anderson, "Chapter 1: Statistical Portrait of the U.S. Black Immigrant Population," Pew Research Center, April 9, 2015, http://www.pewsocialtrends.org/2015/04/09/chapter-1-statistical-portrait-of-the-u-s-black-immigrant-population/ (accessed June 26, 2019).

192 "Half of Canadian Millionaires are Immigrants," *Sault This Week*, June 13, 2013, https://www.saultthisweek.com/2013/06/13/half-of-canadian-millionaires-are-immigrants/wcm/6774bf21-7b09-10d1-dcc9-653d6b228dd8 (accessed August 21, 2019).

193 "It Is Time to Stop Misrepresenting What Is Happening to Migrant Workers in the UAE," *Muftah*, http://muftah.org/it-is-time-to-stop-misrepresenting-what-is-happening-to-migrant-workers-in-the-uae/#.WB8bnNIrK1t (accessed June 26, 2019).

194 Widney Brown and Joe Saunders, eds., "'Bad Dreams': Exploitation and Abuse of Migrant Workers in Saudi Arabia," *Human Rights Watch*, July 15, 2004, https://www.hrw.org/report/2004/07/13/bad-dreams-exploitation-and-abuse-migrant-workers-saudi-arabia (accessed June 26, 2019).

195 Evan Andrews, "Who Invented the internet?" *History.com*, March 14, 2019, http://www.history.com/news/ask-history/who-invented-the-internet (accessed June 26, 2019).

196 Lifeline Support for Affordable Communications, Federal Communications Commission, September 8, 2017, https://www.fcc.gov/consumers/guides/lifeline-support-affordable-communications (accessed June 26, 2019).

197 Monica Anderson, Andrew Perrin, Jingjing Jiang, and Madhumitha Kumar, "10% of Americans Don't Use the Internet. Who Are They?" Pew Research Center, April 22, 2019, http://www.pewresearch.org/fact-tank/2016/09/07/some-americans-dont-use-the-internet-who-are-they/ (accessed June 26, 2019).

198   Report: One in Four Students Enrolled in Online Courses, Online Learning Consortium, Feb-
      ruary 25, 2016, https://onlinelearningconsortium.org/news_item/report-one-four-students-
      enrolled-online-courses// (accessed June 26, 2019).

199   Thuy Mai, ed., Global Positioning System History, NASA, August 7, 2017, https://www.nasa.gov/
      directorates/heo/scan/communications/policy/GPS_History.html (accessed June 26, 2019).

200   Organization and Leadership, National Institutes of Health: Intramural Research Program,
      https://irp.nih.gov/about-us/organization-and-leadership (accessed June 26, 2019).

201   "At A Glance 2016: Tobacco Use: Extinguishing the Epidemic," Centers for Disease Control
      and   Prevention,   https://www.tidewaterortho.com/sites/tidewaterortho.com/files/tobacco-
      aag.pdf (accessed August 21, 2019).

202   Sam Chambers, "War on Smoking," Bloomberg, December 14, 2017, https://www.bloomberg.
      com/quicktake/war-smoking (accessed June 26, 2019).

203   Current Cigarette Smoking among Adults in the United States, Centers for Disease Control
      and Prevention, February 4, 2019, https://www.cdc.gov/tobacco/data_statistics/fact_sheets/
      adult_data/cig_smoking/index.htm (accessed June 26, 2019).

204   David A. Pheiffer, "Ike's Interstates at 50: Anniversary of the Highway System Recalls Eisen-
      hower's Role as Catalyst," Prologue Magazine 38, no. 2 (Summer 2006), https://www.archives.
      gov/publications/prologue/2006/summer/interstates.html (accessed June 26, 2019).

205   Abby Rogers, "15 Mind-Blowing Salaries Pulled in by Corporate America's Top Lawyers," Busi-
      ness Insider, July 1, 2012, http://www.businessinsider.com/15-mind-blowing-salaries-pulled-
      in-by-corporations-top-lawyers-2012-6#marathon-oils-sylvia-kerrigan-earned-3118335-2
      (accessed June 30, 2019).

206   Kristina Rasmussen, "What Did Your State Senator Earn in 2011?" Illinois Policy, April 16,
      2012, https://www.illinoispolicy.org/2011_illinois_state_senate_salaries/ (accessed June 30,
      2019).

207   Chase Peterson-Withorn, "Donald Trump Falls 35 Spots on the Forbes 400," Forbes, October
      4, 2016, http://www.forbes.com/sites/chasewithorn/2016/10/04/donald-trump-falls-35-spots-
      on-the-forbes-400/#1461f4ef3885 (accessed June 30, 2019).

208   "President Asif Ali Zardari 2nd Most Richest Man of Pakistan," Pakistan Daily, October 16,
      2008,   https://web.archive.org/web/20120113183927/http://www.daily.pk/president-asif-ali-
      zardari-2nd-most-richest-man-of-pakistan-6666/ (accessed June 30, 2019).

209   Catherine Clifford, "A Record Number of Americans Are Now Millionaires, New Study
      Shows," CNBC, March 24, 2017, https://www.cnbc.com/2017/03/24/a-record-number-of-
      americans-are-now-millionaires-new-study-shows.html (accessed June 30, 2019).

210   Michael Babad, "Canadians Make Up 3% of the 1%, But 'Dollar' Millionaires Dwindle,"
      The Globe and Mail, June 5, 2017, http://www.theglobeandmail.com/report-on-business/
      top-business-stories/canadians-make-up-3-of-the-1-but-dollar-millionaires-dwindle/arti-
      cle26783583/ (accessed June 30, 2019).

211   Steph Cockroft, "Why Being a Millionaire is Nothing Special," DailyMail.com, August 27, 2015,
      http://www.dailymail.co.uk/news/article-3212354/Why-millionaire-special-One-65-people-
      worth-seven-figures-surge-price-property-stock-markets.html (accessed June 30, 2019).

212   Ansuya Harjani, "Number of Billionaires hits record high in 2014," CNBC, September 17,
      2014, http://www.cnbc.com/2014/09/17/number-of-billionaires-hits-record-high-in-2014.html
      (accessed June 30, 2019).

213   "Is Vladimir Putin the Richest Man in the World at $200 Billion?" Raw Africa, June 21, 2016,
      https://rawafricaonline.com/is-vladimir-putin-the-richest-man-in-the-world-at-200-billion/
      (accessed August 21, 2019).

214   Katie Sanders, "Bill Clinton: 'I had the lowest net worth of any American president in the 20th
      century,'" Punditfact, June 29, 2014, http://www.politifact.com/punditfact/statements/2014/

jun/29/bill-clinton/bill-clinton-i-had-lowest-net-worth-any-american-p/ (accessed June 30, 2019).

215 "George W. Bush: Who America's Next President Is and Where He Stands," *The New York Times*, December 14, 2000, http://www.nytimes.com/2000/12/14/news/george-w-bushwho-americas-next-president-is-and-where-he-stands.html (accessed June 30, 2019).

216 Michael Galvis, "Barack Obama's Net Worth on His 55th Birthday," *Money*, August 4, 2016, http://time.com/money/4439729/barack-obama-net-worth-55th-birthday/ (accessed June 30, 2019).

217 Pivotfarm, "Top Corrupt Leaders in the World," ZeroHedge, July 7, 2015, http://www.zero hedge.com/news/2015-07-07/top-corrupt-leaders-world (accessed June 30, 2019).

218 David A. Fahrenthold and Jonathan O'Connell, "What is the 'Emoluments Clause'? Does It Apply to President Trump?" *The Washington Post*, January 23, 2017, https://www.wash ingtonpost.com/politics/what-is-the-emoluments-clause-does-it-apply-to-president-trump/2017/01/23/12aa7808-e185-11e6-a547-5fb9411d332c_story.html?utm_term=.6742 7d57d0f0 (accessed June 30, 2019).

219 Abubakar Siddique, "Vote-Buying Allegations Cloud Pakistan Senate Elections," *Gandara*, February 21, 2015, http://gandhara.rferl.org/a/pakistan-senate-vote-buying/26861448.html (accessed June 30, 2019).

220 Legit, "Patience Jonathan Hires Thugs To Destabilize Bayelsa" *Legit*, https://www.legit. ng/434652-patience-jonathan-hires-thugs-to-destabilize-bayelsa.html (accessed September 1, 2019).

221 Factors of the Rule of Law, *World Justice Project*, http://worldjusticeproject.org/factors (accessed June 30, 2019).

222 Killid Correspondents, "Afghanistan: Two Justice Systems for Poor and Rich," *Inter Press Service*, July 28, 2009, http://www.ipsnews.net/2009/07/afghanistan-two-justice-systems-for-poor-and-rich/ (accessed June 30, 2019).

223 Shobhan Saxena, "A Billion Indians and Millions of Injustices," *The Times of India*, July 26, 2009, http://timesofindia.indiatimes.com/home/sunday-times/deep-focus/A-billion-Indians-and-millions-of-injustices/articleshow/4820879.cms (accessed June 30, 2019).

224 Ahmad Fakir Muhammad, "Police versus FIR Registration," *Dawn*, December 1, 2009, http://www.dawn.com/news/863875/police-versus-fir-registration (accessed June 30, 2019).

225 Preston Byrne, "A Comparison of American and English Civil Liberties," January 26, 2016, https://prestonbyrne.com/2016/01/06/the-american-english-civil-liberties-comparison-table/ (accessed June 30, 2019).

226 Lisa Mascaro, "GOP Tax Bill Is Latest Example of Senate leader Mitch McConnell Breaking the Norms He Often Espouses," *Los Angeles Times*, December 3, 2017, http://beta.latimes. com/politics/la-na-pol-mcconnell-trump-taxplan-20171203-story.html (accessed July 1, 2019).

227 "Sanders Raises $26M in April and Over $200M Overall," *The Bern Report*, May 1, 2016, http:// thebernreport.com/sanders-raises-26m-april-breaks-200m-raised-campaign/ (accessed August 21, 2019).

228 Keith Ellison, OpenSecrets.org, https://www.opensecrets.org/personal-finances/net-worth ?cid=N00028257&year=2014 (accessed August 21, 2019).

229 Mazhar Abbas, "How Political Parties Manage Their Finances," *The International News*, April 7, 2017, ttps://www.thenews.com.pk/print/197019-How-political-parties-manage-their-financ es (accessed July 1, 2019).

230 Analysis of Sources of Funding of National and Regional Parties—FY 2004–05 to 2014–15, Association for Democratic Reforms, January 24, 2017, https://adrindia.org/content/anal

ysis-sources-funding-national-and-regional-parties-fy-2004-05-2014-15 (accessed July 1, 2019).

231   Understanding Ways to Support Federal Candidates, Federal Election Commission, 2019–20, http://www.fec.gov/pages/brochures/citizens.shtml#how_much (accessed July 1, 2019).

232   "Super Pacs," OpenSecrets.org: *Center for Responsive Politics*, June 27, 2019, https://www.opensecrets.org/pacs/superpacs.php (accessed July 1, 2019).

233   Emmie Martin, "Donald Trump is Officially the Richest US President in History," *Business Insider*, January 23, 2017, http://www.businessinsider.com/donald-trump-richest-us-president-in-history-2017-1 (accessed July 1, 2019).

234   Lauren Carroll, "Is Donald Trump Self-Funding His Campaign? Sort of," *Politifact*, February 10, 2016, http://www.politifact.com/truth-o-meter/statements/2016/feb/10/donald-trump/donald-trump-self-funding-his-campaign-sort/ (accessed July 1, 2019).

235   Tom Hamburger, "The Koch Brothers' Impact on the American Political System," *The Washington Post*, January 15, 2016, https://www.washingtonpost.com/opinions/the-koch-brothers-impact-on-the-american-political-system/2016/01/15/6a3694aa-b579-11e5-9388-466021d971de_story.html?utm_term=.b01d39e83453 (accessed August 21, 2019).

236   "Federal Budget 101: Why Should You Care About the Federal Budget," National Priorities Project, https://www.nationalpriorities.org/budget-basics/federal-budget-101/ (accessed July 1, 2019).

237   "U.S. Military Spending vs. the World," National Priorities Project, https://www.nationalpriorities.org/campaigns/us-military-spending-vs-world/ (accessed July 1, 2019).

238   Lauren Carroll, "Obama: US Spends More on Military Than Next 8 Nations Combined," *Politifact*, January 13, 2016, http://www.politifact.com/truth-o-meter/statements/2016/jan/13/barack-obama/obama-us-spends-more-military-next-8-nations-combi/ (accessed July 1, 2019).

239   Kimberly Amadeo, "US Military Budget, Its Components, Challenges, and Growth: Why Military Spending Is More Than You Think It Is," *The Balance*, April 22, 2019, https://www.the-balance.com/u-s-military-budget-components-challenges-growth-3306320 (accessed July 1, 2019).

240   Walter Pincus, "U.S. Pays Steep Price for Private Security in Iraq," *The Washington Post*, October 1, 2007, http://www.washingtonpost.com/wp-dyn/content/article/2007/09/30/AR2007093001352.html (accessed July 1, 2019).

241   David Isenberg, "Contractors and Cost Effectiveness," Cato Institute, December 23, 2009, https://www.cato.org/publications/commentary/contractors-cost-effectiveness (accessed July 1, 2019).

242   Samuel Weigley, "10 Companies Profiting the Most from War," *USA Today*, March 10, 2013, http://www.usatoday.com/story/money/business/2013/03/10/10-companies-profiting-most-from-war/1970997/ (accessed July 1, 2019).

243   David Isenberg, "Contractors and Cost Effectiveness," Cato Institute, December 23, 2009, https://www.cato.org/publications/commentary/contractors-cost-effectiveness (accessed July 1, 2019).

244   Alexander Cohen, "Defense Contractors Spend Millions to Overturn Limits on Military Spending," *Time*, August 5, 2015, http://time.com/3984453/defense-contractors-lobbying/ (accessed July 1, 2019).

245   Defense: Sector Profile, 2019, OpenSecrets.org: Center for Responsive Politics, https://www.opensecrets.org/lobby/indus.php?id=D (accessed July 1, 2019).

246   Alexander Cohen, "Defense Contractors Spend Millions to Overturn Limits on Military Spending," *Time*, August 5, 2015, http://time.com/3984453/defense-contractors-lobbying/ (accessed July 1, 2019).

247 Javier E. David, "US-Saudi Arabia Seal Weapons Deal Worth Nearly $110 Billion Immediately, $350 Billion over 10 Years," *CNBC*, May 22, 2017, https://www.cnbc.com/2017/05/20/us-saudi-arabia-seal-weapons-deal-worth-nearly-110-billion-as-trump-begins-visit.html (accessed July 1, 2019).

248 2004 Bureau of Justice Statistics survey data, found at https://www.prisonpolicy.org/reports/income.html (accessed June 16, 2020).

249 *Patriot Act with Hasan Minhaj*, Sept. 9, 2019 episode located at https://www.youtube.com/watch?v=km4uCOAzrbM (Accessed on June 16, 2020).

250 Prison Policy Initiative from U.S. Census 2010 Summary File 1 located at https://www.prisonpolicy.org/graphs/raceinc.html?gclid=EAIaIQobChMIrKbN3oLw6QIVQ77ACh3VP-giiEAAYASAAEgISH_D_BwE (Accessed on June 16, 2020).

251 NAACP Criminal Justice Fact Sheet located at https://www.naacp.org/criminal-justice-fact-sheet/ (Accessed on June 16, 2020)

252 A Guide to Private Privatization. The Heritage Foundation. May 24, 1988 located at https://www.heritage.org/political-process/report/guide-prison-privatization (Accessed on June 16, 2020).

253 *Swedish Prison vs United States Prison: How Do They Actually Compare?* The Infographics Show. September 3, 2019, located at https://www.youtube.com/watch?v=OzOfjX0VWCk (Accessed June 16, 2020).

254 Silver, Nate. *Most Police Don't Live in The Cities They Serve*. Five Thirty Eight. August 20, 2014, located at https://fivethirtyeight.com/features/most-police-dont-live-in-the-cities-they-serve/ (Accessed on June 16, 2020).

255 *Diversity in Law Enforcement is Essential to Good Policing*. Muslim Public Affairs Council. September 4, 2014 located at https://www.mpac.org/programs/government-relations/diversity-in-law-enforcement-is-essential-to-good-policing.php#:~:text=Diversity is particularly important if the,department itself has racist undertones. (Accessed on June 16, 2020).

256 Jawando, Michele L., and Chelsea Parsons. *4 Ideas That Could Begin to Reform the Criminal Justice System and Improve Police-Community Relations*. Center for American Progress. December 18, 2014 located at https://www.americanprogress.org/issues/courts/reports/2014/12/18/103578/4-ideas-that-could-begin-to-reform-the-criminal-justice-system-and-improve-police-community-relations/ (Accessed June 17, 2020).

257 Leslie Shaffer, "Why Sri Lanka's Economic Outlook Is Looking Less Rosy," *CNBC*, May 2, 2016, https://www.cnbc.com/2016/05/02/why-sri-lankas-economic-outlook-is-looking-less-rosy.html (accessed June 30, 2019).

258 "2050: Climate Change Will Worsen the Plight of the Poor," Food and Agriculture Organization of the United Nations, September 30, 2009, http://www.fao.org/news/story/en/item/35831/icode/ (accessed June 30, 2019).

RESOURCES

Books

Acemoglu, Daron and James A. Robinson, *Why Nations Fail: The Origins of Power, Prosperity, and Poverty* (New York: Crown Business, 2012).

Carson, Clayborne, *The Autobiography of Martin Luther King, Jr.* (New York: Warner Books, 2001).

Chayes, Sarah, *Thieves of State: Why Corruption Threatens Global Security* (New York: W. W. Norton, 2016).

Chomsky, Noam, *Power systems: Conversations with David Barsamian on Global Democratic Uprisings and the New Challenges to U.S. Empire* (London: Hamish Hamilton, 2014).

Diamond, Jarod, *Guns, Germs, and Steel: The Fates of Human Societies* (New York: W. W. Norton & Company, 1997).

Freedman, Russell, *The War to End All Wars: World War I*, (Boston: Clarion Books, 2013).

Friedman, Thomas L., *Thank You For Being Late: An Optimist's Guide to Thriving in the Age of Accelerations* (London: Penguin Books, 2017).

Hacker, Jacob S., and Paul Pierson, *American Amnesia: How the War on Government Led Us to Forget What Made America Rich* (New York: Simon & Schuster, 2017).

Harris, Sam, *Free Will* (New York: Free Press, 2012).

Hawkins, David R., *Power vs. Force: The Hidden Determinants of Human Behavior* (Carlsbad, Ca: Hay House Inc, 2014).

Kleinfeld, Rachel, *A Savage Order: How the World's Deadliest Countries Can Forge a Path to Security* (New York: Pantheon Books, 2018).

Mayer, Jane, *Dark Money: The Hidden History of the Billionaires Behind the Rise of the Radical Right* (New York: Doubleday, 2017).

Montesquieu, Charles-Louis de Secondat (Baron) *The Spirit of the Laws* (Philadelphia: Mathew Carey, 1802).

Obama, Barack, *The Audacity of Hope: Thoughts on Reclaiming the American Dream*, (New York, NY: Broadway Books, 2007).

Rappaport, Doreen, and Bryan Collier, *Martin's Big Words: The Life of Dr. Martin Luther King, Jr.* (New York: Hyperion Books for Children, 2001).

Rice, Condoleezza, *Democracy: Stories from the Long Road to Freedom* (Ashland, Oregon : Blackstone Audio, 2017).

Notable Websites

Anti-Corruption Authorities
https://www.acauthorities.org/

Human Rights Watch
https://www.hrw.org

Live Science
https://www.livescience.com

National Priorities Project
https://www.nationalpriorities.org

Organization for Economic Co-operation and Development
https://www.oecd.org

The Center for Responsive Politics
https://www.opensecrets.org

Transparency International
http://www.transparency.org/

United Nations
http://www.un.org

War on Want
http://www.waronwant.org

ACKNOWLEDGMENTS

Thanks to Alia, my wife for supporting me in this effort. Thanks to my daughter, Aleezeh, and our son, Moiz.

Thanks to Erika Winston for helping me write this book.

Thanks to friends: Khursheed Siddique, Tom Thomas, Shafqat Ullah, and Yousaf Wazirzada for improving the book.

Finally, thanks to my mother, Qaisra, for instilling the work ethic required to finish this book.

ABOUT THE AUTHOR

Born in Pakistan and a resident of the United States for forty years, Raza Hasan's global perspective has been enhanced by travel to more than thirty countries and his own experiences with the types of adversities faced by common people, for which he believes there is a solution. His strength in thought leadership based on creative systems thinking is fueled by his intellectual curiosity about global politics.

Raza has a BS in Aerospace Engineering and an ME in Electrical Engineering from Iowa State University, and an MBA in Marketing and Strategic Management at the Carlson School of Management at the University of Minnesota. During the early days of the internet, he recognized its potential and changed careers from a future planning role as senior analyst and software engineer at Northwest Airlines to work in product management and product marketing for web-based software product companies.

Raza has presented at the global AGIFORS (The Airline Group of the International Federation of Operational Research Societies) meetings in London, Kuala Lumpur, and Hong Kong. He was selected as one of two Minnesota delegates to meet US Congress members in Washington DC for the nonpartisan Fix the Debt movement. He served a three-year term on the Economic Development Commission for the City of Eagan, Minnesota. He has been an adjunct professor for Quantitative Decision-making for the MBA program at Augsburg University, and for Strategic Management and Quantitative Decision-making at the National American University.

Since 2006 Raza has been president and CEO of TimeSolv Corporation, a SaaS time tracking and billing software solution for law firms and others. He launched the nonprofit, Prosperity for All, with the goal of curbing corruption in third world countries.

Raza lives with his wife Alia in the Twin Cities area of Minnesota.

———————

Learn more by visiting www.prosperityweb.org.

Made in the USA
Coppell, TX
08 May 2022

77550576R00163